BREAKING THROUGH

BREAKING THROUGH

A CANADIAN LITERARY MOSAIC

JOHN BOROVILOS

PRENTICE-HALL CANADA INC.
SCARBOROUGH, ONTARIO

Canadian Cataloguing in Publication Data

Main entry under title:
Breaking through : a Canadian literary mosaic

Includes bibliographical references.
ISBN 0-13-083072-0

1. Multiculturalism - Canada - Literary collections.*
2. Multiculturalism - Canada. 3 . Minorities -
Canada - Literary collections. 4. Minorities -
Canada. 5. Immigrants - Canada - Literary collections.
6. Immigrants - Canada. 7. Canadiain literature.
I. Borovilos, John , date.

PS 8237.M84B7 1989   C810'.8'0355   C89-094992-1
PR9194.52.M84B7 1989

© 1990 by Prentice-Hall Canada Inc., Scarborough, Ontario

Prentice-Hall, Inc., Englewood Cliffs, New Jersey
Prentice-Hall International, Inc., London
Prentice-Hall of Australia, Pty., Ltd., Sydney
Prentice-Hall of India Pvt., Ltd., New Delhi
Prentice-Hall of Japan, Inc., Tokyo
Prentice-Hall of Southeast Asia (PTE) Ltd. Singapore
Editora Prentice-Hall do Brasil Ltda., Rio de Janeiro
Prentice-Hall Hispanoamericana, S.A., Mexico

ISBN 013-0830720

Aquiring Editor: David Steele
Project Editor: Jennifer Taylor
Production Editor: Kateri Lanthier
Manufacturing Buyer: Crystale Sheehan
Interior Design: Steve Eby
Cover Design: Gail Ferreira Ng-A-Kien
Composition: CompuScreen Typesetting Ltd.
Cover Painting: Claude Breeze, *Canadian Atlas: The Great Divide*(1974)

Printed and bound in Canada by Webcom Limited
1 2 3 4 5 6 W 94 93 92 91 90 89

CONTENTS

ESSAYS AND ARTICLES   167

STUDENT HANDBOOK

ACKNOWLEDGMENTS

If we perceive learning to be a many-sided collaborative effort, then the creation of a book is the embodiment of that principle. In that respect, I am indebted to my own "small group" at Prentice-Hall who encouraged me, cajoled me, and finally pushed me to "break through" and produce the anthology you are reading. I am particularly grateful to the insights, intelligence, and constructive criticism of my editors, David Steele and Jennifer Taylor. I am also grateful and perhaps more than a little fortunate to have had in my life a variety of inspired teachers who taught me how to read and write with sensitivity and compassion: in particular, Northrop Frye and my other professors at Victoria College who taught me how to see things clearly and to see them whole; and Jimmy Britton who taught me the value of expressive language and "entry points" in students' language development.

DEDICATION

to my immigrant parents, Anastasios and Eleni,
who struggled to give me a better life,

and, to my wife, Anita, and children, Tas,
Alexa, and Adam,
who love me

To the Student

"Something there is that doesn't love a wall. . ."

So wrote the American poet Robert Frost, as he attempted in poetic and symbolic form to visualize for us the barriers that human beings often create, barriers that can lead to misunderstandings, distrust and distortions. They are walls that have been erected, consciously or unconsciously, by people's unfounded fears and ignorance—ignorance based on a lack of knowledge of and a lack of communication with people who may, on the surface and from a distance, seem different. In time, the real differences may become grotesquely exaggerated while the similarities become increasingly obscure.

If we break down these walls and look clearly at the other side, the distrust and distortions will largely vanish—to be replaced by trust and truth. Good, vivid literature that powerfully evokes universal human truths while acknowledging specific differences helps all of us to reach a greater understanding of human nature, motivation, and conflict, and thus helps us to break through those walls--particularly as they might exist within the rich mosaic that is Canada.

As you read through the literature in this anthology—all written by Canadians or writers who have lived in Canada—you will experience in a very direct way the feelings and thoughts of writers and characters at crucial moments in their lives. Through their words, you will begin to feel and think as these characters and authors do. By placing yourself in their shoes and by bringing your own experiences to your reading, your own feelings will be broadened and your own perceptions sharpened. In effect, your understanding of human nature—its joys and laughter, its grief and tears—will deepen.

Through short stories, poetry, personal and formal essays, and journalistic articles, you will be travelling on a journey towards deeper understanding, insight, and reconciliation. At the end of the selections, the Student Handbook will act as a friendly guide on your literary journey. The biographical sketches and specific "Entry Points" and the many general activities will involve you even more actively in exploring and sharing the great themes, feelings, and stylistic motivators of the works in this anthology. These activities will also help your critical thinking to evolve. Further, the thematic cross-referencing of the selections and the additional resources listed will extend your understanding and pleasure as well as suggest ideas and materials for your writing notebooks and folders, oral seminars, small group work, and independent learning projects and essays.

Now it's up to you. Take the journey with open-eyed determination and courage, and see those walls for what they are. Break through those walls and end in triumph as you acknowledge the similarities and celebrate the differences of *all* the people in Canada's mosaic.

JOHN BOROVILOS

SHORT STORIES

I'm talking about Canada as a state of mind, as the space you inhabit not just with your body but with your head. It's that kind of space in which we find ourselves lost. What a lost person needs is a map of the territory, with his own position marked on it so he can see where he is in relation to everything else. Literature is not only a mirror; it is also a map, a geography of the mind.

Margaret Atwood, Survival

What I Learned from Caesar

Guy Vanderhaeghe

The oldest story is the story of flight, the search for greener pastures. But the pastures we flee, no matter how brown and blighted—these travel with us; they can't be escaped.

My father was an immigrant. You would think this no penalty in a nation of immigrants, but even his carefully nurtured, precisely colloquial English didn't spare him much pain. Nor did his marriage to a woman of British stock (as we called it then, before the vicious-sounding acronym Wasp came into use). That marriage should have paid him a dividend of respectability, but it only served to make her suspect in marrying him.

My father was a lonely man, a stranger who made matters worse by pretending he wasn't. It's true that he was familiar enough with his adopted terrain, more familiar than most because he was a salesman. Yet he was never really *of* it, no matter how much he might wish otherwise. I only began to understand what had happened to him when I, in my turn, left for greener pastures, heading east. I didn't go so far, not nearly so far as he had. But I also learned that there is a price to be paid. Mine was a trivial one, a feeling of mild unease. At odd moments I betrayed myself and my beginnings; I knew that I lacked the genuine ring of a local. And I had never even left my own country.

Occasionally I return to the small Saskatchewan town near the Manitoba border where I grew up. To the unpractised eye of an easterner the countryside around that town might appear undifferentiated and monotonous, part and parcel of that great swath of prairie that vacationers drive through, pitying its inhabitants and deploring its restrooms, intent only on leaving it all behind as quickly as possible. But it is just here that the prairie verges on parkland, breaking into rolling swells of land, and here, too, that it becomes a little greener and easier on the eye. There is still more sky than any country is entitled to, and it teases the traveller into believing he can never escape it or find shelter under it. But if your attention wanders from that hypnotic expanse of blue and the high clouds drifting in it, the land becomes more comfortable as prospects shorten, and the mind rests easier on attenuated distances. There is cropland: fields of rye, oats, barley, and wheat; flat, glassy sloughs shining like mirrors in the sun; a solitary clump of trembling poplar; a bluff that gently climbs to nudge the sky.

When I was a boy it was a good deal bleaker. The topsoil had blown off the fields and into the ditches to form black dunes; the crops were withered and burnt; there were no sloughs because they had all dried up. The whole place had a thirsty look. That was during the thirties when we were dealt a doubly cruel hand of drought and economic depression. It was not a time or place that was kindly to my father. He had come out of the urban sprawl of industrial Belgium some twenty-odd years before, and it was only then, I think, that he was beginning to come to terms with a land that must have seemed forbidding after his own tiny country, so well tamed and marked by man. And then this land played him the trick of becoming something more than forbidding; it became fierce, and fierce in every way.

It was in the summer of 1931, the summer that I thought was merely marking time before I would pass into high school, that he lost his territory. For as long as I could remember I had been a salesman's son, and then it ended. The company he worked for began to feel the pinch of the depression and moved to merge its territories. He was let go. So one morning he unexpectedly pulled up at the front door and began to haul his sample cases out of the Ford.

"It's finished," he said to my mother as he flung the cases on to the lawn. "I got the boot. I offered to stay on—strictly commission. He wouldn't hear of it. Said he couldn't see fit to starve two men where there was only a living for one. I'd have starved that other sonofabitch out. He'd have had to hump his back and suck the hind tit when I was through with him." He paused, took off his fedora and nervously ran his index finger around the sweatband. Clearing his throat, he said, "His parting words were 'Good luck, Dutchie!' I should have spit in his eye. Jesus H. Christ himself wouldn't dare call me Dutchie. The bastard."

Offence compounded offence. He thought he was indistinguishable, that the accent wasn't there. Maybe his first successes as a salesman owed something to his naivety. Maybe in good times, when there was more than enough to go around, people applauded his performance by buying from him. He was a counterfeit North American who paid them the most obvious of compliments, imitation. Yet hard times make people less generous. Jobs were scarce, business was poor. In a climate like that, perceptions change, and perhaps he ceased to be merely amusing and became, instead, a dangerous parody. Maybe that district manager, faced with a choice, could only think of George Vander Elst as Dutchie. Then again, it might have been that my father just wasn't a good enough salesman. Who can judge at this distance?

But for the first time my father felt as if he had been exposed. He had never allowed himself to remember that he was a foreigner, or if he had, he persuaded himself he had been wanted. After all, he was a northern European, a Belgian. They had been on the preferred list.

He had left all that behind him. I don't even know the name of the town or the city where he was born or grew up. He always avoided my questions about his early life as if they dealt with a distasteful and criminal past that was best forgotten. Never, not even once, did I hear him speak Flemish. There were never any of the lapses you might expect. No pet names in his native language for my mother or myself; no words of endearment which would have had the comfort of childhood use. Not even when driven to one of his frequent rages did he curse in the mother tongue. If he ever prayed, I'm sure it was in English. If a man forgets the cradle language in the transports of prayer, love, and rage—well, it's forgotten.

The language he did speak was, in a sense, letter-perfect, fluent, glib. It was the language of wheeler-dealers, and of the heady twenties, of salesmen, high-rollers, and persuaders. He spoke of people as live-wires, go-getters, self-made men. Hyphenated words to describe the hyphenated life of the seller, a life of fits and starts, comings and goings. My father often proudly spoke of himself as a self-made man but this description was not the most accurate. He was a remade man. The only two pictures of him which I have in my possession are proof of this.

The first is a sepia-toned photograph taken, as nearly as I can guess, just prior to his departure from Belgium. In this picture he is wearing an ill-fitting suit, round-toed, clumsy boots, and a cloth cap. The second was taken by a street photographer in Winnipeg. My father is walking down the street, a snap-brim fedora slanting rakishly over one eye. His suit is what must have been considered stylish then—a three-piece pin-stripe—and he is carrying an overcoat casually over one arm. He is exactly what he admired most, a "snappy dresser", or, since he always had trouble with his p's, a "snabby dresser". The clothes, though they mark a great change, aren't really that important. Something else tells the story.

In the first photograph my father stands rigidly with his arms folded across his chest, unsmiling. Yet I can see that he is a young man who is hesitant and afraid; not of the camera, but of what this picture-taking means. There is a reason why he is having his photograph taken. He must leave something of himself behind with his family so he will not be forgotten, and carry something away with him so that he can remember. That is what makes this picture touching; it is a portrait of a solitary, an exile.

In the second picture his face is blunter, fleshier; nothing surprising in that, he is older. But suddenly you realize he is posing for the camera—not in the formal, European manner of the first photograph but in a manner far more unnatural. You see, he is pretending to be entirely natural and unguarded; yet he betrays himself. The slight smile, the squared shoulder, the overcoat draped over the arm, all are calculated bits of a composition. He has seen the camera from a block away. My father wanted to be caught in exactly this negligent, unassuming pose, sure that it would capture for all time his prosperity, his success, his adaptability. Like most men, he wanted to leave a record. And this was it. And if he had coached himself in such small matters, what would he ever leave to chance?

Guy Vanderhaeghe / 5

That was why he was so ashamed when he came home that summer. There was the particular shame of having lost his job, a harder thing for a man then than it might be today. There was the shame of knowing that sooner or later we would have to go on relief, because being a lavish spender he had no savings. But there was also the shame of a man who suddenly discovers that all his lies were transparent, and everything he thought so safely hidden had always been in plain view. He had been living one of those dreams. The kind of dream in which you are walking down the street, meeting friends and neighbours, smiling and nodding, and when you arrive at home and pass a mirror you see for the first time you are stark naked. He was sure that behind his back he had always been Dutchie. For a man with so much pride a crueller epithet would have been kinder; to be hated gives a man some kind of status. It was the condescension implicit in that diminutive, its mock playfulness, that made him appear so undignified in his own eyes.

And for the first time in my life I was ashamed of him. He didn't have the grace to bear an injustice, imagined or otherwise, quietly. At first he merely brooded, and then like some man with a repulsive sore, he sought pity by showing it. I'm sure he knew that he could only offend, but he was under a compulsion to justify himself. He began with my mother by explaining, where there was no need for explanation, that he had had his job taken from him for no good reason. However, there proved to be little satisfaction in preaching to the converted, so he carried his tale to everyone he knew. At first his references to his plight were tentative and oblique. The responses were polite but equally tentative and equally oblique. This wasn't what he had hoped for. He believed that the sympathy didn't measure up to the occasion. So his story was told and retold, and each time it was enlarged and embellished until the injustice was magnified beyond comprehension. He made a damn fool of himself. This was the first sign, although my mother and I chose not to recognize it.

In time everyone learned my father had lost his job for no good reason. And it wasn't long before the kids of the fathers he had told his story to were following me down the street chanting, "No good reason. No good reason." That's how I learned my family was a topical joke that the town was enjoying with zest. I suppose my father found out too, because it was about that time he stopped going out of the house. He couldn't fight back and neither could I. You never can.

After a while I didn't leave the house unless I had to. I spent my days sitting in our screened verandah reading old copies of *Saturday Evening Post* and *Maclean's.* I was content to do anything that helped me forget the heat and the monotony, the shame and the fear, of that longest of summers. I was thirteen then and in a hurry to grow up, to press time into yielding the bounty I was sure it had in keeping for me. So I was killing time minute by minute with those magazines. I was to enter high school that fall and that seemed a prelude to adulthood and independence. My father's misfortunes couldn't fool me into believing that maturity didn't mean the strength to plunder at will. So when I found an old Latin grammar of my mother's I began to read that too. After all, Latin was the arcane language of the professions, of lawyers and doctors, those divinities owed immediate and unquestioning respect. I decided I would become either one, because respect could never be stolen from them as it had been from my father.

That August was the hottest I can remember. The dry heat made my nose bleed at night, and I often woke to find my pillow stiff with blood. The leaves of the elm tree in the front yard hung straight down on their stems; flies buzzed heavily, their bodies tip-tapping lazily against the screens, and people passing the house moved so languidly they seemed to be walking in water. My father, who had always been careful about his appearance, began to come down for breakfast barefoot, wearing only a vest undershirt and an old pair of pants. He rarely spoke, but carefully picked his way through his meal as if it were a dangerous obstacle course, only pausing to rub his nose thoughtfully. I noticed that he had begun to smell.

One morning he looked up at me, laid his fork carefully down beside his plate and said, "I'll summons him."

"Who?"

"Who do you think?" he said scornfully. "The bastard who fired me. He had no business calling me Dutchie. That's slander."

"You can't summons him."

"I can," he said emphatically. "I'm a citizen. I've got rights. I'll go to law. He spoiled my good name."

"That's not slander."

"It is."

"No it isn't."

"I'll sue the bastard," he said vaguely, looking around to appeal to my mother, who had left the room. He got up from the table and went to the doorway. "Edith," he called, "tell your son I've got the right to summons that bastard."

Her voice came back faint and timid, "I don't know, George."

He looked back at me. "You're in the same boat, sonny. And taking sides with them don't save you. When we drown we all drown together."

"I'm not taking sides," I said indignantly. "Nobody's taking sides. It's facts. Can't you see. . .," but I didn't get a chance to finish. He left, walked out on me. I could hear his steps on the stairway, tired, heavy steps. There was so much I wanted to say. I wanted to make it plain that being on his side meant saving him from making a fool of himself again. I wanted him to know he could never win that way. I wanted him to win, not lose. He was my father. But he went up those steps, one at a time, and I heard his foot fall distinctly, every time. Beaten before he started, he crawled back into bed. My mother went up to him several times that day, to see if he was sick, to attempt to gouge him out of that room, but she couldn't. It was only later that afternoon, when I was reading in the verandah, that he suddenly appeared again, wearing only a pair of undershorts. His body shone dully with sweat, his skin looked grey and soiled.

"They're watching us," he said, staring past me at an empty car parked in the bright street.

Frightened, I closed my book and asked who was watching us.

"The relief people," he said tiredly. "They think I've got money hidden somewhere. They're watching me, trying to catch me with it. The joke's on them. I got no money." He made a quick, furtive gesture that drew attention to his almost naked body, as if it were proof of his poverty.

"Nobody is watching us. That car's empty."

"Don't take sides with them," he said, staring through the screen. I thought someone from one of the houses across the street might see him like that, practically naked.

"The neighbours'll see," I said, turning my head to avoid looking at him.

"See what?" he asked, surprised.

"You standing like that. Naked almost."

"There's nothing they can do. A man's home is his castle. That's what the English say, isn't it?"

And he went away laughing.

Going down the hallway, drawing close to his door that always stood ajar, what did I hope? To see him dressed, his trousers rolled up to mid-calf to avoid smudging his cuffs, whistling under his breath, shining his shoes? Everything as it was before? Yes. I hoped that. If I had been younger then and still believed that frogs were turned into princes with a kiss, I might even have believed it could happen. But I didn't believe. I only hoped. Every time I approached his door (and that was many times a day, too many), I felt the queasy excitement of hope.

It was always the same. I would look in and see him lying on the tufted pink bedspread, naked or nearly so, gasping for breath in the heat. And I always thought of a whale stranded on a beach because he was such a big man. He claimed he slept all day because of the heat, but he only pretended to. He could feel me watching him and his eyes would open. He would tell me to go away, or bring him a glass of water; or, because his paranoia was growing more marked, ask me to see if they were still in the street. I would go to the window and tell him, yes, they were. Nothing else satisfied him. If I said they weren't, his jaw would shift from side to side unsteadily and his eyes would prick with tears. Then he imagined more subtle and intricate conspiracies.

I would ask him how he felt.

"Hot," he'd say, "I'm always hot. Can't hardly breathe. Damn country," and turn on his side away from me.

My mother was worried about money. There was none left. She asked me what to do. She believed women shouldn't make decisions.

"You'll have to go to the town office and apply for relief," I told her.

"No, no," she'd say, shaking her head. "I couldn't go behind his back. I couldn't do that. He'll go himself when he feels better. He'll snap out of it. It takes a little time."

In the evening my father would finally dress and come downstairs and eat something. When it got dark he'd go out into the yard and sit on the swing he'd hung from a limb of our Manitoba maple years before, when I was a little boy. My mother and I would sit and watch him from the verandah. I felt obligated to sit with her. Every night as he settled himself onto the swing she would say the same thing. "He's too big. It'll never hold him. He'll break his back." But the swing held him up and the darkness hid him from the eyes of his enemies, and I like to think that made him happy, for a time.

He'd light a cigarette before he began to swing, and then we'd watch its glowing tip move back and forth in the darkness like a beacon. He'd flick it away when it was smoked, burning a red arc in the night, showering sparks briefly, like a comet. And then he'd light another and another, and we'd watch them glow and swing in the night.

My mother would lean over to me and say confidentially, "He's thinking it all out. It'll come to him, what to do."

I never knew whether she was trying to reassure me or herself. At last my mother would get to her feet and call to him, telling him she was going up to bed. He never answered. I waited a little longer, believing that watching him I kept him safe in the night. But I always gave up before he did and went to bed too.

The second week of September I returned to school. Small differences are keenly felt. For the first time there was no new sweater, or unsharpened pencils, or new fountain pen whose nib hadn't spread under my heavy writing hand. The school was the same school I had gone to for eight years, but that day I climbed the stairs to the second floor that housed the high school. Up there the wind moaned more persistently than I remembered it had below, and intermittently it threw handfuls of dirt and dust from the schoolyard against the windows with a gritty rattle.

Our teacher, Mrs. MacDonald, introduced herself to us, though she needed no introduction since everyone knew who she was—she had taught there for over ten years. We were given our texts and it cheered me a little to see I would have no trouble with Latin after my summer's work. Then we were given a form on which we wrote a lot of useless information. When I came to the space which asked for Racial Origin I paused, and then, out of loyalty to my father, numbly wrote in "Canadian".

After that we were told we could leave. I put my texts away in a locker for the first time—we had had none in public school—but somehow it felt strange going home from school empty-handed. So I stopped at the library door and went in. There was no school librarian and only a few shelves of books, seldom touched. The room smelled of dry paper and heat. I wandered around aimlessly, taking books down, opening them, and putting them back. That is, until I happened on Caesar's *The Gallic Wars*. It was a small, thick book that nestled comfortably in the hand. I opened it and saw that the left-hand pages were printed in Latin and the right-hand pages were a corresponding English translation. I carried it away with me, dreaming of more than proficiency in Latin.

When I got home my mother was standing on the front step, peering anxiously up and down the street.

"Have you seen your father?" she asked.

"No," I said. "Why?"

She began to cry. "I told him all the money was gone. I asked him if I could apply for relief. He said he'd go himself and have it out with them. Stand on his rights. He took everything with him. His citizenship papers, baptismal certificate, old passport, bank book. 'Everything', I said. 'Everyone knows you. There's no need.' But he said he needed proof. Of what? He'll cause a scandal. He's been gone for an hour."

We went into the house and sat in the living-room. "I'm a foolish woman," she said. She got up and hugged me awkwardly. "He'll be all right."

We sat a long time listening for his footsteps. At last we heard someone come up the walk. My mother got up and said, "There he is." But there was a knock at the door.

I heard them talking at the door. The man said, "Edith, you better come with me. George is in some trouble."

My mother asked what trouble.

"You just better come. He gave the town clerk a poke. The constable and doctor have him now. The doctor wants to talk to you about signing some papers."

"I'm not signing any papers," my mother said.

"You'd better come, Edith."

She came into the living-room and said to me, "I'm going to get your father."

I didn't believe her for a minute. She put her coat on and went out.

She didn't bring him home. They took him to an asylum. It was a shameful word then, asylum. But I see it in a different light now. It seems the proper word now, suggesting as it does a refuge, a place to hide.

I'm not sure why all this happened to him. Perhaps there is no reason anyone can put their finger on, although I have my ideas.

But I needed a reason then. I needed a reason that would lend him a little dignity, or rather, lend me a little dignity; for I was ashamed of him out of my own weakness. I needed him to be strong, or at least tragic. I didn't know that most people are neither.

When you clutch at straws, anything will do. I read my answer out of Caesar's *The Gallic Wars*, the fat little book I had carried home. In the beginning of Book I he writes, "Of all people the Belgae are the most courageous. . . ." I read on, sharing Caesar's admiration for a people who would not submit but chose to fight and see glory in their wounds. I misread it all, and bent it until I was satisfied. I reasoned the way I had to, for my sake, for my father's. What was he but a man dishonoured by faceless foes? His instincts could not help but prevail, and like his ancestors, in the end, on that one day, what could he do but make the shadows real, and fight to be free of them?

The Hockey Sweater

Roch Carrier

The winters of my childhood were long, long seasons. We lived in three places—the school, the church and the skating-rink—but our real life was on the skating-rink. Real battles were won on the skating-rink. Real strength appeared on the skating-rink. The real leaders showed themselves on the skating-rink. School was a sort of punishment. Parents always want to punish children and school is their most natural way of punishing us. However, school was also a quiet place where we could prepare for the next hockey game, lay out our next strategies. As for church, we found there the tranquillity of God: there we forgot school and dreamed about the next hockey game. Through our daydreams it might happen that we would recite a prayer: we would ask God to help us play as well as Maurice Richard.

We all wore the same uniform as he, the red, white and blue uniform of the Montreal Canadiens, the best hockey team in the world; we all combed our hair in the same style as Maurice Richard, and to keep it in place we used a sort of glue—a great deal of glue. We laced our skates like Maurice Richard, we taped our sticks like Maurice Richard. We cut all his pictures out of the papers. Truly, we knew everything about him.

On the ice, when the referee blew his whistle the two teams would rush at the puck; we were five Maurice Richards taking it away from five other Maurice Richards; we were ten players, all of us wearing with the same blazing enthusiasm the uniform of the Montreal Canadiens. On our backs, we all wore the famous number 9.

One day, my Montreal Canadiens sweater had become too small; then it got torn and had holes in it. My mother said: 'If you wear that old sweater people are going to think we're poor!' Then she did what she did whenever we needed new clothes. She started to leaf through the catalogue the Eaton company sent us in the mail every year. My mother was proud. She didn't want to buy our clothes at the general store; the only things that were good enough for us were the latest styles from Eaton's catalogue. My mother didn't like the order forms included with the catalogue; they were written in English and she didn't understand a word of it. To order my hockey sweater, she did as she usually did; she took out her writing paper and wrote in her gentle schoolteacher's hand: 'Cher Monsieur Eaton, Would you be kind enough to send me a Canadiens' sweater for my son who is ten years old and a little too tall for his age and Docteur Robitaille thinks he's a little too thin? I'm sending you three dollars and please send me what's left if there's anything left. I hope your wrapping will be better than last time.'

Monsieur Eaton was quick to answer my mother's letter. Two weeks later we received the sweater. That day I had one of the greatest disappointments of my life! I would even say that on that day I experienced a very great sorrow. Instead of the red, white and blue Montreal Canadiens sweater, Monsieur Eaton had sent us a blue and white sweater with a maple leaf on the front—the sweater of the Toronto Maple Leafs. I'd always worn the red, white and blue Montreal Canadiens sweater; all my friends wore the red, white and blue sweater; never had anyone in my village ever worn the Toronto sweater, never had we even seen a Toronto Maple Leafs sweater. Besides, the Toronto team was regularly trounced by the triumphant Canadiens. With tears in my eyes, I found the strength to say:

'I'll never wear that uniform.'

'My boy, first you're going to try it on! If you make up your mind about things before you try, my boy, you won't go very far in this life.'

My mother had pulled the blue and white Toronto Maple Leafs sweater over my shoulders and already my arms were inside the sleeves. She pulled the sweater down and carefully smoothed all the creases in the abominable maple leaf on which, right in the middle of my chest, were written the words 'Toronto Maple Leafs'. I wept.

'I'll never wear it.'

'Why not? This sweater fits you . . . like a glove.'

'Maurice Richard would never put it on his back.'

'You aren't Maurice Richard. Anyway, it isn't what's on your back that counts, it's what you've got inside your head.'

'You'll never put it in my head to wear a Toronto Maple Leafs sweater.'

My mother sighed in despair and explained to me:

'If you don't keep this sweater which fits you perfectly I'll have to write to Monsieur Eaton and explain that you don't want to wear the Toronto sweater. Monsieur Eaton's an *Anglais*; he'll be insulted because he likes the Maple Leafs. And if he's insulted do you think he'll be in a hurry to answer us? Spring will be here and you won't have played a single game, just because you didn't want to wear that perfectly nice blue sweater.'

So I was obliged to wear the Maple Leafs sweater. When I arrived on the rink, all the Maurice Richards in red, white and blue came up, one by one, to take a look. When the referee blew his whistle I went to take my usual position. The captain came and warned me I'd be better to stay on the forward line. A few minutes later the second line was called; I jumped onto the ice. The Maple Leafs sweater weighed on my shoulders like a mountain. The captain came and told me to wait; he'd need me later, on defense. By the third period I still hadn't played; one of the defensemen was hit in the nose with a stick and it was bleeding. I jumped on the ice: my moment had come! The referee blew his whistle; he gave me a penalty. He claimed I'd jumped on the ice when there were already five players. That was too much! It was unfair! It was persecution! It was because of my blue sweater! I struck my stick against the ice so hard it broke. Relieved, I bent down to pick up the debris. As I straightened up I saw the young vicar, on skates, before me.

'My child,' he said, 'just because you're wearing a new Toronto Maple Leafs sweater unlike the others, it doesn't mean you're going to make the laws around here. A proper young man doesn't lose his temper. Now take off your skates and go to the church and ask God to forgive you.'

Wearing my Maple Leafs sweater I went to the church, where I prayed to God; I asked him to send, as quickly as possible, moths that would eat up my Toronto Maple Leafs sweater.

Translated by Sheila Fischman

The Rink

Cyril Dabydeen

George sits there. Thinking of skating down the rink with the ease of Guy LaFleur; he, a black, black man doing this thing with ease. But the more he thinks about it, the more it begins to boggle his mind. He's thinking too that he, an islander who has come to this country to establish roots, must really learn to skate; this same skating that looks so easy because he'd stand by the boards right there and watch people, especially the young ones, floating down the ice in the hockey rink as if they had skates on their feet from the day they were born. Such an amazing thing it was. More than once he felt really ashamed of himself not being able to skate. How could a grown man living in Canada have difficulty doing such a simple thing? George is determined more than ever now. He imagines going down the ice once more, doing twists and turns.

But it seems more difficult to do than he imagines, for right then as he makes another attempt to get up from the ice, nervousness overtakes him, making him more uncomfortable in the skates by the minute the longer he has them on. At once too his heels begin to ache, burning at the ankles as well. Yet with determination he struggles to get up while he still imagines going down the ice. He steps out a few feet now; away from the boards; he sees himself going closer to the other end of the rink. This skating thing is one helluva thing to do, he says to himself, gritting his teeth.

He's really taking his time now, trying his damndest not to fall again. He remembers falling down twice yesterday, once hitting his head heavily and nearly being knocked out. This time it won't happen again; he's taking greater care, is yet more determined than ever. At the same time he's thinking, too, of Boysie coming to visit him at two o'clock in the morning; Boysie should be ashamed of himself, knocking at his door at that ungodly hour, thinking he's still back on the island. Sure, lots of other islanders often do the same, behaving without responsibility: as if they have no civilization with them. George moans a little, even as he steps out farther, becoming more confident now. Indeed, skating is an easy thing after all. He's about to smile.

But he looks ahead then too, at the few kids by the sideboards who're looking at him, studying his every move. And for a moment he imagines being one of them, being born and bred right here in Canada, in this cold, cold place. Would the cold really bother him as much as it does now if he were born right here? George doesn't really know. He takes another tentative step forward now, even as he turns and looks sideways at the kids and forces a smile, sort of. Another deliberate step, even though still tentative. George begins to feel the skates really heavy on his legs now, as if his feet are cast in iron, making him really uncomfortable. Again he looks up, mechanically sort of, this time to see the kids smiling; maybe they're really encouraging him. But his ankles are really burning now.

Yet another move forward, even as he's fully aware of the kids watching and smiling at him with increased interest. For a second, the skates feel different, almost like something fanciful in a dream, just as he'd once imagined before. Yet another step forward.

As if encouraged, the kids come closer to the boards, almost in his line of vision; these same apple-cheeked, fluffy-headed-and-handsome kids, all smiling and making him really self-conscious now. Suddenly George dares not move. He's even afraid to look up now. Something is about to happen, something he fears. It's as if his legs are moving apart of their own accord, diagonally sort of. George's heart beats faster. One of the kids bursts out laughing, nearly upsetting him fully this time. A flood of embarrassment rushes through him, like a sudden wave. George is now only five feet from the opposite end; and he's trying his damndest to make it, which he knows he must do now. He stretches out both hands, ready to hold on to anything, to something, for support. And he looks at the kids, their eyes gleaming almost, these same kids who're smiling fully; even as he tries to smile himself as a way of hiding shame. Ah, no one's going to stop him now. He'll make it. Not even Ida, his wife, will stop him; the same Ida who's been laughing at him, telling him that he—an islander—will never be able to skate since he wasn't born with ice in his veins. George asked her, "What d'you mean by that, woman?" He was angry. But Ida laughed, loudly, her typical island laughter which had echoed all around her. She added, "George, you're different, man. We are different. We've come from a hot, hot climate. We weren't born with ice in our veins as I've done told you before!" George had replied almost immediately, with anger burning in him. "But we . . . I—I want to be a—" He stopped and looked at her accusingly, questioningly. He blurted out now, "That's why I came here!" He was incoherent, he knew. Ida had a way of making him very incensed. Now he knew she wasn't even listening to him. Maybe Ida was satisfied with the way things were, still wanting to remain an islander in Canada without ever changing.

The kids laugh again, now leaning forward over the boards almost, as they are really very close to him and are watching a strange show in which he—George—is on centre stage. A few seconds pass by, while George, as if by a miracle, recovers his grip. Holding onto the boards once again, he remains standing there, a little proud, thinking: he doesn't want to be like other black immigrants in Canada. He wants to integrate; fully; and he believes that before long he'll be skating like the best of the native born-and-bred Canadians. At once, he stretches out a leg again, willing himself to go out, thinking still—what's the point of living in a new country if you have no intention of conforming with its ways even though they are foreign ways? He wishes Ida would understand that sometimes. Just then he falls—*bradacks*!

At once George scurries and wriggles on the ice, spinning like a top next, eager as he is to get up, and hoping that none of the kids sees him. But the kids are already laughing, uncontrollably. George twists and scrapes, gets up and goes down once more, then up again, and once more on the ground. The kids' shrill laughter rings in the air. It's as if Ida and Boysie are also laughing with them now. The whole damn Caribbean island laughing with them too! George is not sure what to do now. In sheer frustration, he sits on the ice, casually sort of; and he looks back at them, smiling; grinning too from ear to ear to hide his increasing discomfort.

More kids appear now, laughing, some pointing to him for the benefit of the others who are still coming into the arena. George, really play-acting now, continues his grin, even though deep down he wishes he wasn't in this predicament. Now he senses the kids are watching him as if he's some sort of a performer indeed: he, acting solely for their benefit. Now they're rattling the sideboards in their excitement. George reddens. The kids come closer, some leaning over the sideboards, looking down at him. One says, "Get up, Mister." Another adds in a voice of encouragement, "Start again."

But George merely sits on the ice, as if that's all he can do now. Yet he keeps smiling his smile of embarrassment. He wishes now he never put on the blasted skates; and he grits his teeth in silent anger beneath his smiles, even as he simultaneously feels the cold seeping up under his pants. And he looks directly at these same apple-cheeked faces in agony. At once he realizes that the kids are really giving him their sympathy and encouragement, all in one: in a way too, telling him that it's no shameful thing for a man who's learning to skate to be sitting flat on the ice the way he's doing now. Once more George tries getting up; but he's having difficulty. And still with their uncontrollable laughter, the kids cluster around him, again offering encouragement. But George feels more of the cold seeping up; and at once he begins thinking that this place isn't a cricket field he's sitting on, but sheer ice! Yet he remains there, immobile: as in a sort of daze . . . even as he thinks of Boysie laughing again at him (just like Ida did); Boysie laughing the same old laugh, telling him loud and clear, "What a damn fool you are, man. You's learnin' to skate! You know full well that this ain't your kinda sport. Why you doan play cricket instead, man? Why not, eh?" Boysie's laugh echoes all around him, whirring in every cell of his brain. Another moment George imagines Ida laughing, too—she and Boysie laughing together, having fun at his expense.

Willing himself, George turns his attention to the kids once more—even as he sits there and looks at their winter clothes: at their gloves and red-and-blue toques. No doubt they're wondering why he doesn't get up now like any other easily would. He surveys their innocent-as-babes faces, wondering if they've ever seen a black man such as he, fully grown and learning to skate, now flat on the ice. What a ridiculous picture he must make.

Immediately he wants to shout out to them, telling them to leave him alone. Instead, he merely continues sitting there, in a way knowing that if he tries once more, he'll quickly fall again. But George also knows that he can't sit there forever. On an impulse he tries getting up; but he's unable to budge now.

What's the matter? Boysie's image again, saying now: "Man, this ain't a cricket field. This ain't like standing up straight-straight and hitting the ball on *de off side* across the green like Garfield Sobers or Clive Lloyd an' watching it shooting down to the boundary for four!"

At once George wants to tell the kids that; to tell that he, sitting-down George, used to be one of the best batsmen on the island, and of how the crowd used to cheer him loudly like thunder ringing through your ears. Oh, the sweet-sweet applause. Smiling, George reminisces happily. Right then one of the kids comes up and tries to pull him up. Then another comes, assisting. In no time three others, all around him, urging him to get up. And George, realizing he needs their help, heaves, thankful now for their assistance. In a final struggle, with skates and all, he pulls himself up. Aah! He feels the bump at the back of his head, which he remembers is the result of his falling down heavily the week he'd begun to learn to skate. He thanks the kids for their help, even though he simultaneously swears under his breath. Once more the kids laugh, a little louder this time, with satisfaction and amusement—as they look at him standing with legs splayed out, once again like a pregnant woman's.

George decides he's had enough for one day. But he will come again tomorrow, intent on becoming a skater, no matter what. Despite the taunts of Boysie. Or Ida. Or the kids. George is still swearing under his breath because of the realization of his ineptitude; swearing more than he used to as a grown-up man dreaming of coming to Canada and waiting four long years for his immigration papers to be processed. Briefly he thinks of his mother he's left behind: to whom he used to regularly send letters with a ten-dollar bill in the envelope each time and imagining the excitement on his mother's face when she opened the envelope with the bill falling out and landing on the ground like manna from heaven; but he'd stopped sending money upon realizing that his mother wasn't really receiving any (some *orangutan* postman in the district was stealing his hard-earned cash!) He remembers, too, only three months after he'd married Ida how he'd stopped writing letters to his mother, all because he'd discovered her snooping around in his pockets to read the letters before the envelope was sealed, in a way trying to censor everything he wrote. Was it because she didn't want him to have anything to do with the island again?

After much contemplating, George had decided to chart his own course, Ida or not. He'd decided to be a real Canadian, thinking that when he returned to the island, on vacation, he'd be flashing hundred-dollar bills before his mother's watery eyes and be telling her in his best-acquired Canadian accent that he isn't the same short-pants, barefooted fella who used to walk about the streets with a piece of raw sugar-cane sticking out of his mouth as if he was born like that, like someone having really evolved from sugar-cane as some of the native Indians believed. No siree! There'll be a real gleam in his mother's eyes, as he'll be telling her all the progress he has made. Yes, he—black as he is—will do just that. And smiling, George figures he'll be wearing collar and tie from morning to night since he'll no longer be working with his hands but with his God-given brains as man is meant to work in the first place.

Ida greets him at the door. "Well, George, you're back early today." George looks at the beautiful woman standing before him, his own wife, who's been trying to put him off his plan of action. He's about to smile, and to tell her to wait and see, that before long he'll skate as the best of the same people she's so fond of watching on TV. Instead, George looks at the skates in his hand dangling like a bunch of steel lobsters he has caught by the sea; and he remembers sitting down on the ice with his bottom freezing, with the kids laughing all around him. How can he forget that. Ignoring Ida, George walks straight past her to the storeroom to put the skates away.

Ida follows behind. George, sensing her presence, is suddenly angry, because he knows that she's about to mock and tease him now. Maybe she has become crochety since she became pregnant. As he bends down to put the skates away, he looks longingly at them one more time (as if he's been used to wearing these same things all his life like cricket pads). But Ida's closeness, in a way, still irks. And once more the skates begin to appear now like a pair of ridiculous boots which only a strange breed of people wear; people who want to punish themselves for nothing at all. But this feeling is temporary, for just then George hears applause coming to his ears, just as before, the difference now being that he imagines he's in the NHL. And it's almost the same sound as when he's hitting the cricket ball a mighty blast in the field and watching it race down to the boundary for four. More applause splitting his ears, happily. He looks up at Ida and grins. But Ida, her lips pursed, says:

"Is it true, George? I mean, are you really skating now?" "Yes, woman!" he wants to shout to her. Instead, he mutters, not loudly enough, and self-consciously too, the sound coming out of his lips like a grunt; and he's not sure of what he's really saying now. But Ida begins to lambaste him:

"But, George, you can't blasted well be able to skate! You, a black-black man doing a white thing. It isn't the sport fo' you, man!"

George angrily faces her. Yet he knows he must keep his cool because only uncivilized people lose their temper, who shout and swear like mad people even. And he's saying to her with his cold-cold civilized eyes, *Leave me alone woman. Leave me alone to do my thing in my own blasted way! Leave me, Ida, I done tell yuh!* But Ida begins to laugh in his face, telling him again that he'll never be good enough, no matter what. George is no longer able to stand the irony in her voice. She's saying this thing loudly now. "You's one helluva black man who's gonna be different in this country! You hear me, George?" And, looking at her, George sees real pain in her eyes. For a while, as if not knowing what to do, how else to react, he smiles, an odd sort of smile, because he knows full well too that there's nothing else a man can do against the onslaught of a woman's tongue, a woman born-an'-bred on the island. He looks a little sheepishly at her, studying her serious face, like some sort of pity and terror written all over it now, confusing him; for he's never seen his woman looking like this before: yes, the same beautiful woman he's married to—now looking serious, and ugly too.

Throughout supper George wonders if Ida is right. What if he'll never be taken seriously in this country, no matter how hard he tries; no matter if he goes on taking evening courses all his life as he struggles to better himself, eager as he is to match up with the best people, those same ones he and Ida often meet in the offices and stores and everywhere else, who look professional and who in one way or another sometimes make him feel inferior. And George tries to focus his mind on the rink again, as if this is the real solution, trying to imagine once more skating down with ease and joyful rhythm from one end to another. Slowly he puts food into his mouth, without speaking. Ida too isn't speaking.

In bed that night, Ida turns and twists. George is also awake, thinking. Ida asks in the unbearable silence, "What's going through your mind, George?" "Nothing," he lies. She turns again, once more to her side, still unable to sleep, this same soon-to-be-heavy-bodied woman bearing his child. A three-month thing already, George is thinking, turning around right then and patting her stomach a little, then putting an arm out to caress her: to feel the living thing planted there at the same time, like some sort of miracle. Then he remembers Boysie's face: Boysie laughing and saying, "Man, George, your first-born's gonna be a genius, gonna be my God-child too. Ha-ha." George had laughed then as well, because he'd been drinking rum and coke. That was only a month ago. But now, at once almost, George makes up his mind that no *island-orangutan* is going to be the God-father of his child. He wants someone responsible, a native born-and-bred Canadian. Ida still twists and turns. She asks, "Are you thinking about our child, George?"

George doesn't answer right away. He only becomes more aware of her burgeoning roundness, the smoothness of her flesh under her pink nightgown, the same nightgown he'd bought for her on her last birthday. He rests a hand against her wide-awake heart (so he tells himself) which is now beating rapidly, so rapidly that he can almost hear it. And George thinks right then of a daughter being born, a child with a stout heart, this same child who'll make him (and Ida too) very proud. Ah, he imagines taking her to learn how to skate. This child's bound to learn easily because it'll be something she'll be doing every day at the rink among a number of other kids like her. Yes, there'll be no stopping her. He smiles. But the smile quickly fades because he remembers falling down earlier that day, and the kids all around him, laughing.

"Get up! Get up!" they encourage, one pulling his arm.

"Go on, sir, get up. You can make it!"

George feels more embarrassed than ever because he knows that the longer he's on the ground the more embarrassing it'll be for him; the more too he'll invite others to come an' watch him making a fool of himself.

"Get up, it's easy to do!" George hears the voice of his own child now: a black child, talking to him, urging him to get up, repeatedly. George isn't sure what's happening, as he sits there, almost bewildered. Right then he looks around and sees a large crowd of people (mostly adults), all looking at him—at him alone—who're now ready to applaud him. George pulls himself upright with the assistance of this same black child, and stands with pride. Turning, he looks at the crowd and bows. Then he looks in the middle of the rink, and there he sees this same child, his daughter, with her skates on, all alone—doing this miraculous thing as if she was born with skates on, pirouetting around to the further applause of everyone. By the boards, George applauds too, marvelling at this child he and Ida brought into the world, who's skating with such grace and ease. He's really pleased now, smiling and applauding . . . thinking . . . again, and again, and laughing too.

"George, you okay?" he hears Ida's voice.

But he's still chuckling inside, not wanting to stop this feeling inside him, welling up like a tide, making him not sure if he's still dreaming or is fully awake.

"You sure you're okay, George?" Ida turns once more, to his side. "Remember, Boysie's coming to see us again, soon. Maybe you should take him with you to learn to skate. The two o' you." Ida smiles, as he senses, still in her half-asleep state. She continues to mutter, "This skating, George, maybe you're very determined, are you not?" It's as if she's now waiting for an answer, turning and looking at him, now wide awake. George is thinking, and grinning too, at the same time. He's saying close to her ears, "Yes, Ida, I'm going to take Boysie to learn how to skate. It's something he's bound to know how to do. After all, this child, our newborn in a few months' time, this child right inside you now, she's gonna skate better than both of us. Ha-ha." George is unable to suppress the gladness now overtaking him, while Ida presses closer to him and looks fully at him in the dark with her eyes brimful with tears of her own sweet joy.

Input

Laura Bulger

T hen, the man asked her to be seated. He glanced at her legs, which she immediately crossed, the knee showing below a very tight short skirt. It had not been intentional. It was the only woollen skirt she had that was in good shape; it happened to match the blouse of blue silk, a reminder of more prosperous times. He moved to the large swivel chair behind the mahogany desk and sat down. His hands together, as if in prayer, he touched his fingers to the tip of his chin with an air of concentration. Impatient, she waited and noticed the very small teeth showing through a forced grin, the rapid flutter of the eyelids behind the lenses. At last, in a nasal voice he introduced himself.

—My name is Jack Bumbleby. I am the director.

She was tense, but feigned a timid smile.

Feeling confident when she had applied for the job, now she was ready to submit to the questioning. The expectations of the future boss were unknown. (She felt optimistic, though.) Hands still together, the director started by asking her reasons for the interest in the said position. That or any other, she thought, without feeling any loyalty or preference, that is, as long as it paid well and had good working conditions.

Till then she had not succeeded in finding work in spite of knowing several languages, having travelled widely and attended university, a fact she omitted in her job applications. After all a good secretary is not required to analyze or reflect critically. Let's keep things in perspective! Too many qualifications might even be a disadvantage. *Overqualified. Overeducated. Overexposed.* They always found an excuse to turn her down. Other drawbacks were the language, rather stilted with traces of a European accent and, of course, lack of experience. She had completed a six-month course in typing and stenography. She had also acquired the art of answering the telephone and organizing papers, by stapling some on the right, others on the left—those secrets of the indispensable secretary who remains unnoticed while serving coffee. She had made an effort to forget the polished education of which her mother still spoke with an authoritarian voice. Boastful snobbery is out of place in a world indifferent to the confusion of old lineages. Pretentions are paid for, either with cash or credit cards. And these cannot be obtained without the guarantee of a monthly salary.

She showed interest, great interest indeed, in the position and the firm in question. The director continued the interrogation and note taking. Why? When? How? Sometimes repeating himself, perhaps looking for contradictions. Perhaps because he had not understood. She tried to guess the intentions hidden behind the metal-rimmed glasses. She noticed the picture of a happy blond child on his desk. At that very moment, her own son must be waiting for her at the school, eagerly expecting her arrival.

Now, she had to concentrate on the director's questions. At least she had passed the first test, which gave her some hope. The man cleared his throat and then excused himself in order to make a call. Although straightforward, he was courteous.

On the wall, behind the desk, hung a picture. An abstract. A labyrinth of orange, yellow and red. What bad taste, she thought, but it gave colour to the sombre office. The picture reminded her of a confusing past. Those art exhibitions which she never missed. She was then a student at university. Crammed classes, hastily-taken notes empty of meaning, games of memory. Extinct civilizations. Lively conversations in the cafés. That local ambiance dominated by personalities from a naive provincial universe. A tradition forever rooted in a future without hope. The weariness of the everyday which by late afternoon turns to repressed anguish. The frustration confined to a narrow space which does not permit one to go on without having to shove and curse. And so immersed was she in those thoughts that the director's fragmented sentences and laconic sounds went unnoticed.

When he finished the call, he looked up as if to examine her. (This, by the way, always causes a certain uneasiness.) Embarrassed, he told her he still had to ask some questions of a personal nature. Privacy is a right in this country, she was sure of that, no one dared invade it. There are laws that protect the individual against such transgressions. But ... did she have anything to hide? Absolutely nothing. She decided to co-operate. No, this was her second marriage. The first had ended in divorce. It had dissolved amidst recriminations and threats. From one day to next he had become a stranger, violent and emotional, really another person, after returning from the war. One day she was forced to shut the door in his face. Scandal in the family. She could endure the mistreatment no longer. She also had to protect the child, who began to suffer the effects of the environment, the misunderstanding, the abusive language. In the end, although torn to shreds, she had won. With the second, it was not for love. She needed someone. He liked the boy and treated her well. He was self-made, pragmatic. They had married so that both of them, she and her son, could emigrate. Her family sighed with relief when they saw her settled again notwithstanding her husband's obscure beginnings. It had put an end to the gossip. Her friends envied her luck. (She was, of course, omitting this and adding that.) Now, what she really wanted was security and stability for herself and her child. She wanted to start all over with hope in the future and, deep inside, something was telling her she would succeed.

Meanwhile the director had removed his glasses and was listening in silence. He had stopped scribbling. Wearily, he stroked his forehead and she understood that everything had been said. She arranged her skirt and waited. The man put on his glasses again and came around to sit on the edge of the desk, right in front of her, his right leg dangling. He wore grey socks and black laced shoes. The pants had no cuffs but had a perfect crease. He had a blue blazer, a shirt with fine stripes and a red tie. He looked impeccable, she thought, apparently more at ease, more open. She also noticed the well-manicured delicate hands of a careful prudent man. In other words, the director was a human being. She would like to work there for him. He asked her whether she was interested in accompanying him abroad, if the occasion arose. Short trips, perhaps. She said yea, she was available anytime, ready to work and do whatever was necessary. She realized she was a little anxious, showing too much interest. Enough had been said, she thought. The director must have understood because he grinned as she spoke. Apologetically, he mentioned he had to interview the other candidates and consult with members of the board before giving her a definite answer. She assumed that was a formality. (Under the circumstances it's better not to show hostility.) The man asked her to wait in the next room where a secretary would fill in a form for her to sign, if that was all right, of course. He put out his hand and she said goodbye without ever turning her back to him, as if on stage.

A Scandinavian-looking girl came to meet her and asked if she wanted coffee. She said no, thanks, and the other began to type the information handed to her by the director. Her fingers flew over the keyboard of the computer which grunted assent.

It was a pleasant office. Close to the permanently sealed window grew a domestic figtree. The light was diffused blue as in a space-ship. On the little screen of the monitor data on the recent interview began to appear. She could not read it from a distance but she knew her life would depend on the "info" which the computer would spit out, thanks to the efficiency of the blonde secretary who suddenly tore off a sheet and presented it to her to be signed. She read it in amazement.

Name: Magalhaes Da Silva, Maria do Rosario
Sex: Female   Marital Status: married
Legal immigrant
Country of Origin: Portugal
Education: Secondary school, fluency in spoken and written English, French, Italian, German and Portuguese, Secretarial course
Experience: none
References:. . . .

There was a space reserved for further information in case the candidate was accepted. She couldn't believe it. Half an hour of a conversation reduced to that! Absurd. She felt like laughing and crying at the same time. With a bright smile, pen in hand, the girl was standing there. OK? Yes, the information was correct. She was going to add she hoped the director would remember their conversation because, really, that sheet said next to nothing. But it wasn't worthwhile. She put her name to it. Still radiant, the secretary removed the paper from her hand and showed her the door.

This time she didn't even turn to say goodbye; she was dying to get out of there. The grunts from the computer bothered her.

A Class of New Canadians

Clarke Blaise

Norman Dyer hurried down Sherbrooke Street, collar turned against the snow. "Superb!" he muttered, passing a basement gallery next to a French bookstore. Bleached and tanned women in furs dashed from hotel lobbies into waiting cabs. Even the neon clutter of the side streets and the honks of slithering taxis seemed remote tonight through the peaceful snow. *Superb*, he thought again, waiting for a light and backing from a slushy curb: a word reserved for wines, cigars, and delicate sauces; he was feeling superb this evening. After eighteen months in Montreal, he still found himself freshly impressed by everything he saw. He was proud of himself for having steered his life north, even for jobs that were menial by standards he could have demanded. Great just being here no matter what they paid, looking at these buildings, these faces, and hearing all the languages. He was learning to be insulted by simple bad taste, wherever he encountered it.

Since leaving graduate school and coming to Montreal, he had sampled every ethnic restaurant downtown and in the old city, plus a few Levantine places out in Outremont. He had worked on conversational French and mastered much of the local dialect, done reviews for local papers, translated French-Canadian poets for Toronto quarterlies, and tweaked his colleagues for not sympathizing enough with Quebec separatism. He attended French performances of plays he had ignored in English, and kept a small but elegant apartment near a colony of *émigré* Russians just off Park Avenue. Since coming to Montreal he'd witnessed a hold-up, watched a murder, and seen several riots. When stopped on the street for directions, he would answer in French or accented English. To live this well and travel each long academic summer, he held two jobs. He had no intention of returning to the States. In fact, he had begun to think of himself as a semi-permanent, semi-political exile.

Now, stopped again a few blocks farther, he studied the window of Holt Renfrew's exclusive men's shop. Incredible, he thought, the authority of simple good taste. Double-breasted chalk-striped suits he would never dare to buy. Knitted sweaters, and fifty-dollar shoes. One tanned mannequin was decked out in a brash checkered sportscoat with a burgundy vest and dashing ascot. Not a price tag under three hundred dollars. Unlike food, drink, cinema, and literature, clothing had never really involved him. Someday, he now realized, it would. Dyer's clothes, thus far, had all been bought in a chain department store. He was a walking violation of American law, clad shoes to scarf in Egyptian cottons, Polish leathers, and woolens from the People's Republic of China.

He had no time for dinner tonight; this was Wednesday, a day of lectures at one university, and then an evening course in English as a Foreign Language at McGill, beginning at six. He would eat afterwards.

Besides the money, he had kept this second job because it flattered him. He was a god two evenings a week, sometimes suffering and fatigued, but nevertheless an omniscient, benevolent god. His students were silent, ignorant, and dedicated to learning English. No discussions, no demonstrations, no dialogue.

I love them, he thought. They need me.

He entered the room, pocketed his cap and earmuffs, and dropped his briefcase on the podium. Two girls smiled good evening.

They love me, he thought, taking off his boots and hanging up his coat; I'm not like their English-speaking bosses.

I love myself, he thought with amazement even while conduct-ing a drill on word order. I love myself for tramping down Sherbrooke Street in zero weather just to help them with noun clauses. I love myself standing behind this podium and showing Gilles Carrier and Claude Veilleux the difference between the past continuous and the simple past; or the sultry Armenian girl with the bewitching half-glasses that "put on" is not the same as "take on"; or telling the dashing Mr. Miguel Mayor, late of Madrid, that simple futurity can be expressed in four different ways, at least.

This is what mastery is like, he thought. Being superb in one's chosen field, not merely in one's mother tongue. A respected performer in the lecture halls of the major universities, equipped by twenty years' research in the remotest libraries, and slowly giving it back to those who must have it. Dishing it out suavely, even wittily. Being a legend. Being loved and a little feared.

"Yes, Mrs. David?"

A *sabra**: freckled, reddish hair, looking like a British model, speaks with a nifty British accent, and loves me.

"No," he smiled, "*I were* is not correct except in the present subjunctive, which you haven't studied yet."

The first hour's bell rang. In the halls of McGill they broke into the usual groups. French Canadians and South Americans into two large circles, then the Greeks, Germans, Spanish, and French into smaller groups. The patterns interested Dyer. Madrid Spaniards and Parisian French always spoke English with their New World co-linguals. The Middle Europeans spoke German together, not Russian, preferring one occupier to the other. Two Israeli men went off alone. Dyer decided to join them for the break.

Not *sabras*, Dyer concluded, not like Mrs. David. The shorter one, dark and wavy-haired, held his cigarette like a violin bow. The other, Mr. Weinrot, was tall and pot-bellied, with a ruddy face and thick stubby fingers. Something about him suggested truck-driving, perhaps of beer, maybe in Germany. Neither one, he decided, could supply the name of a good Israeli restaurant.

"This is really hard, you know?" said Weinrot.

"Why?"

"I think it's because I'm not speaking much of English at my job."

"French?" asked Dyer.

"French? Pah! All the time Hebrew, sometimes German, sometimes little Polish. Crazy thing, eh? How long you think they let

**sabra: native-born Israeli.*

me speak Hebrew if I'm working in America?"

"Depends on where you're working," he said.

"Hell, I'm working for the Canadian government, what you think? Plant I work in—I'm engineer, see—makes boilers for the turbines going up North. Look. When I'm leaving Israel I go first to Italy. Right away-bamm I'm working in Italy I'm speaking Italian like a native. Passing for a native."

"A native Jew," said his dark-haired friend.

"Listen to him. So in Rome they think I'm from Tyrol—that's still native, eh? So I speak Russian and German and Italian like a Jew. My Hebrew is bad, I admit it, but it's a lousy language anyway. Nobody likes it. French I understand but English I'm talking like a bum. Arabic I know five dialects. Danish fluent. So what's the matter I can't learn English?"

"It'll come, don't worry," Dyer smiled. *Don't worry, my son*; he wanted to pat him on the arm. "Anyway, that's what makes Canada so appealing. Here they don't force you."

"What's this *appealing*? Means nice? Look, my friend, keep it, eh? Two years in a country I don't learn the language means it isn't a country."

"Come on," said Dyer. "Neither does forcing you."

"Let me tell you a story why I come to Canada. Then you tell me if I was wrong, O.K.?"

"Certainly," said Dyer, flattered.

In Italy, Weinrot told him, he had lost his job to a Communist union. He left Italy for Denmark and opened up an Israeli restaurant with five other friends. Then the six Israelis decided to rent a bigger apartment downtown near the restaurant. They found a perfect nine-room place for two thousand kroner a month, not bad shared six ways. Next day the landlord told them the deal was off. "You tell me why," Weinrot demanded.

No Jews? Dyer wondered. "He wanted more rent," he finally said.

"More—you kidding? More we expected. *Less* we didn't expect. A couple with eight kids is showing up after we're gone and the law in Denmark says a man has a right to a room for each kid plus a hundred kroner knocked off the rent for each kid. What you think of that? So a guy who comes in *after* us gets a nine-room place for a thousand kroner *less*. Law says no way a bachelor can get a place ahead of a family, and bachelors pay twice as much."

Dyer waited, then asked, "So?"

"So, I make up my mind the world is full of communismus, just like Israel. So I take out applications next day for Australia, South Africa, U.S.A., and Canada. Canada says come right away, so I go. Should have waited for South Africa."

"How could you?" Dyer cried. "What's wrong with you anyway? South Africa is fascist. Australia is racist."

The bell rang, and the Israelis, with Dyer, began walking to the room.

"What I was wondering, then," said Mr. Weinrot, ignoring Dyer's outburst, "was if my English is good enough to be working in the United States. You're American, aren't you?"

It was a question Dyer had often avoided in Europe, but had rarely been asked in Montreal. "Yes," he admitted, "your English is probably good enough for the States or South Africa, whichever one wants you first."

He hurried ahead to the room, feeling that he had let Montreal down. He wanted to turn and shout to Weinrot and to all the others that Montreal was the greatest city on the continent, if only they knew it as well as he did. If they'd just break out of their little ghettos.

At the door, the Armenian girl with the half-glasses caught his arm. She was standing with Mrs. David and Miss Parizeau, a jolly French-Canadian girl that Dyer had been thinking of asking out.

"Please, sir," she said, looking at him over the tops of her tiny glasses, "what I was asking earlier—*put on*—I heard on the television. A man said *You are putting me on* and everybody laughed. I think it was supposed to be funny but *put on* we learned means get dressed, no?"

"Ah—*don't put me on*," Dyer laughed.

"I yaven't erd it neither," said Miss Parizeau.

"To put some*body* on means to make a fool of him. To put some*thing* on is to wear it. O.K.?" He gave examples.

"Ah, now I know," said Miss Parizeau. "Like bull-shitting somebody. Is it the same?"

"Ah, yes," he said, smiling. French Canadians were like children learning the language. "Your example isn't considered polite. 'Put on' is very common now in the States."

"Then maybe," said Miss Parizeau, "we'll ave it ere in twenty years." The Armenian giggled.

"No—I've heard it here just as often," Dyer protested, but the girls had already entered the room.

He began the second hour with a smile which slowly soured as he thought of the Israelis. America's anti-communism was bad enough, but it was worse hearing it echoed by immigrants, by Jews, here in Montreal. Wasn't there a psychological type who chose Canada over South Africa? Or was it just a matter of visas and slow adjustment? Did Johannesburg lose its Greeks, and Melbourne its Italians, the way Dyer's students were always leaving Montreal?

And after class when Dyer was again feeling content and thinking of approaching one of the Israelis for a restaurant tip, there came the flood of small requests: should Mrs. Papadopoulos go into a more advanced course; could Mr. Perez miss a week for an interview in Toronto; could Mr. Giguère, who spoke English perfectly, have a harder book; Mr. Côté an easier one?

Then as he packed his briefcase in the empty room, Miguel Mayor, the vain and impeccable Spaniard, came forward from the hallway.

"Sir," he began, walking stiffly, ready to bow or salute. He wore a loud, gray checkered sportscoat this evening, blue shirt, and matching ascot-handkerchief, slightly mauve. He must have shaved just before class, Dyer noticed, for two fresh daubs of antiseptic cream stood out on his jaw, just under his earlobe. He stepped closer. "Sir?"

"What's on your mind, then?"

"Please—have you the time to look on a letter for me?"

He laid the letter on the podium.

"Look *over* a letter," said Dyer. "What is it for?"

"I have applied," he began, stopping to emphasize the present perfect construction, "for a job in Cleveland, Ohio, and I want to know if my letter will be good. Will an American, I mean—"

"Why are you going there?"

"It's a good job."

"But Cleveland—"

"They have a blackman mayor, I have read. But the job is not in Cleveland."

"Let me see it."

Most honourable Sir: I humbly beg consideration for a position in your grand company . . .

"Who are you writing this to?"

"The president," said Miguel Mayor.

I am once a student of Dr. Ramiro Gutierrez of the Hydraulic Institute of Sevilla, Spain . . .

"Does the president know this Ramiro Gutierrez?"

"Oh, everybody is knowing him," Miguel Mayor assured, "he is the most famous expert in all Spain."

"Did he recommend this company to you?"

"No—I have said in my letter, if you look—"

An ancient student of Dr. Gutierrez, Salvador del Este, is actually a boiler expert who is being employed like supervisor is formerly a friend of mine . . .

"Is he still your friend?"

Whenever you say come to my city Miguel Mayor for talking I will be coming. I am working in Montreal since two years and am now wanting more money than I am getting here now . . .

"Well . . ." Dyer sighed.

"Sir—what I want from you is knowing in good English how to interview me by this man. The letters in Spanish are not the same to English ones, you know?"

I remain humbly at your orders . . .

"Why do you want to leave Montreal?"

"It's time for a change."

"Have you ever been to Cleveland?"

"I am one summer in California. Very beautiful there and hot like my country. Montreal is big port like Barcelona. Everybody mixed together and having no money. It is just a place to land, no?"

"Montreal? Don't be silly."

"I thought I come here and learn good English but where I work I get by in Spanish and French. It's hard, you know?" he smiled. Then he took a few steps back and gave his cuffs a gentle tug, exposing a set of jade cuff links.

Dyer looked at the letter again and calculated how long he would be correcting it, then up at his student. How old is he? My age? Thirty? Is he married? Where do the Spanish live in Montreal? He looks so prosperous, so confident, like a male model off a page of *Playboy*. For an instant Dyer felt that his student was mocking him, somehow pitting his astounding confidence and wardrobe, sharp chin, and matador's bearing against Dyer's command of English and mastery of the side streets, bistros, and ethnic restaurants. Mayor's letter was painful, yet he remained somehow competent. He would pass his interview, if he got one. What would he care about America, and the odiousness he'd soon be supporting? It was as though a superstructure of exploitation had been revealed, and Dyer felt himself abused by the very people he wanted so much to help. It had to end someplace.

He scratched out the second "humbly" from the letter, then folded the sheet of foolscap. "Get it typed right away," he said. "Good luck."

"Thank you, sir," said his student, with a bow. Dyer watched the letter disappear in the inner pocket of the checkered sportscoat. Then the folding of the cashmere scarf, the draping of the camel's-hair coat about the shoulders, the easing of the fur hat down to the rims of his ears. The meticulous filling of the pigskin gloves. Mayor's patent leather galoshes glistened.

"Good evening, sir," he said.

"*Buenas noches*," Dyer replied.

He hurried now, back down Sherbrooke Street to his daytime office where he could deposit his books. Montreal on a winter night was still mysterious, still magical. Snow blurred the arc lights. The wind was dying. Every second car was now a taxi, crowned with an orange crescent. Slushy curbs had hardened. The window of Holt Renfrew's was still attractive. The legless dummies invited a final stare. He stood longer than he had earlier, in front of the sporty mannequin with a burgundy waistcoat, the mauve and blue ensemble, the jade cuff links.

Good evening, sir, he could almost hear. The ascot, the shirt, the complete outfit, had leaped off the back of Miguel Mayor. He pictured how he must have entered the store with three hundred dollars and a prepared speech, and walked out again with everything off the torso's back.

I want that.

What, sir?

That.

The coat, sir?

Yes.

Very well, sir.

And *that.*

Which, sir?

All that.

"Absurd man!" Dyer whispered. There had been a moment of fear, as though the naked body would leap from the window, and legless, chase him down Sherbrooke Street. But the moment was passing. Dyer realized now that it was comic, even touching. Miguel Mayor had simply tried too hard, too fast, and it would be good for him to stay in Montreal until he deserved those clothes, that touching vanity and confidence. With one last look at the window, he turned sharply, before the clothes could speak again.

Details from the Canadian Mosaic

C.D. Minni

Mario dreamed of running barefoot across a beach to tell his grandfather, to tell him they were going to Canada. The old man sat in the lee of a red-brick church that stood half on the paving, half on the shore. He was mending his fishing nets, removing the weakened outer edges. The harbour shone like an oily green mirror; the town shone with whitewash and the bright awnings of shops . . .

He dreamed of baggage piled in the street, green trunks and bulging suitcases fastened with rope. He sat on one of the trunks, waiting. The house was crowded with relatives, friends and neighbours, but they did not miss him until later. "Mario? Where's Mario?" He was embraced, kissed, crushed, tears on his cheeks. It was time to go. The bus to Naples pulled out of the village square, down a street of vine-hung balconies and out along the rocky coast, north. Oleanders flowered blood-red in crags; below, the sea flashed an incredible blue. The bus passed nondescript towns like his own, olive groves, twisted railroad tracks, scars of war . . .

He dreamed of a ship, a Greek liner, and of how passengers in native costumes squatted in a circle on deck, clapping hands rhythmically, yelling, as one of them danced in their center. He was learning new words, passports, emigration, disembarkation . . . But then it seemed that he was, with the shifting quality of dreams, on a train rattling across frozen prairies where snow drifted, and he was celebrating his ninth birthday with his parents in the restaurant car . . .

He dreamed, but he woke to the shrill cry of gulls in a room surrounded by green trunks, and he remembered: the bus, the ship, the train. All of them now unreal as if he had indeed dreamed them. But he was here. Destination: one of his new words. He smelled coffee and heard voices downstairs.

One of the suitcases was open, and he saw that his mother had already laid out clean clothes for him. He dressed: knee trousers with stockings and a blue shirt, for today he was to sign up at school.

He went to the window and pushed up the sash. It was drizzling, and the wind blew from the Ocean. The Pacific, his teacher had called it on the last day. She had suspended the regular lesson and asked the class to take out their geography books and look up where Mario was going. Everyone was awed that he was going so far away.

Now, gulls circled against the grey sky, crying ruefully, sped seaward or alighted on warehouses and men's bunkhouses built on pilings over the shore. There was, he saw, scarcely space for a town on this inlet. The rain-beaten houses climbed the mountain-side in haphazard rows up to the forest's edge. Across the inlet was the pulp mill, where his father worked, its chimney belching out smoke. Men, carrying black lunchbuckets, were crossing over the wooden bridge. They reminded him of ants, each burdened with a grain of wheat.

In the street below, his small brother was already exploring the neighbourhood.

Mario went into the bathroom and drew water to wash. His mother came in and made him scrub his ears until they squeaked. She had prepared a big Canadian breakfast; these were their first real home meals, and they had sat down to it when his small brother ran inside in bewilderment.

"Hey, no one knows how to talk in this place!"

He looked so funny standing there that they could not help but laugh—at his turned-up nose, at his child's logic, at their own strangeness.

"Mario is going to school to learn," his father said and fetched their coats.

Only three weeks ago, in his native village, it was spring. Orange trees and roses bloomed in gardens behind stone houses. Now, here, in a yard daffodils pushed bravely through leftover snow, but the wind was cold. Mario turned up his coat collar as he followed his father through unfamiliar streets, past strange wood-frame houses, work of carpenters with hammer and nails.

Up ahead surrounded by a steel fence was the schoolyard. He heard shouting and the whack of a bat, but only weeks later knew the game was called baseball.

In the principal's office he waited, sitting, while registration papers were filled. The principal was a tall man with a polished dome of a head, and he motioned for the boy to follow him. Down a corridor. Up some stairs. Knocked on a door. Room number 6. A teacher with silver hair.

She introduced him to the class, a new student—from Italy. Some giggled, and for the first time he became conscious of his clothes. But he took an empty seat and received workbooks and pencils.

Some subjects he could do even on that first day—arithmetic, art, gym. Others puzzled him. At recess another boy showed him where the washroom was, then left. He was alone until the bell rang. He walked home alone. The teacher began to keep him in after school to learn English. By the time he left, the schoolyard was almost empty, except for a few boys. Usually the same boys.

Three of them came up to him one day, shouting: "Hey dummy! Cat got your tongue?" When he tried to run, they blocked his way, surrounding him. "Where'd ya get the funny getup, eh?" They began to pull at his clothes, and he heard his blue shirt rip. Then he was pushed, knocked down, kicked. He swore at them. "What say?"

"Aw, leave him alone," one said. He had red hair and blue jeans.

In that moment of distraction Mario stood up. The three were laughing at him as if at a joke, and this hurt him most. He threw his arithmetic book. It caught one of the boys in the face; blood gushed from his nose. The others seized him, one holding back his arms, another raising his fist. Mario saw the arm arch, the fist like a hammer, and before knowing it he had kicked with force, connecting with genitals. There was a yelp of pain as the boy buckled and clutched his pants. Mario, having twisted free, ran, his breath like a hot wire in his throat. When he looked back, they were staring after him.

C.D. Minni / 43

The next morning they were waiting for him. He brandished his arithmetic book as they surrounded him. One of them had red hair and blue jeans, and his face cracked into a grin as he extended a hand.

"Friends?" he said.

Were they his friends?

But they shook.

"Bruce," he said.

"Mario."

"Friends. OK?"

"OK."

His exploit had won him respect in the schoolyard. But on Saturday his father took him to the Bay store and bought him Canadian clothes, his first blue jeans. He wore them when he danced around the May pole and when he signed up for Little League baseball.

With his friend Bruce he explored the woods above the town, saw a black bear, competed and lost in the marbles championships, and fished off the wharf. He told Bruce that his grandfather was a fisherman.

"Ya? What'd he catch?"

"Everything. Octopus even."

"Really?"—with sudden interest.

"Sure. You eat octopus with bread and olives."

"Yetch!"

He asked Bruce where his grandparents lived.

"In the city," his friend said. "In a home."

"Home?"

"You know, for old folks."

He did not know. In his native village families were large, embracing uncles, cousins and especially grandparents. It puzzled him that there should be no old people in this town.

He had also made other discoveries. One: the pulp mill was the pulse of the town which adjusted to—or complained about—the rhythm of its changing work shifts. Two: his friends seemed to live on hot dogs, potato chips, peanut butter and Cokes. Three: though he was changing, his parents remained foreign. His mother especially needed protection. He became her companion and interpreter—at the store, the post office, the bank, even the church.

The school holidays had begun. The weather turned fine. Bruce asked him if they wanted to be best friends, and together they planned new adventures. They went cycling. They built a tree house where on the wings of imagination anything was possible. They made a raft and sailed it down the Mississippi. They never missed the Saturday twenty-cent matinee where they bought crackerjacks and candy bars, and they collected and traded comics—especially Superman and Batman—with the treasured DC sign.

His coach had told him that he had a good pitching arm, and he spent hours in the schoolyard developing his technique. The Giants were going to win the Little League trophy that year, and he was drawn into the excitement. The fans cheered when he walked to the pitcher's mound. They cheered Mike.

He did not know at what point he had become Mike. One day looking for a suitable translation of his name and finding none, he decided that Mike was closest. By the end of summer, he was Mario at home and Mike in the streets.

It was Mike who pitched a five-hitter for the Giants, Mike who in August watched the salmon run upstream to spawn and Mike who returned to school in September. At Christmas he received his first pair of skates and toque on his head, planned to learn hockey. When he dreamed, it was of Rocket Richard or three-speed bikes or a girl named Gwendolyn who sat behind him in Grade Five . . .

It is by luck that I find a parking place. There is a crowd. Children are running everywhere. Some line up at a truck that is dispensing free ice cream. Dignitaries, from the provincial and municipal governments, are shaking hands with leaders of the Italian-Canadian community. Speeches are made. Cameras click.

The sun is warm, and the park's sunken gardens are a riot of colours. There is music, accordions and mandolins, and a troupe in gay folk costumes is performing, twirling in a dance, linking arms, breaking and reforming. A kaleidoscope of colours and patterns.

The music, a sea-song, draws me like a hooked fish. It plays on the stereo of my memory. And I—Mike, Mario—am again running barefoot across the beach to the red-brick church where Grandfather is mending his nets.

He hooks his toes into the net, anchoring it to the ground, lifts a section with his left bronzed hand until the edge pulls tight and with his right hand rips away the line of cable and cork floats. Next, he cuts about a foot of the mesh behind the ripped edge, drops the net, lifts his foot, brings up another section of the edge and starts all over again. The strip of discarded mesh settles in a neat pile near his idle foot.

The Glass Roses

Alden Nowlan

Every night for six weeks the wind had risen to gale force as soon as the sun went down. Lying on his straw-filled bunk, Stephen heard it howl under the eaves of the bunkhouse, batter the tarpapered walls and make despondent, blowing sounds in the snow-weighted boughs of the spruces. He drew the dirty army blankets tighter under his chin. The sound alone was enough to make him shiver.

In the sooty obscurity of a gas lantern, four men played cards beside the pot-bellied wood stove. They were burly, red-faced men in wool work pants and checkered jackshirts. Each night since Stephen had joined the pulp-cutting crew, and through each of the days when snow kept them from work, they had played Auction 45's. Like everything else they did, their card playing was serious and purposeful. They spoke only when they made their bids. To Stephen, watching them from his upper bunk, it seemed they sat frozen for hours, moving only their hands. Enviously he studied their faintly humped backs and ox-like shoulders. He thought despairingly of his own willowy fifteen-year-old body. The more he observed the easy strength of these men, the oftener he worked himself into aching exhaustion at the end of a pulpsaw, the more certain he was that he could never become a man.

The huskiest and most solemn of the card players was the foreman of the crew of six who occupied the bunkhouse. This man was Stephen's father. "You got to start actin' like a man if you want to hold down a man's job," he had warned. "There ain't no room for kids in the pulp woods." The boy winced, remembering the too-familiar squint of doubt, the hard knots of disappointment above the cold grey eyes.

A gust shook the camp and made the white flame of the lantern flicker. Beside him in the bunk, the Polack stirred, moaning, in his sleep. Stephen raised himself on an elbow and shook his shoulder. With a muffled groan he jerked awake.

"I guess you was havin' a nightmare," Stephen whispered.

The Polack ran his fingers through his dishevelled hair.

"Yes."

His eyes, which seemed to focus on the other side of the room, were so bleak with fear that Stephen swung around and looked in the same direction. He saw only the greasy, unbarked slabs of the wall.

The Polack chuckled. He had such nightmares almost every night, but the fear seemed to leave him as soon as he was wholly awake. "It is strange, the things one remembers," he murmured.

As they always did, Stephen and the Polack spoke too low for the others to hear. In talking with the others, the Polack garbled his sentences as though his mouth were full of cotton wool. Stephen had stood speechless with astonishment when, on their second day as partners at the edge of the northwest clearing, he had first heard him speak English coherently.

"Yeah?" Stephen invited. His fascination with tales of far places had attracted him to the Polack. But he felt that his interest in such stories was childish: an aspect of the boyish daydreaming that he was expected to scorn now that he was becoming a man. Apprehensively he glanced over the edge of the bunk to assure himself that none of the others overheard.

The Polack lay back on the sour-smelling pillows and gazed at the newspaper-lined ceiling.

His voice made Stephen's flesh tingle as at the approach of sleep.

"In our house in Tarnopol, there were glass roses. Pretty little flowers made of red glass. My mother was very proud of them. She would let no one touch them. . . . When the first bombs fell, farther down the street, the glass roses were shaken from the mantel and they fell on the floor and broke in a million pieces." He raised himself on his elbows to roll a cigarette. "That is a very silly thing for one to remember."

Stephen thought for a long moment. "I don't think it's silly," he said.

"There is not much room in the world for glass roses," the Polack said gently, blowing purple tobacco smoke toward the ceiling.

The card players rose from their benches. One by one they went outdoors to urinate. Each time the door opened, Stephen's flesh goose-pimpled in the clutch of the cold. His father and the others grunted and spat in the stove, then pulled off their boots and pants and climbed into their bunks. The last man extinguished the lantern. In the darkness Stephen thought of glass roses and listened to the wail of the ten-below-zero wind.

The cook, whose quarters were separated from the bunkhouse by a partition of rough boards, woke the men at five-thirty. After eating their breakfast of pork and pancakes by lanternlight, they gathered up their saws and axes and started in pairs for their various stations in the woods. The first mustard-coloured streaks of daylight were appearing on the black-forested, snow-shrouded horizon.

The wind had fallen somewhat, but it was still raw enough to lacerate Stephen's temples. The cold gnawed at his legs and forced watery mucus from his nostrils. Head down, he walked beside the Polack in the deep-rutted logging road.

"Sometimes I think this country does not like people," the Polack shouted above the wind.

Stephen laughed, almost in embarrassment. The Polack was the only foreigner he had ever known, and he often said things no ordinary pulp-cutter would have dreamt of saying.

"Or perhaps it is only that God made this country to teach man humility," the Polack yelled, his voice a flapping wisp in the wind.

Stephen laughed again. As they went deeper into the woods, great spruce and fir trees broke the force of the wind. In a way, Stephen reflected, it was fun to be with the Polack. When he worked with the other men, they spoke only when it was necessary to give commands or criticism. But he knew his father despised the Polack and he suspected that they had been consigned together as the crew's clumsiest and weakest members.

The day's work began. Stephen chopped a notch in a spruce. Each time his axe struck the tree, showers of snow poured from the branches and sifted down his neck. Twice he misjudged his stroke and hit the trunk with the handle, the shock of it burning his wrists. The axe made him feel stupid and ridiculous. It did not belong to him. He could not think of himself as a woodsman. In using the axe, he was pretending to be something he was not, something he might never be. When his father worked an axe, it was as though the blade grew out of his arm.

He and the Polack took hold of opposite ends of the saw and knelt by the tree. On the first stroke Stephen exerted too much pressure and the blade buckled.

"You try too hard, kid," the Polack murmured. "You act as if the saw were the most important thing in the world."

"Maybe."

"The world would not come to an end if it took us all day to cut this one tree down."

"I guess not."

Stephen decided glumly that foreigners did not know when to keep their mouths shut. The Polack grinned. Purring, the saw sank slowly into the frozen wood.

As they cut deeper, the weight of the tree lay heavy on the blade. Stephen closed his eyes, the better to concentrate on the effort of bringing the saw back each time the Polack pulled it away from him. He thought of the dozens of trees they would have to fell before the end of the day, the millions of trees he would have to fell before he died. For as long as he lived, he would kneel beside a tree, a slave to the monotonous rhythm of the pulpsaw.

"Gently, now, gently," the Polack admonished.

"Look, I don't need no advice," Stephen gritted. "You take care of your end of the saw and I'll look after mine. Okay?"

The Polack grinned again. After ten minutes of sawing, the tree creaked like a dry hinge and gave away. Snow rose like the smoke of an explosion when it struck the ground.

They chopped off limbs and sawed the tree into four-foot lengths. "I'm sorry I made you angry," the Polack said.

Stephen blinked and looked away. In his world, men did not tender apologies.

"It don't matter," he mumbled.

"Today when we eat lunch I will tell you about Cracow."

"Cracow," Stephen said, liking the sound of the word.

"Cracow," the Polack repeated.

He paused for a moment before completing his saw stroke.

"Once I was there and saw the cathedral."

Stephen let go of the saw and beat his mittened hands together. "What was it like—the cathedral?"

"Very beautiful. You would like to hear about it, eh?"

"Yes," Stephen said, feeling a little twinge of guilt. He was a man now. Men did not tell one another fairy tales about cathedrals. But his father and the men at the bunkhouse need never know—

"I was only eight years old when I saw Cracow. My oldest brother was in the cavalry. He had red things on his shoulders—epaulettes—and he wore a sabre. That day there was a parade for the president." The Polack sighed. "He was killed on the first day of the war, my brother. They were very pretty, but not much good against tanks, those cavalrymen."

"Sabres," Stephen said, "Jesus." He was thinking of the yelling, sabre-wielding horsemen he had seen in movies. The Polack ran his hand through thick black hair.

"Now we must get back to work," he said. "At noon I will tell you about the cathedral."

For a few minutes they sawed in silence.

"Look," Stephen stammered suddenly.

"Yes, what should I look at, eh?"

"Oh, I don't mean, look. I mean, well, I'm sorry I got mad at you."

He flushed, feeling childish and ludicrous, wishing he had kept his mouth shut.

"We are friends then?"

"Yeah."

Convinced that he had been guilty of a babyish weakness, Stephen began sawing furiously.

By noon their sandwiches were frozen as hard as cedar shingles. Squatting behind a windbreak of logs, they speared them on slivers of pine and held them over a small fire until they were fried in the fat of margarine and bologna. They drank boiled tea out of tin mugs without removing their mittens.

As they ate, the Polack talked of an ancient city and of a cathedral with spires and domes. He told of bearded, black-robed priests and of chanting monks and of altar boys who carried burning incense through the streets during holy-day processions. Stephen sat enthralled, scarcely noticing the Canada Jays, white and mouse-grey like the colour of winter, though they flew almost close enough to snatch the food from his hands.

"I was very small then," the Polack said. "I was nine when the Russians came to Tarnopol. When the Germans came, I was twelve."

Stephen chewed sizzling bologna. "I'd like to see Poland," he said. "I'd like to see Poland and France and Italy. I'd like—" He left the sentence unfinished. He was not certain what he felt.

The Polack moved closer to the fire. The evergreens bowed, as though in resignation, before the wind. "I am not Polish," he said. "I am Ukrainian."

"You ain't a Polack then?" Stephen asked in bewilderment.

The Polack shrugged. "Yesterday the Ukrainians were called Poles. Today they are called Russians. Me, I am either a Polack or a Canadian."

For a few minutes they ate in silence.

"My name is Leka," the Polack said abruptly.

"Leka," Stephen repeated.

"Now I think we had better forget about the cathedrals and begin to think of the pulpwood. Your father, the foreman, says we cut the least of any pair of choppers in the woods."

"Yeah, I know," Stephen said bitterly.

Suddenly the Polack reached out and pinched the boy's cold-reddened cheek.

"Don't be so sad, little one," he smiled.

Stephen stood up and kicked snow over the fire.

"Tomorrow perhaps I will tell you about Wiesbaden."

"Wiesbaden, is that in Poland?"

"Wiesbaden is in Germany. During the war I worked there: making hand grenades for the Germans. Every April we were given a holiday in honour of Hitler's birthday." The Polack laughed. "When the planes came, the British and Americans, we used to hope some of their bombs would hit the factory. But they never did."

The Polack smiled at Stephen as though in some mysterious way he were pitying him, rather than himself.

"No, I don't think I want to talk about Wiesbaden. I will tell you more about Tarnopol and my mother's glass roses. It is better to talk about things like that." The Polack rolled a cigarette and scratched a match on the zipper of his windbreaker.

"The roses that got smashed," Stephen said.

"Eh? Yes, the roses that got smashed." He picked up his axe and selected a tree. "They were very pretty, those little glass roses, I need only close my eyes and I can see them."

"But they got smashed," Stephen insisted.

The Polack's axe thudded home. "In the morning, when the sun came up, the first little shafts of light would strike those roses. You see, the mantel was opposite the window. Yes, they were very beautiful. . . ."

The tree notched, Stephen fetched the pulpsaw. The Polack spat out his cigarette and knelt opposite him. Stephen shut his eyes and forced the blade into the obdurate wood.

"Gently, now, gently," the Polack counselled.

Now there was neither time nor energy for talk. By mid-afternoon Stephen slumped and staggered with weariness. Dull pains nagged his shoulders, hips and calves. But more crushing than the weariness was the conviction that he was a weakling. He could not believe that his father, or any of the other choppers, knew tiredness such as his. Sometimes he wondered if he suffered from a wasting disease. He almost hoped that this was so, for then his weakness would be thought less shameful.

With darkness settling around them, they trudged back to the camp. Only pride kept Stephen from throwing himself down as soon as he entered the bunkhouse. Noticing his father's sharp, searching look, he clenched his teeth and straightened.

The men washed their hands and faces in cold water, then filed into the cookhouse. As always the room smelled of fat and boiled tea. The choppers winked at one another as the Polack crossed himself before beginning on his hard-boiled eggs and fried potatoes.

"Guess the Polack don't trust you," one of the men said to the cook.

The cook did not smile. Like most woods cooks, he frowned on conversation at the table. The Polack gave no sign that he heard. Meeting his father's eyes, Stephen grinned guiltily.

When the choppers had finished their dessert of stewed prunes and drained their coffee mugs, they shuffled back to the bunkhouse. They sat on benches beside the stove and rolled their after-supper cigarettes. Stephen's father pulled on his mackinaw. "Come out here a minute will you, Stephen?" he growled. "I want you to give me a hand with something."

"Yeah, sure." He leapt to his feet, then looked around in embarrassment: he did not want the men to notice the nervous alacrity with which he responded to his father's commands. After all, he was no little boy to be cowed into obedience. Putting on his windbreaker and cap, he followed his father into the night.

The man stood in the shelter of the tool shed. The world was a maelstrom of darkness and wind.

"I wanted to talk to you alone for a minute."

"Sure."

"You seem to be gettin' awful chummy with that Polack," his father declared abruptly.

"Huh?" Stephen gaped in astonishment. The wind striped his back like an alder switch. "He ain't no special friend of mine," he said, not sure whether or not he lied.

"Some of the men's laughin' about him pattin' and pokin' you. I don't like to hear anybody laughin' at my son."

It wasn't true. The Polack did not "pat and poke" him. Then, uneasily, he recalled that the Polack often *did* pinch his cheek or throw an arm across his shoulder. Usually he was only half-aware of these gestures. His father fidgeted when he had to shake hands. But little casual caresses were part of the Polack's speech.

"Them Wops and Bohunks and Polacks has gotta lotta funny ideas. They ain't our kinda people. You gotta watch them."

"Yeah." The wind hurled pellets of frozen snow against his face.

"If he bothers you, let me know and I'll kick the guts outta him."

"Yeah."

"This work ain't too hard for you, is it?"

He wants me to quit, Stephen thought. He wants to shame me into quitting.

"No, it ain't too hard for me. Not by a God damn sight."

"Don't be afraid of hard work. Work never killed nobody."

"No, I guess it never did," Stephen said, shivering.

"Just make that Polack keep his hands off you."

"Yeah."

"I've seen fellers like him before."

"Yeah."

"Well, we better go in. It's cold enough to break the stones."

Inside, Stephen climbed into his bunk. In a little while the Polack climbed in beside him. Eyeing him dubiously, Stephen edged away until his back pressed against the cold, splintery beams where the wall joined the ceiling. The card players went to their seats by the stove. Before the first game was finished, the Polack fell asleep. The wind howled until Stephen expected it to wrench the roof from the camp. When the Polack began to tremble and moan, Stephen hesitated for a long time before he reached out to wake him.

School, the First Day

Barbara Sapergia

The hard wood pressed against his knees, the desk was made for a child. Doamne!* It must be nearly time to go home. His muscles were stiff from sitting so long, and he ached to stand and stretch them.

There wasn't enough air to breathe. The school had been closed up all summer, and the open windows hadn't cleared out the stuffy smell of varnish and dust. A breeze from the window reached him, and he smelled the sweet sage and grass. Already Nicu saw himself walking home across the hills, leaving the school behind. He thought of the dark stallion running free across the hills.

The desk was built for a child, and he was almost a man. He ran his fingers over the desk top. He didn't like the feel of the wood, stained dark so you couldn't see the grain through the thick varnish. It felt tacky against his fingers, as if it had never been cleaned from the years of sticky fingers. Someone had carved letters into the wood, and he traced these with his finger. He didn't know what the letters meant.

Tata said they were lucky to live near a school. This was Sweet Grass School, the oldest school in the badlands, except for the school in Coteau.

He couldn't remember ever being so hungry. It felt like the sides of his stomach were pressing together, trying to get something to work on. He saw himself walking, fast, over the hills. He was angry, he wanted to leave this school. He didn't understand anything. All day he'd watched the teacher writing on the big slate on the wall at the front of the room, and he hadn't learned a thing.

Doamne: my goodness.

He was the biggest boy in the school. Except for Jame
John Chisholm, Margaret's brothers. They didn't want her to
to him. She smiled at him once, but they didn't like it. ⌐
Chisholm boys didn't look like Margaret at all. They were sand
haired and barrel-chested like their father and their faces already
had a set, suspicious cast like his. John was the older one, about
seventeen years old, but James was louder and stronger. They
laughed when Nicu made mistakes in English.

Luba didn't seem to understand anything either. She was afraid
to answer the teacher. Miss Scrimshaw had asked Luba what was
her name. "I have fifteen year," she had answered. All the
children laughed, and Nicu's face burned with shame. "I asked
what is your name, what are you *called*?" the teacher said. Then
Luba understood, and told the teacher her name. The Chisholm
boys snickered, as if there was something wrong with the name.

He would have to get up soon, his back was getting so stiff. It
must be nearly time. The teacher stood at the front of the room,
leading the grade fours and fives in their reading. They would
stand up and read in turn from a little book. It made no sense to
him at all. Nicu's desk was at the very back of the room, along the
windows. He stared out the window, at the hills outside, the little
barn beside the school, the wooden toilets.

In the middle of the morning, the teacher let them go outside
to play. For a moment he had thought it was lunch time, but no,
not yet. It was called *re-cess*. That was when they found the toilets.
He hadn't known there would be two, but he saw all the girls
went to one place, all the boys to another.

At recess they played ball. On what looked like a big square
worn into the grass, but was called a diamond. You tried to hit a
ball with a big round stick called a bat. If you hit the ball, you ran
around the diamond. The corners were called first base, second
base, and third base, and you could stop at any one of them. If
you made it back to where you started, then you were home. His
first turn at bat, Nicu swung three times without hitting the ball.
This meant he was out. A little girl had gone out before him, so
he knew what it was, thank God. Knew enough to put the bat
down and take the little girl's place in the field out past third base.

Then Margaret hit the ball over second base. Nicu was ashamed that she could do it and he couldn't. Then it was Luba's turn, and she also managed to hit the ball, but it only dribbled along the grass, and she was put out too. The tall red-haired girl who took the bat next patted Luba's arm and spoke to her. She was called Beryl Langford, and she didn't laugh at foreigners.

Then James Chisholm was up. Nicu watched the way he planted his feet, the way he held his arms and shoulders, as he made practice swings with the bat. Then the ball shot towards him, and James swung with all his force, hitting the ball far past the fielders. A little boy in denim overalls ran down the hill after it, while James ran all around the diamond. This was called a home run.

Finally it was Nicu's turn again, and this time he was sure he could do it. He saw that James Chisholm was throwing the ball to him, and frowned. James had changed places with another boy. He stood talking with his brother until the other children yelled at them to get going, then they both laughed, and James got ready to throw.

The first pitch was too high, but Nicu wanted to hit so badly that he swung wildly at it and missed. He got ready again, planting his feet and swinging the bat. James took his time getting ready to throw, then the ball was whizzing straight at Nicu's face, and he stepped back and half turned. The ball caught him hard on the shoulder. He fought to hold back tears of pain and anger. He wanted to rush right over and fight with James, but he couldn't.

"James!" Margaret was yelling. "You be careful!"

Nicu got ready to hit again, trying to forget the throbbing in his shoulder. This time the ball came fast, but it was right across the plate. He was ready, he hit it as hard as he could. There was a loud crack and pains shooting up in his arms. He had actually broken the bat. James had caught the weak hit and thrown it to first before Nicu could drop the shattered stub of the bat. And then the bell was ringing, calling them back to school, and he was so ashamed.

All the students were put in grades, according to how much they knew. Margaret and her brothers were in grade twelve, the highest grade. Her brothers must be two or three years older than her, why were they all in the same grade?

When it came time to put him and Luba into grades, Nicu could hardly look up. He knew nothing of the things that were taught here. Even the littlest children knew more. But the teacher just said they wouldn't decide right away. "We'll wait and see how you do." Maybe they could learn really fast. But how? He wanted to scream. How could he learn fast if he didn't even know what the teacher was talking about? He didn't want to look stupid in front of Margaret Chisholm. Better to quit.

Who needed to know these things anyway? He could do a man's work already. Maybe he couldn't do things with numbers, but he knew how many sheep they had, how many lambs. Why did he need to know those other things? His learning was in his hands, his learning was from Tata.

Maica Domnolui,* it must be nearly time to go home. He was so hungry his stomach was hurting, and he hadn't even done any work today. They'd had mamaliga* and cold lamb for lunch, but that seemed like ages ago. The other children had stared at the mamaliga. "*Mush!*" one little girl had said and giggled. Christ, he didn't care what the teacher said, he was going to have to get up, he couldn't stand it a moment longer.

Then children were walking past his desk towards the door, moving all together as if someone had given them a signal. They were all talking at once. School was over! Luba looked at him hesitantly, afraid to get out of her desk. He got up, nodding at her to do the same. All his muscles felt stiff and shrunken, and he stretched them to make sure they would still work. They followed the other children out of the school while the teacher stood at the front of the room, wiping the writing off the big slate.

It felt so good to be in the moving air again, to feel his legs striding under him. He wanted to walk as fast as he could, to get home again almost before he could think about it. He had never thought about time before. Now he knew that a day is a very long time. Tata had bought a small clock from Coteau, so they would know the time to leave for school. It stood on the table in the living room, making a loud ticking noise.

Maica Domnolui: mother of God. Mamaliga: cornmeal mush.

When they walked into the kitchen, there was mama making supper as usual, and Gheorghe sleeping in his cradle. Nicu felt happy just seeing them. It seemed a very long time since he'd left in the morning. Mama looked worried, as if she expected that already they would be changed by the things they had learned. As if they had gone into a world where she could never follow. Tata was coming up from the barn. He came into the kitchen too, and smiled at them. He looked so nice standing there, that Nicu wanted to put his arms around Tata and hug him. But he better tell him right away.

"I'm not going to school any more, Tata," he said, trying to speak firmly, like a man.

"Oh," said Tata, "and why is this?" Luba just watched him. She was helping mama, who was frying the little pancakes spread with jam to eat after their cabbage rolls. Nicu could see the finished ones on a plate in the warming oven, and he longed to grab one and gulp it down.

"Because it is of no use to me," Nicu replied. "And I'm too far behind. Even the little children know more than I do." Everyone watched him.

"You are sure it is of no use to you?" Tata asked.

"Yes, I'm sure. I can do a man's work already."

"No." Tata spoke very quietly. "You're wrong."

"But I can work!"

"In this country it is very important for people to read and write. That is how everything is done here."

"But Tata—"

"Listen to me! Everything you do here, you must have a paper. A paper to come into this country, a paper to be born, a paper to get married. A paper to show who owns land, and who owns houses, and horses. If you cannot read papers, everyone will cheat you!" Tata did not say, you have to have a paper when someone dies, but Nicu remembered.

"But Tata, they laugh at us! They laugh at how we talk."

Tata looked sad. "Listen. You know I won't force you. But I'll tell you something. I left the old country. In our old village there, no one knows how to read or write, or count things on paper. Only the priest. We have to pay the priest to help us."

"Then a man came to our village. In Canada, he says, all children can go to school. Me, I don't know. It's too late. But if you will just learn now, my children, then we will all know. Your children will know, and their children. Our family will never be ignorant again." Nicu could not speak. "I'm telling you, Nicu, a man who wants to take care of himself, he has to know how to read."

Nicu knew Tata was remembering Trian. He had no answer.

"Luba," Tata said, "you don't like school either?"

"No."

"But will you try for a little while?"

"Yes, Tata, for a little while."

"And Nicu? You will try too?"

"All right," Nicu said. "I will try too."

Hunky

Hugh Garner

I t was a hot August morning. The sun, still low against the horizon, was a white-hot stove lid that narrowed the eyes into slits and made the sweat run cold along the spine. The sky was as high and blue as heaven, and the shade-giving cumulus wouldn't form until noon. Before us lay the serried rows of tobacco plants, armpit high and as dull green as bile. Along with Hunky and the other members of the priming gang I sat in the grass at the edge of the Ontario field waiting for the stoneboat to arrive from the farmyard. The noise of the tiny tractor coming down the dusty track from the yard hid the scratching sound of the grasshoppers in the hedge.

Hunky, to give him the name he called himself, was the gang's pace-setter and also my room-mate in the disused tool shed where we bunked. He sat in the grass, effortlessly touching the toes of his sneakers with the palms of his hands, a redundant exercise considering the limbering up we were getting from our work in the fields. Hunky was proud of his physique, and had a bug about physical fitness, and he practised every evening with a set of weights he had put together from an old Ford front axle with the wheels attached. He believed in health and strength as some believe in education. He had said to me on my first evening at the farm, 'Me, I'm a poor D.P. No brains, only strong back. Keep strong, always find job.' There was enough truth in his philosophy to make me feel a little ashamed of my own softness, but even more ashamed of the education and training I'd thrown away over the years.

When Kurt arrived on the tractor, he pulled the boat with its high boxed sides into the aisle between the fourth and fifth rows of the new field. When he glanced back at us we got to our feet, my protesting muscles and sinews stiff from the twelve hours of disuse that bridged the time between the morning and the evening before. Without a word we walked to our rows and crouched between them, tearing off the sand leaves like destructive ants, and cradling them in the crook of our other arm. We shuffled ahead on our haunches through a world suddenly turned to jungle, along a sandy aisle that promised an ephemeral salvation at the other end of the field.

Hunky was soon several yards ahead of me, his gilded shoulders bobbing and weaving two rows away, his crewcut nodding up and down between the plants. When he crossed my aisle on his way to the stoneboat he would give me an encouraging wink. The pride he felt in his speed and skill was apparent in his stride and in the way he flaunted his wide armful of green and yellowing leaves before the straw boss, Kurt. At the opposite side of the tractor, McKinnon, Frenchy Coté, and Old Man Crumlin were farther back than Hunky and I. Kurt fidgeted on the tractor seat, trying to hurry them with angry glances when he caught their eye.

When I reached the end of my rows Hunky was stretched out in the shade of the tobacco, his head resting in the sand. With an indolent finger he was tracing the rivulets of sweat that ran along his throat. When he saw me he sat up.

'You do good for new man, George,' he said.

'Yeah,' I answered, throwing myself on the grass.

'You come to farm too late this summer. Better to be here for suckerin'. Taking suckers first make it better to prime after. Loose up muscles,' he said. He stretched out an arm that showed the mice running under the chocolate tan of his skin.

'I think you're right, Hunky.'

'How many years are you, George?'

'Forty-five at the last count.'

He shook his head solemnly. 'Priming is young man's job. How you get job with Vandervelde?'

'The usual way. From the slave market in Simcoe.'

'Why you take job on tobacco, George?'

I didn't want to go into that. My domestic and financial fall from grace would have taken all morning to tell. 'I needed the money.'

'Yes,' he said soberly. Then he brightened up. 'How old is Hunky, George?'

I pushed myself up on an elbow and looked him over. 'I'd say twenty-four, twenty-five.'

'Twenty-t'ree, George. Born nineteen and t'irty-five.' Then proudly, 'I got papers.'

I smiled and lay down again. I thought of the rows upon rows still to be primed of sand leaves, the lowest leaves on the plant. After the sand leaves were gone the work would become easier, as we harvested the leaves higher and higher on the stalk. It was a promise that kept me going almost as much as my desperate need of the money.

'Time to go, George,' Hunky said, getting up.

I stood up as Kurt disengaged the tractor from the loaded stoneboat, hitched on to an empty one that had been waiting at the end of the field, and pulled it into an aisle midway between the next ten rows. He waited impatiently until the five of us began working again, then rehitched the tractor to the loaded boat and drove back towards the yard, where the leaf-handlers and tyers were waiting.

Hunky was right; priming tobacco is a young man's job. This was my third day at the Vandervelde farm, and I was surprised I had lasted so long. The beginning of each day was a torture that became an aching hell by evening. Fifteen years of losing jobs on newspapers is no training for manual labour. Though I was sweating heavily, I could no longer smell the exuded alcohol, which was something I was glad of.

At noon hour Mrs. Vandervelde banged the stick around the brake-drum to call us to dinner, and we stumbled up the dusty road, following the tractor and stoneboat to the house. Hunky ran ahead as he always did, to shower under the crude pipe that was rigged behind the kilns. As I passed I could see him behind the gunny sack curtains, his face raised into the guttering stream of water. I just washed my hands.

The table was set out in the yard, under the shade of an oak tree. The two male tyers, and the woman leaf-handlers, Frenchy Coté's wife and another French Canadian girl, were already eating. I don't know too much about Belgian cooking, but the Vandervelde farm was not the place to make a study of it. We had boiled beef again for the third straight day, with boiled turnips and potatoes. Marie Vandervelde, the eighteen-year-old daughter of the farmer, strained against her dress as she ladled the food onto our plates. We swallowed it as fast as we could, before the flies could beat us to it.

Hunky came to the table in a minute or two, the water running out of his hair and forming glycerine drops on his shoulders. Marie rubbed against him as she filled his plate. He gave her a shy smile, then disregarded the flies as he bowed his head and crossed himself before he ate. There were plates of doughnuts under cheesecloth covers, but I settled for a mug of coffee. My admiration for Hunky was slightly soured with envy. I wished I'd had a son like him, if I'd had a son. I couldn't even remember ever being as young and healthy myself.

The Vanderveldes, the North Carolina tobacco curer called Joe, and Kurt Gruenther, all ate in the kitchen; the rest of us ate in the yard unless it was raining. As we sipped our second coffee, smoked, and talked together in either English or French, Maurice Vandervelde came through the kitchen doorway and walked down the slope of the yard to the table.

'Kurt tells me you're not getting all the sand leaves,' he said.

All the primers but Hunky looked up at him.

'From now on I want every leaf primed,' he said, standing there with his hands on his fat hips like a Belgian burgomaster. 'Crumlin, and you too Taylor,' he said, looking at me. 'I want every leaf. You can go over the rows again after supper. I want them plants stripped.'

'No leafs left on plants,' Hunky said, fixing the boss with his eye. He took an insolent bite of doughnut and washed it down with coffee.

Vandervelde stared down at him, while two white spots appeared on his cheeks. He said, 'I didn't say nothing about *your* rows.'

Hunky asked, 'Why Kurt not say nothing in the field?'

They remained facing each other for a long minute, held apart by something more than fear or respect. 'Don't forget what I told you,' Maurice said, then swung around on his heel and walked back to the house.

Before we started priming in the afternoon, Hunky walked to the tractor and had a long argument in German with Kurt. Kurt got down from the machine and followed Hunky along the rows we'd primed that morning. When they came back, Hunky was carrying ten or twelve limp yellow leaves. He threw them into the boat with an angry gesture, before disappearing into the tobacco and beginning work.

Nothing was said about the priming at supper, and Maurice stayed in the house. The men each took a shower behind the kilns, and the two French Canadian girls were allowed to use the bath in the house because it was Saturday night. After my shower I put my shorts and extra shirt to soak in a pail. Then I lay on my bunk with the shed door open, watching Hunky lifting his weights in the yard. I heard the laughing chatter of the two girls as they got into Frenchy's car, then watched it pull down the road in the direction of Simcoe with Frenchy at the wheel.

Hunky showered and shaved, then took his white shirt and beige-coloured slacks from the hanger beneath his jacket.

'You stayin' here, George?' he asked.

'Yeah, Hunky. I think I'll stay away from towns for a while.'

'You want a couple of dollars, George?' he asked. 'I go now to get my money up at house.'

'No thanks. I've got enough for tobacco and papers for next week. That's all I need.'

'Hokay. See you Monday morning. You feel good by Monday, you see, George.' He laughed.

'I want to thank you for what you did today. If it hadn't been for you, Crumlin and I would have had to go over our rows tonight.'

'Was nothing, George. Gruenther try to make trouble, is all. He not make trouble for Hunky though. No siree, not for Hunky.' We both laughed at the preposterous thought.

'Are you going away for the weekend?' I asked.

'Sure t'ing. Go to Delhi. Stay with Polish family. Go to church.' He pulled a small book from his pocket and showed it to me. The printing was in Polish, but it was half-filled with columns of figures and weekly dates. Most of the figures were for small amounts of money, and it showed a total of $350. 'Polish people credit union,' he explained. 'After save for couple years, buy tobacco farm. Tonight I put in fifty dollars, make four hundred, eh, George?'

'You're a rich man, Hunky.'

'No important, George. More better to be healthy, eh?' He laughed, slapped me on the shoulder, and left the shed. I watched him take his old bicycle from the barn and wheel it to the house. He disappeared inside for a few minutes, then came out and rode away in the direction of Delhi.

The slight evening breeze dropped with the setting of the sun. McKinnon and Crumlin, who bunked in the barn, dropped by to ask me if I wanted anything from the crossroads store about a mile down the road. I gave McKinnon enough money to get me a package of makings, but turned down their invitation to accompany them.

After a while I gave up trying to feel sorry for myself, and thinking how stupid I'd been to end up this way, priming tobacco. I got up and walked across the yard. In the dark the farm had the shadowed realism of a stage set, the big frame house with its windbreak of poplars, the oak tree dominating the yard, the barn, and greenhouse and, behind them, the five tall kilns. Numbers 1, 2 and 3 were belching oily smoke from their chimneys as the tobacco slowly cured.

As I circled the house, listening to the cicadas in the poplars and the cadenced beep of a predatory nighthawk somewhere in the darkening sky above, I heard Maurice shouting inside the house. I was too far away to hear the words, or even understand the language, but I could see the fat form of the boss through the livingroom window, pointing a finger at Marie and shouting. Kurt was standing against the door wearing a self-satisfied smirk. Mrs. Vandervelde was remonstrating with her husband, and holding him by the arm. I knew they were discussing Hunky. I turned around and walked towards the kilns.

Joe the curer was sitting in a tilted chair propped against No. 4 kiln, listening to a hillbilly program on his portable radio. He was mumbling to himself and keeping time with his feet. He nodded to me but said nothing. In a moment or two Kurt Gruenther came from the direction of the house, said hello to Joe but not to me, and bent over and peered into the fire-box of No. 3. He spent most of his evenings around the kilns, ambitious to become a curer himself. I went back to the tool shed.

It was some time later when I heard the screen door bang at the house. I looked through the doorway of the shed and saw young Marie come out on the porch and stand there crying. She was soon joined by Kurt, and the two of them sat together on the porch steps. Once, I heard her giggle, and I knew that her tears when her father had been shouting at her had been protective ones.

She wasn't the girl Hunky should think of marrying, but who was I to think of anything like that? What she did when Hunky was away was her own business. I'd woke up a couple of times in the late evening and found Hunky missing from his bunk, and once I'd seen him returning from the fields with Marie. I mused on the thought that the affairs of the young are the envies of the middle-aged. I got undressed and climbed beneath the blanket.

During the next week we finished the sand leaves, and began priming higher up on the plants. Almost imperceptibly the pain and stiffness of the first few days disappeared. I found myself even looking forward to the meals, which showed me my physical cure was almost complete. Sometimes I went most of the day without thinking of a drink.

The weather held good for priming. There was a heavy dew in the morning, which evaporated shortly after we reached the fields. All the day the scorching sun burned down on the tobacco, tinting the sea-green leaves with lighter hues, yellowing their edges and bringing them to ripeness. Midway during the morning and afternoon Marie came out to the field, carrying a pail of barley water and a dipper, which she set down at the end of the rows. Kurt always stepped down from the tractor to talk to her and take the first drink. The girl laughed a little too loudly at his jokes, her eye roving down the aisle where Hunky was working. After she had stretched her stay as long as she could she would walk back towards the house, her step a little less hurried than when she came.

In the early evenings Hunky and I generally sat on the steps of the shed and talked. He told me about his childhood, which wasn't a childhood at all, but had been spent on a German farm during the war. I knew from hints he dropped that his parents had been put to death in the gas chambers in a German concentration camp. From things he told me I came to realize that physical fitness and strength were not youthful fads with him, but were the legacy of a time when to be weak or ill meant death.

His ambitions were the modest ones of most immigrants: to buy a place of his own, marry, and have children. He placed great stress on the fact that he hoped to become a Canadian citizen in the fall. His longing for citizenship was not only gratitude and patriotism towards the country that had given him asylum, but a craving for status as a recognized human being.

He seemed very thoughtful one evening, and finally he said, 'I never know the good life, George.'

'Some of us never do, Hunky.'

'After October things change though, eh? I have Canadian passport then, eh, George.'

'Sure. You'll be okay then.'

'I never before have passport. Never.'

He reached into the inside pocket of his jacket hanging on the wall and pulled out a piece of folded paper, its folds blackened from constant opening and its outside surfaces yellowed with age and exposure. It was an immigration clearance from a displaced persons camp near Martfeld, Lower Saxony. Now I remembered his pride when he had told me, a week before, that he had papers. This flimsy thing was Hunky's only proof that his life had a beginning as well as a present. It was all that connected this big, quiet, honest, muscular human being with the rest of documented humanity. I read his name, Stanislaw Szymaniewski, and beneath it his birthplace, Piotrków, Poland. Beside the printed question, 'Date of birth?' was typed July 24, 1935.

'My name is hard for Canadian to say, eh?' Hunky asked. 'Hunky not so hard, eh, George?'

I suddenly realized Hunky is a good name, depending on how it is said. It made me smile a little bitterly to myself to think how he had acquired it. It had probably been some native-born jerk in a railroad bunk-car or construction boarding-house somewhere who had named him that. Whoever he was, he must have been abashed when Hunky adopted the sarcastic epithet as his own.

The harvest was going well, but there was a tension in the air. Vandervelde came out to the fields more and more as the days passed. He would stand beside the tractor and talk to Kurt, while the little German's eyes would stare at us balefully from his small, dark, pinched face, trying to hurry us with an unspoken threat. One quarter of the barn floor was piled high with the cured tobacco, and the five kilns throbbed with the heat from their flues day and night as the leaves dried and cured.

'What's the matter with Vandervelde?' I asked Hunky one night.

'He's scared. Plant too big crop. He owe big mortgage on farm. Have to borrow money from Gruenther for seed last spring."

'From Kurt?'

'Sure. Kurt want Marie, so lend father money. Maurice give him share of crop. Now both scared." He laughed.

'Hunky.'

'Yeah, George?'

'Do you like Marie a lot?'

'Sure. She good strong girl, like girl in old country. She—'

'Has she said she'll marry you?' I blurted out.

He stared at me, and there was a hint of sorrow in his sudden anger.

'You think I not good enough for her, George?'

'I didn't say that,' I said, turning away.

'We go to dances in the spring, or a movie-picture in Simcoe. Why you ask that, George?'

'Nothing. I've noticed she likes you better than Kurt.'

'Sure,' he said, smiling again with youthful assurance. 'Her father not like me, though.'

'I can see that, too.'

'He try to make Marie stop meeting me,' he said, laughing once again.

I looked at Hunky and wanted to tell him what I thought, but I couldn't. I hoped he never would marry Marie, but for opposite reasons than her father's. He was too good for her, too naïve and unspoilt to let a girl like that break him down. She wore her dresses too tight, and cut her hair too short, and laughed too easily to ever settle down as the wife of an immigrant farmer. Some day she would take off for the city with a good-looking harvest hand, or run away with a salesman of waterless cookers. She was too ripe to stay on the tree but not quite ripe enough yet to go bad. Hunky deserved a better deal from a life that up to then had dealt him only deuces. He was so sure, so youthfully sure, that his health and strength would get him out of any situation. How could I warn him that life wasn't that uncomplicated, that youth and strength were no match for a young woman's wiles and an older man's hatred? He would have to learn it himself, as we have all had to learn at one time or another.

'Maurice want Marie to marry Kurt,' he said. 'I got no money. I'm only poor Polish D.P.'

'But Vandervelde and Gruenther are immigrants too.'

'Sure, but got citizenship.'

My thoughts about the girl, and his constant harping about passports, 'papers', and becoming a citizen, made me angry. He seemed to think that once he received his papers he would no longer be an unschooled labourer: that in some magic way it would make him the equal of anyone in the country.

'Citizenship! I'm a citizen and what has it got me! You'd think it was the most important thing in the world!' I shouted.

He said quietly, 'When you have none, George, it is most important thing.'

When I cooled down I asked, 'Where are you going after the harvest?'

'I got job in Beachville—in limestone quarry. Polish friend work there.'

'Are you thinking of taking Marie with you?'

He laughed and slapped his thigh. 'Sure t'ing, George! What

Maurice say to dat, eh?'

I had a pretty good idea.

Hunky walked to the side of the shed and picked up his home-made bar bells. From my seat on the steps I saw Marie standing on the porch watching him, straining forwards in her dress as he was straining as he hefted the bar. It was like watching a piece of taut elastic that is about to break. I went inside again and rolled a cigarette.

The following evening as we hung tobacco in No. 2 kiln, old man Crumlin reached too far for a lath of tobacco and fell from the peak to the earthen floor, breaking his wrist on the way down on a horizontal two-by-four. Maurice Vandervelde ranted and cursed, almost accusing Crumlin of falling just to spite him. He claimed he didn't have enough gas in his car to drive him to the hospital in Simcoe, and Frenchy Coté had to take him in his. The rest of us worked until dark, filling the kiln, though Hunky did the work of two men.

It was getting late in the season, and help was scarce. From then on there were only four of us in the priming crew, and Kurt refused to get down from the tractor to give us a hand. Despite Kurt's weasel glances and Vandervelde's curses, Hunky refused to increase the pace.

'We not run along rows, Maurice,' he said to the boss one day. 'Want tobacco in, get more men.'

Vandervelde spat out something in Flemish, turned around and walked from the field. It was only the shortage of help that prevented him from firing Hunky on the spot. From then on we had to fill an extra boat each day, and the sun was setting by the time we'd hung a kiln in the evening.

One noon hour as we sat at the dinner-table, Vandervelde came into the yard with a junk dealer, and pointed to a pile of old irrigation pipe and worn-out appliances near the bar. The dealer backed his truck through the gate, and looked towards the table for some help in loading it.

The boss cried, 'Hey, some of you give this man a hand with this stuff.'

McKinnon and one of the tyers rose to their feet, but Hunky

shouted, 'We get paid for work in fields, not load junk.' The two men sat down again.

I had been trying to think of who Hunky reminded me of, and now it came to me. It was an old Scots syndicalist I'd met on a road gang in B.C. in the early years of the depression. He had been a Wobbly, with the guts and dignity of his convictions, long before the trade unions and bargaining tables made his kind an anachronism. 'Direct action is all the bosses understand,' he used to say.

Vandervelde glared at Hunky, before his fat face cracked with a mean little smile. He called Kurt from the house, and the two of them helped the junkman load his truck. Then the boss walked to the side of the tool shed and picked up Hunky's bar bells. He carried them to the truck and threw them in. 'You can have these for nothing,' he said to the man, while Kurt laughed at the joke. I glanced at Hunky. He was eating a piece of pie with studied unconcern, but his face was white beneath his tan.

By Saturday there were only a few days' priming left, and one half of the barn was piled high with the cured tobacco. Instead of being cheered by this, Vandervelde became more nervous and irritable than ever. He had caught McKinnon smoking in the barn, and with much cursing had moved him in with the two tyers, who slept in a lean-to against the farmhouse. Once, he spied Marie talking to Hunky at supper, and called her to the house. As she passed him in the doorway he slapped her across the head.

The weather had been too good to last, and there was electricity in the air. Joe's radio reported a low pressure area moving northeast from the Mississippi Valley, through Illinois, Indiana, and Michigan, and expected in Ontario by early evening. The front was accompanied by heavy thunderstorms and a chance of hail.

Hunky lay on his bunk, stripped to his shorts. He had been unusually quiet since talking with Marie as we came in from the field. Suddenly he said, 'Maurice gone to Delhi to try borrow money from Growers' Association. Got no cash or insurance, only tobacco in barn.'

'How do you know?'

'Marie tell me,' he said. 'Not get pay tonight.'

'We'll get it tomorrow.'

'No, George. Have to wait till tobacco is bought. By then is too long for us to wait.' He began pacing up and down the floor of the shed. 'I know Vandervelde. He's fat pig. Not want to pay us wages.'

'What can we do?'

'I find out if he got money in Delhi tonight,' he said.

After he dressed he rode off in the quick gathering darkness in the direction of Delhi. Down in the southwest sky the lightning was flashing pink along the horizon. A strange stillness, broken only by the accelerated chirp of the crickets, fell on everything around.

The storm struck about an hour later, sucking the wind from the east at first, then gusting sheets of rain from the west against the side of the shed. The lightning, white and sulphurous now, flashed through every crack in the walls, and the thunder banged sharply overhead before rolling off into the sky. As quickly as it had come, the storm died off to the east, leaving a residue of gently spattering rain and a breeze that was as clean and cool as new-washed sheets. Before the rain stopped, I heard Vandervelde's car being driven into the yard. The barn door was unlocked, and the car driven inside. Then the door was locked again.

On Sunday, as those of us who had stayed at the farm were eating dinner, a provincial police car pulled up at the gate and two policemen walked up to the house. They talked with Maurice for several minutes at the door, then walked to their car. Joe the curer told me during the afternoon that Hunky had been killed the night before on the road by a hit-and-run motorist. The police had been checking to find if he had worked at Vandervelde's.

Hunky dead! It didn't seem possible, unless God had played a senseless joke upon the world. Why would it have to be Hunky, riding along on his bike during the storm of the night before, who had to die? Hunky, the Polack kid with the overwhelming desire to become a Canadian. Hunky, who had had enough pain and sorrow already to do the rest of us a lifetime. Hunky, who crossed himself at meals and went to mass. Boy, that was some heavenly joke all right!

At suppertime the others began to jabber about what a good boy Hunky had been, and Frenchy Coté's wife began to sniffle. I left the table, not wanting to talk to them about Hunky, or listen to their indifferent eulogies. Harvest hands are like hobos, their friendships as casual as the mating of a pair of flies.

The next evening after work I asked Maurice if he'd drive me to Delhi.

'I'm not going to Delhi,' he said. 'What do *you* want to go there for?'

'To see a friend,' I said.

'Who, Stan the Polack?' he asked, laughing his fat ugly laugh.

Though I knew he could kill me with one hand I suddenly wanted to smash his face. I wanted a miracle that would allow me to reach up and pull his face down to where my boots could crush it. I turned away with a hatred for my size, and a frustration I hadn't felt for years.

'My car has a flat tire,' Vandervelde shouted after me as I walked away. I pretended not to have heard him.

After supper I walked to the back of the barn and peered through a crack in the boards. The boss's car was parked in the middle of the floor, beside the roof-high pile of yellow cured tobacco. There was no sign of a flat tire, but its left front fender was loose and its left headlight broken, as if it had struck something coming from the opposite direction along the road.

Hunky's jacket was still hanging in a corner of the shed. I reached into the inside pocket and pulled out his D.P. camp release. I thought how proud he had been of his 'papers', and I shoved it into my own pocket, determined not to leave it for strangers to find. I knew that Hunky's friends and the Polish credit union officials in Delhi would look after the funeral. If I couldn't get there to see him for the last time, I'd go to Simcoe and try to forget him.

Frenchy Coté was driving Joe the curer into Simcoe for an evening off, and I bummed a ride into town with him. Kurt was taking care of the kilns.

My evening there was a failure. I tried a couple of beer parlours, but couldn't stand the noise and laughter. The more I tried to forget my friend the more I thought of him. I was sure Hunky had been right when he said we'd have to wait weeks for our pay. I thought of laying charges against Vandervelde, but changed my mind. Who would listen to a harvest stiff in the middle of the tobacco country? I'd end up on the wrong end of a vag charge myself.

I went to a bootlegger's and bought two bottles of cheap wine, one of which I drank there. I kept remembering Hunky's remark, 'I never know the good life, George.' It was the tortured cry of the whole bottom half of humanity.

I walked out to the highway with my bottle, and flagged down a car, driven by a young fellow going to St. Thomas. He let me out where the road to the farm led north from the highway. I drank the bottle and then set out across the fields towards Vandervelde's. I had some brave, drunken idea that I would stand up to the boss and tell him what I knew, then laugh at him as he had laughed at Hunky.

I cut across the fields and had almost reached the farmyard when I saw Marie coming down the path. I hid myself in the hedge, and saw Kurt cutting across towards her from the kilns. When he joined her they went towards the fields, her arm around his waist. They were all rotten, and just accusing Maurice was not enough. I had to hurt them all, for Hunky's sake.

A half-hour later I returned to the junction of the side road and the highway and waited for Frenchy to come along. When he did, I flagged him down. I told Frenchy and Joe that I'd been given a lift that far by a young man driving to St. Thomas.

We had almost reached the farm before we met Kurt, running down the road and glancing back every now and then across his shoulder. It was then that we first saw the pillar of whitened smoke hanging over the farmyard.

We pulled up in the yard alongside the fire truck from a small village to the south of us. The barn and two kilns were gutted, nothing remaining but a portion of the barn floor, a few char-coaled posts, and the still-steaming frame of Vandervelde's automobile. Joe jumped out of Frenchy's car and looked at the fireboxes of the other three kilns; the oil feedcocks on all of them had been turned on full, and the tobacco ruined.

The fire chief was telling Maurice that the fire had jumped from the kilns to the barn. Nobody told him any different, although I knew that the breeze was coming from the opposite direction.

Mrs. Vandervelde and Marie stood in the kitchen doorway, alternately sobbing and staring fearfully at Maurice, who stood in the middle of the yard, not laughing now, but opening and shutting his fat mouth like a landed carp.

The next morning before anyone else was up I walked between the rear of the gutted barn and the cracked and broken greenhouse. On the ground was a half-burned piece of document paper. By bending close I could read the beginning of a name typed along a dotted line: Stanislaw Szym . . . I crushed it into the mud with my foot. In a way you could call it Hunky's epitaph. But even that didn't seem enough. Not by a goddam long shot!

The Broken Globe

Henry Kreisel

S ince it was Nick Solchuk who first told me about the opening
in my field at the University of Alberta, I went up to see him
as soon as I received word that I had been appointed. He lived in
one of those old mansions in Pimlico that had once served as
town houses for wealthy merchants and aristocrats, but now
housed a less moneyed group of people—stenographers, students,
and intellectuals of various kinds. He had studied at Cambridge
and got his doctorate there and was now doing research at the
Imperial College and rapidly establishing a reputation among the
younger men for his work on problems which had to do with the
curvature of the earth.

His room was on the third floor, and it was very cramped, but
he refused to move because he could look out from his window
and see the Thames and the steady flow of boats, and that gave
him a sense of distance and of space also. Space, he said, was what
he missed most in the crowded city. He referred to himself,
nostalgically, as a prairie boy, and when he wanted to demonstrate
what he meant by space he used to say that when a man stood
and looked out across the open prairie, it was possible for him to
believe that the earth was flat.

'So,' he said, after I had told him my news, 'you are going to
teach French to prairie boys and girls. I congratulate you.' Then
he cocked his head to one side, and looked me over and said:
'How are your ears?'

'My ears?' I said. 'They're all right. Why?'

'Prepare yourself,' he said. 'Prairie voices trying to speak
French—that will be a great experience for you. I speak from
experience. I learned my French pronunciation in a little one-
room school in a prairie village. From an extraordinary girl, mind

you, but her mind ran to science. Joan McKenzie—that was her name. A wiry little thing, sharp-nosed, and she always wore brown dresses. She was particularly fascinated by earthquakes. "In 1755 the city of Lisbon, Portugal, was devastated. 60,000 persons died; the shock was felt in Southern France and North Africa; and inland waters of Great Britain and Scandinavia were agitated." You see, I still remember that, and I can hear her voice too. Listen: "In common with the entire solar system, the earth is moving through space at the rate of approximately 45,000 miles per hour, toward the constellation of Hercules. Think of that, boys and girls." Well, I thought about it. It was a lot to think about. Maybe that's why I became a geophysicist. Her enthusiasm was infectious. I knew her at her peak. After a while she got tired and married a solid farmer and had eight children.'

'But her French, I take it, was not so good,' I said.

'No,' he said. 'Language gave no scope to her imagination. Mind you, I took French seriously enough. I was a very serious student. For a while I even practised French pronunciation at home. But I stopped it because it bothered my father. My mother begged me to stop. For the sake of peace.'

'Your father's ears were offended,' I said.

'Oh, no,' Nick said, 'not his ears. His soul. He was sure that I was learning French so I could run off and marry a French girl. . . . Don't laugh. It's true. When once my father believed something, it was very hard to shake him.'

'But why should he have objected to your marrying a French girl anyway?'

'Because,' said Nick, and pointed a stern finger at me, 'because when he came to Canada he sailed from some French port, and he was robbed of all his money while he slept. He held all Frenchmen responsible. He never forgot and he never forgave. And, by God, he wasn't going to have that cursed language spoken in his house. He wasn't going to have any nonsense about science talked in his house either.' Nick was silent for a moment, and then he said, speaking very quietly, 'Curious man, my father. He had strange ideas, but a strange kind of imagination, too. I couldn't understand him when I was going to school or to the university. But then a year or two ago, I suddenly realized that the

Henry Kreisel / 79

shape of the world he lived in had been forever fixed for him by some medieval priest in the small Ukrainian village where he was born and where he received an education of sorts when he was a boy. And I suddenly realized that he wasn't mad, but that he lived in the universe of the medieval church. The earth for him was the centre of the universe, and the centre was still. It didn't move. The sun rose in the East and it set in the West, and it moved perpetually around a still earth. God had made this earth especially for man, and man's function was to perpetuate himself and to worship God. My father never said all that in so many words, mind you, but that is what he believed. Everything else was heresy.'

He fell silent.

'How extraordinary,' I said.

He did not answer at once, and after a while he said, in a tone of voice which seemed to indicate that he did not want to pursue the matter further, 'Well, when you are in the middle of the Canadian West, I'll be in Rome. I've been asked to give a paper to the International Congress of Geophysicists which meets there in October.'

'So I heard,' I said. 'Wilcocks told me the other day. He said it was going to be a paper of some importance. In fact, he said it would create a stir.'

'Did Wilcocks really say that?' he asked eagerly, his face reddening, and he seemed very pleased. We talked for a while longer, and then I rose to go.

He saw me to the door and was about to open it for me, but stopped suddenly, as if he were turning something over in his mind, and then said quickly, 'Tell me—would you do something for me?'

'Of course,' I said. 'If I can.'

He motioned me back to my chair and I sat down again. 'When you are in Alberta,' he said, 'and if it is convenient for you, would you—would you go to see my father?'

'Why, yes,' I stammered, 'why, of course. I—I didn't realize he was still . . .''

'Oh, yes,' he said, 'he's still alive, still working. He lives on his farm, in a place called Three Bear Hills, about sixty or seventy miles out of Edmonton. He lives alone. My mother is dead. I have a sister who is married and lives in Calgary. There were only the two of us. My mother could have no more children. It was a source of great agony for them. My sister goes to see him sometimes, and then she sometimes writes to me. He never writes to me. We—we had—what shall I call it—differences. If you went to see him and told him that I had not gone to the devil, perhaps . . .' He broke off abruptly, clearly agitated, and walked over to his window and stood staring out, then said, 'Perhaps you'd better not. I—I don't want to impose on you.'

I protested that he was not imposing at all, and promised that I would write to him as soon as I had paid my visit.

I met him several times after that, but he never mentioned the matter again.

I sailed from England about the middle of August and arrived in Montreal a week later. The long journey West was one of the most memorable experiences I have ever had. There were moments of weariness and dullness. But the very monotony was impressive. There was a grandeur about it. It was monotony of a really monumental kind. There were moments when, exhausted by the sheer impact of the landscape, I thought back with longing to the tidy, highly cultivated countryside of England and of France, to the sight of men and women working in the fields, to the steady succession of villages and towns, and everywhere the consciousness of nature humanized. But I also began to understand why Nick Solchuk was always longing for more space and more air, especially when we moved into the prairies, and the land became flatter until there seemed nothing, neither hill nor tree nor bush, to disturb the vast unbroken flow of land until in the far distance a thin, blue line marked the point where the prairie merged into the sky. Yet over all there was a strange tranquillity, all motion seemed suspended, and only the sun moved steadily, imperturbably West, dropping finally over the rim of the horizon, a blazing red ball, but leaving a superb evening light lying over the land still.

I was reminded of the promise I had made, but when I arrived in Edmonton, the task of settling down absorbed my time and energy so completely that I did nothing about it. Then, about the middle of October, I saw a brief report in the newspaper about the geophysical congress which had opened in Rome on the previous day, and I was mindful of my promise again. Before I could safely bury it in the back of my mind again, I sat down and wrote a brief letter to Nick's father, asking him when I could come out to visit him. Two weeks passed without an answer, and I decided to go and see him on the next Saturday without further formalities.

The day broke clear and fine. A few white clouds were in the metallic autumn sky and the sun shone coldly down upon the earth, as if from a great distance. I drove south as far as Wetaskiwin and then turned east. The paved highway gave way to gravel and got steadily worse. I was beginning to wonder whether I was going right, when I rounded a bend and a grain elevator hove like a signpost into view. It was now about three o'clock and I had arrived in Three Bear Hills, but, as Nick had told me, there were neither bears nor hills here, but only prairie, and suddenly the beginning of an embryonic street with a few buildings on either side like a small island in a vast sea, and then all was prairie again.

I stopped in front of the small general store and went in to ask for directions. Three farmers were talking to the storekeeper, a bald, bespectacled little man who wore a long, dirty apron and stood leaning against his counter. They stopped talking and turned to look at me. I asked where the Solchuk farm was.

Slowly scrutinizing me, the storekeeper asked, 'You just new here?'

'Yes,' I said.

'From the old country, eh?'

'Yes.'

'You selling something?'

'No, no,' I said. 'I—I teach at the University.'

'That so?' He turned to the other men and said, 'Only boy ever went to University from around here was Solchuk's boy. Nick. Real brainy young kid, Nick. Two of 'em never got on together. Too different. You know.'

They nodded slowly.

'But that boy of his—he's a real big-shot scientist now. You know them addem bombs and them hydrergen bombs. He helps make 'em.'

'No, no,' I broke in quickly. 'That's not what he does. He's a geophysicist.'

'What's that?' asked one of the men.

But before I could answer, the little storekeeper asked excitedly, 'You know Nick?'

'Yes,' I said, 'we're friends. I've come to see his father.'

'And where's he now? Nick, I mean.'

'Right now he is in Rome,' I said. 'But he lives in London, and does research there.'

'Big-shot, eh,' said one of the men laconically, but with a trace of admiration in his voice, too.

'He's a big scientist, though, like I said. Isn't that so?' the storekeeper broke in.

'He's going to be a very important scientist indeed,' I said, a trifle solemnly.

'Like I said,' he called out triumphantly. 'That's showing 'em. A kid from Three Bear Hills, Alberta. More power to him!' His pride was unmistakable. 'Tell me, mister,' he went on, his voice dropping, 'does he remember this place sometimes? Or don't he want to know us no more?'

'Oh, no,' I said quickly. 'He often talks of this place, and of Alberta, and of Canada. Some day he plans to return.'

'That's right,' he said with satisfaction. He drew himself up to full height, banged his fist on the table and said, 'I'm proud of that boy. Maybe old Solchuk don't think so much of him, but you tell him old Mister Marshall is proud of him.' He came from behind the counter and almost ceremoniously escorted me out to my car and showed me the way to Solchuk's farm.

I had about another five miles to drive, and the road, hardly more now than two black furrows cut into the prairie, was uneven and bumpy. The land was fenced on both sides of the road, and at last I came to a rough wooden gate hanging loosely on one hinge, and beyond it there was a cluster of small wooden buildings. The largest of these, the house itself, seemed at one time to have been ochre-coloured, but the paint had worn off and it now looked curiously mottled. A few chickens were wandering about, pecking at the ground, and from the back I could hear the grunting and squealing of pigs.

I walked up to the house and, just as I was about to knock, the door was suddenly opened, and a tall, massively built old man stood before me.

'My name is . . .' I began.

But he interrupted me. 'You the man wrote to me?' His voice, though unpolished, had the same deep timbre as Nick's.

'That's right,' I said.

'You a friend of Nick?'

'Yes.'

He beckoned me in with a nod of his head. The door was low and I had to stoop a bit to get into the room. It was a large, low-ceilinged room. A smallish window let in a patch of light which lit up the middle of the room but did not spread into the corners, so that it seemed as if it were perpetually dusk. A table occupied the centre, and on the far side there was a large wood stove on which stood a softly hissing black kettle. In the corner facing the entrance there was an iron bedstead, and the bed was roughly made, with a patchwork quilt thrown carelessly on top.

The old man gestured me to one of the chairs which stood around the table.

'Sit.'

I did as he told me, and he sat down opposite me and placed his large calloused hands before him on the table. He seemed to study me intently for a while, and I scrutinized him. His face was covered by a three-days' stubble, but in spite of that, and in spite of the fact that it was a face beaten by sun and wind, it was clear that he was Nick's father. For Nick had the same determined mouth, and the same high cheek bones and the same dark, penetrating eyes.

At last he spoke. 'You friend of Nick.'

I nodded my head.

'What he do now?' he asked sharply. 'He still tampering with the earth?'

His voice rose as if he were delivering a challenge, and I drew back involuntarily. 'Why—he's doing scientific research, yes,' I told him. 'He's . . .'

'What God has made,' he said sternly, 'no man should touch.'

Before I could regain my composure, he went on, 'He sent you. What for? What he want?'

'Nothing,' I said, 'Nothing at all. He sent me to bring you greetings and to tell you he is well.'

'And you come all the way from Edmonton to tell me?'

'Yes, of course.'

A faint smile played about his mouth, and the features of his face softened. Then suddenly he rose from his chair and stood towering over me. 'You are welcome in this house,' he said.

The formality with which he spoke was quite extraordinary and seemed to call for an appropriate reply, but I could do little more than stammer a thank you, and he, assuming again a normal tone of voice, asked me if I cared to have coffee. When I assented he walked to the far end of the room and busied himself about the stove.

It was then that I noticed, just under the window, a rough little wooden table and on top of it a faded old globe made of cardboard, such as little children use in school. I was intrigued to see it there and went over to look at it more closely. The cheap metal mount was brown with rust, and when I lifted it and tried to turn the globe on its axis, I found that it would not rotate because part of it had been squashed and broken. I ran my hand over the deep dent, and suddenly the old man startled me.

'What you doing there?' Curiosity seemed mingled with suspicion in his voice and made me feel like a small child surprised by its mother in an unauthorized raid on the pantry. I set down the globe and turned. He was standing by the table with two big mugs of coffee in his hands.

'Coffee is hot,' he said.

I went back to my chair and sat down, slightly embarrassed.

'Drink,' he said, pushing one of the mugs over to me.

We both began to sip the coffee, and for some time neither of us said anything.

'That thing over there,' he said at last, putting down his mug, 'that thing you was looking at—he brought it home one day—he was a boy then—maybe thirteen-year-old Nick. The other day I found it up in the attic. I was going to throw it in the garbage.

But I forgot. There it belongs. In the garbage. It is a false thing.' His voice had now become venomous.

'False?' I said. 'How is it false?'

He disregarded my question. 'I remember,' he went on, 'he came home from school one day and we was all here in this room—all sitting around this table eating supper, his mother, his sister and me and Alex, too—the hired man like. And then sudden like Nick pipes up, and he says, we learned in school today, he says, how the earth is round like a ball, he says, and how it moves around and around the sun and never stops, he says. They learning you rubbish in school, I say. But he says, no, Miss McKenzie never told him no lies. Then I say she does, I say, and a son of mine shouldn't believe it. Stop your ears! Let not Satan come in!' He raised an outspread hand and his voice thundered as if he were a prophet armed. 'But he was always a stubborn boy— Nick. Like a mule. He never listened to reason. I believe it, he says. To me he says that—his father, just like that, I believe it, he says, because science has proved it and it is the truth. It is false, I cry, and you will not believe it. I believe it, he says. So then I hit him because he will not listen and will not obey. But he keeps shouting and shouting and shouting. "She moves," he shouts, "she moves, she moves!"'

He stopped. His hands had balled themselves into fists, and the remembered fury sent the blood streaming into his face. He seemed now to have forgotten my presence and he went on speaking in a low murmuring voice, almost as if he were telling the story to himself.

'So the next day, or the day after, I go down to that school, and there is this little Miss McKenzie, so small and so thin that I could have crush her with my bare hands. What you teaching my boy Nick? I ask her. What false lies you stuffing in his head? What you telling him that the earth is round and that she moves for? Did Joshua tell the earth to stand still, or did he command the sun? So she says to me, I don't care what Joshua done, she says, I will tell him what science has discovered. With that woman I could get nowhere. So then I try to keep him away from school, and I lock him up in the house, but it was no good. He got out, and he run to the school like, and Miss McKenzie she sends me a letter to say she will sent up the inspectors if I try to keep him away from the school. And I could do nothing.'

His sense of impotence was palpable. He sat sunk into himself as if he were still contemplating ways of halting the scientific education of his son.

'Two, three weeks after,' he went on, 'he comes walking in this door with a large paper parcel in his hand. Now, he calls out to me, now I will prove it to you, I will prove that she moves. And he tears off the paper from the box and takes out this—this thing, and he puts it on the table here. Here, he cries, here is the earth, and look, she moves. And he gives that thing a little push and it twirls around like. I have to laugh. A toy, I say to him, you bring me a toy here, not bigger than my hand, and it is supposed to be the world, this little toy here, with the printed words on coloured paper, this little cardboard ball. This Miss McKenzie, I say to him, she's turning you crazy in that school. But look, he says, she moves. Now I have to stop my laughing. I'll soon show you she moves, I say, for he is beginning to get me mad again. And I go up to the table and I take the toy thing in my hands and I smash it down like this.'

He raised his fists and let them crash down on the table as if he meant to splinter it.

'That'll learn you, I cry. I don't think he could believe I had done it, because he picks up the thing and he tries to turn it, but it don't turn no more. He stands there and the tears roll down his cheeks, and then, sudden like, he takes the thing in both his hands and he throws it at me. And it would have hit me right in the face, for sure, if I did not put up my hand. Against your father, I cry, you will raise up your hand against your father. Asmodeus! I grab him by the arm, and I shake him and I beat him like he was the devil. And he makes me madder and madder because he don't cry or shout or anything. And I would have kill him there, for sure, if his mother didn't come in then and pull me away. His nose was bleeding, but he didn't notice. Only he looks at me and says, you can beat me and break my globe, but you can't stop her moving. That night my wife she make me swear by all that's holy that I wouldn't touch him no more. And from then on I never hit him again nor talk to him about this thing. He goes his way and I go mine.'

He fell silent. Then after a moment he snapped suddenly, 'You hold with that?'

'Hold with what?' I asked, taken aback.

'With that thing?' He pointed behind him at the little table and at the broken globe. His gnarled hands now tightly interlocked, he leaned forward in his chair and his dark, brooding eyes sought an answer from mine in the twilight of the room.

Alone with him there, I was almost afraid to answer firmly. Was it because I feared that I would hurt him too deeply if I did, or was I perhaps afraid that he would use violence on me as he had on Nick?

I cleared my throat. 'Yes,' I said then. 'Yes, I believe that the earth is round and that she moves. That fact has been accepted now for a long time.'

I expected him to round on me but he seemed suddenly to have grown very tired, and in a low resigned voice he said, 'Satan has taken over all the world.' Then suddenly he roused himself and hit the table hard with his fist, and cried passionately, 'But not me! Not me!'

It was unbearable. I felt that I must break the tension, and I said the first thing that came into my mind. 'You can be proud of your son in spite of all that happened between you. He is a fine man, and the world honours him for his work.'

He gave me a long look. 'He should have stayed here,' he said quietly. 'When I die, there will be nobody to look after the land. Instead he has gone off to tamper with God's earth.'

His fury was now all spent. We sat for a while in silence, and then I rose. Together we walked out of the house. When I was about to get into my car, he touched me lightly on the arm. I turned. His eyes surveyed the vast expanse of sky and land, stretching far into the distance, reddish clouds in the sky and blue shadows on the land. With a gesture of great dignity and power he lifted his arm and stood pointing into the distance, at the flat land and the low-hanging sky.

'Look,' he said, very slowly and very quietly, 'she is flat, and she stands still.'

It was impossible not to feel a kind of admiration for the old man. There was something heroic about him. I held out my hand and he took it. He looked at me steadily, then averted his eyes and said, 'Send greetings to my son.'

I drove off quickly, but had to stop again in order to open the wooden gate. I looked back at the house, and saw him still standing there, still looking at his beloved land, a lonely, towering figure framed against the darkening evening sky.

The Story of Nil

Gabrielle Roy

Quite often I asked my small pupils to sing together. One day, in the midst of their rather colourless voices, I could make out one that was clear, vibrant and astonishingly accurate. I had the group stop and let Nil go on alone. What a ravishing voice, and how precious to me, who had never had much of an ear for music!

From then on I would ask: "Nil, will you give the note?"

He would do so without coaxing and without pride—a child born to sing as others are born to pout.

The rest, my flight of sparrows, took off in his wake, soon following rather well; for besides his rare talent, Nil seemed able to pass it on to the others. We listened to him and believed we too could sing.

My music hour was the envy of the teachers in neighbouring classrooms.

"What's going on? We're getting a concert from your room every day now!"

They couldn't believe it, for I had never before shone as a singing teacher.

Our old inspector was stupefied when he came around.

"What's this? Your children are singing a thousand times better than other years!"

Then he stopped staring suspiciously at me, and asked to have them sing once more; the first thing I knew he was off in a happy reverie in which he seemed not even to remember that he was a school inspector.

Shortly after this visit I had another from our principal, who said in a faintly sarcastic way:

"I understand your children are such fine singers this year. I'm very curious to hear these little angels. Would you ask them to perform for me?"

Our principal was a little man made somewhat taller by his crest of blond hair, combed up in the middle like the picture of Monsieur Thiers in the dictionary. His dress, which was that of our teaching brothers at the time, was also very impressive: a black frock-coat and a white, starched dickey.

I had the pupils come close in a compact group, with Nil, one of the smallest, almost hidden in the middle. I made a little sign to him. He gave the starting tone just loudly enough to be heard by those around him. A wire vibrating harmoniously somewhere near! And the choir took off with such zest and in such perfect unison that I thought: Even the principal must be dazzled by this!

At any rate the mocking smile vanished quickly from his face. In its place appeared, to my amazement, the same expression of happy reverie, as if he had forgotten that he was a manager always busy running his school.

Hands behind his back, he wagged his head gently in rhythm with the tune and even when the song was ended kept on listening to it in his mind a moment longer.

But he had spotted the captivating voice. He brought Nil out of the group, looked long and attentively at him, and patted him on the cheek.

As I accompanied him to the door, he said:

"Well, with your thirty-eight sparrows you've caught a meadowlark this year. Do you know the lark? Let him sing and there's not a heart but is lightened!"

I suppose I was too young myself to know what a lightened heart was. But I soon had some idea of it.

That day had started very badly, under a driving autumn rain. The children arrived at school wet, sniffling and ill-humoured, with enormous muddy feet that soon turned my schoolroom, which I loved to see sparkling clean, into a kind of stable. As soon as I went to pick up a still-intact clod of black earth, two or three children would make a point of crushing others with their toes, scattering them in the aisles, watching me slyly all the while. I hardly recognized my pupils in these little rebels who would have risen against me at the drop of a hat, and perhaps they didn't recognize in me their beloved school mistress of yesterday. What had happened to turn us into something resembling enemies?

Some of our most experienced colleagues blamed the moments before the storm, the children's delicate nerves being strained by the atmospheric tension; and some said it was the long school days following weekends or holidays. After that taste of freedom the return to school was like going back to jail; and they grew quite disobedient, and all the more excitable, fidgety and impossible because they felt in their bones, poor things, that their revolt against the adult world had not the slightest chance of ultimate success.

It was my turn to have one of those dreadful days when the teacher seems to be there to do nothing but scold, and the children to comply, and all the sadness in the world settles into this place which can be so happy at other times.

As the bad weather kept up, instead of working off this excess nervousness in the open air we had to go to the gym in the basement, where shoes were loud on the hard floor. The children fought about nothing. I had to treat split lips and bloody noses.

Afterwards, fresh from a visit to the toilets, the children left their desks one after the other to ask permission to go down again. Impossible to continue with my lesson in that traffic! One would leave, another would just be coming back, the door would open, a draught would blow scribblers to the floor and they'd be picked up covered with dirt, and the door would slam: another child was going out. Suddenly I could take no more. "No! That will do! There's a limit after all."

Now it happened that without thinking, but as if I had done it on purpose, my "no" fell on little Charlie, a gentle child, quite guileless, whom his mother purged two or three times a year with a mixture of sulphur and molasses. Relegated to his desk, Charlie couldn't hold in very long. The odour gave him away to his neighbours, little monsters who pretended to be shocked, and shouted from where they sat, as if it wasn't obvious enough: "Charlie did it in his pants." In haste I had to write a note to his mother whom I knew to be vindictive, while Charlie stood at my desk, his legs apart, whimpering with shame.

I hadn't long to wait for the consequences. Charlie had been gone a half-hour when the principal showed his head in the high glass of the door and gestured that he wanted to speak to me. It was a serious business when he called us out to the corridor. Charlie's mother, he told me, had phoned. She was so furious that he had trouble persuading her not to sue me. Laugh if you please, there was such a thing as parents suing a teacher for less than that, and I was accused of having obliged Charlie's mother to re-wash his underwear, which she had done only yesterday.

I tried to present the facts from my point of view, but the principal remarked with some severity that it was better to let the whole class go to the toilet for nothing than to prevent one child in real need.

Perhaps because I was ashamed of myself, I tried to make the children ashamed at having shown their worst possible side all day. They weren't in the least contrite; quite the contrary—they seemed very pleased with themselves indeed, for the most part.

I went and sat down, completely discouraged. And the future descended on me, making all my years to come resemble this one day. I could see myself in twenty, thirty years, still in the same place, worn down by my task, the very image of the "oldest" of my present colleagues whom I found so pitiful; and thinking of them, my pity turned on myself. It goes without saying that the children took advantage of my dejection to chase each other up and down the aisles and add to the tumult. My glance fell on little Nil. While almost all the children were running amok, he was at his desk, trying to concentrate on his drawing. Apart from singing, what interested him most was to draw a cabin, always the same cabin, surrounded by curious animals, with chickens as tall as his cows.

I called to him, I think as if for help:

"Nil, come here a second."

He came running. He was a funny little manikin and always oddly dressed. On this day a pair of men's braces, barely short-ened, held up pants that were too big, their crotch hanging to his knees. His boots must have been just as oversized, for I heard them clatter as he ran up. With his mop of tow-coloured hair and his square head, flat on the top, he looked like a good little kulak determined to get an education. In fact, when he wasn't singing he was the last one in the class that you'd take for a meadowlark.

He leaned toward me affectionately.

"What do you want?"

"To talk to you. Tell me, who taught you to sing so well?"

"My mother."

I had glimpsed her once when the report cards were given out: a gentle, embarrassed smile, high cheekbones like Nil's, fine, penetrating eyes under her snow-white kerchief, a timid shadow who left as she had come, in silence. Did she know more than a few words apart from her own Ukrainian tongue?

"So she teaches you in Ukrainian?"

"Why, sure!"

"Do you know many Ukrainian songs?"

"Hundreds!"

"So many?"

"Well, at least ten . . . or twelve."

"Would you sing us one?"

"Which one?"

"Any one you like."

He took up a firm stand as if to resist the wind, his feet wide apart, his head thrown back, his eyes already shining, in a transformation more radical than I had ever seen—the first time he had sung at school in his mother's language: a little rustic turned into one possessed by music. His body swayed to a catchy rhythm, his shoulders went up, his eyes flamed, and a smile from time to time parted his slightly fleshy lips. With raised hand he seemed to point with a graceful gesture at some pretty scene in the distance, and you couldn't help following the gesture to see what it was he found so pleasing. I couldn't tell which was better: listening to him with my eyes closed, to enjoy that splendid voice without distraction; or watching him sing, so lively, so playful, as if he were ready to rise from the earth.

When this delightful song was ended we were in another world. The children had gradually gone back to their seats. I was no longer in despair about my future. Nil's singing had turned my heart inside out like a glove. Now I was confident about life.

I asked Nil: "Have you any idea what the song's about?"

"Sure I have!"

"Could you explain it to us?"

He launched into the story:

"There's a tree. It's a cherry tree in bloom. In the country my mother comes from there's lots of them. This cherry tree, it's in the middle of a field. Some young girls are dancing around it. They're waiting for the boys that are in love with them."

"What a lovely story!"

"Yes, but it's going to be sad," said Nil, "for one of the boys was killed in war."

"Oh, that's too bad!"

"No, because that gives a chance to another fellow who was secretly in love with her, and he's the good guy."

"Oh! Fine! But where did your mother learn these songs?"

"In that country, before they left, when she was a little girl. Now she says that's all we have left from the Ukraine."

"And she's hurrying to get all that into your little head so it's your turn to keep it?"

He looked at me gravely to be very sure of what I had said, then he smiled affectionately.

"I won't lose a one," he said. And then, "Would you like me to sing another one?"

My mother had broken a hip about three months before. She had been immobilized in a plaster corset for a long time. The doctor had finally removed it and asserted that she would be able to walk if she persevered. She made a great effort every day, but couldn't manage to move her bad leg. I had seen her losing hope during the last week or two. I would catch her sitting in her armchair by the window looking at the outdoors with an expression of heartrending regret. I would scold her so that she wouldn't think I was worried about her. Lively, active and independent as she was, what would her life be if she spent the rest of it a cripple? The horror I had felt one day at the thought of being chained for a lifetime to my teacher's desk gave me a glimpse of her feelings at the prospect of never leaving her prisoner's lookout at the window.

Gabrielle Roy / 95

One day I had the notion of bringing Nil home to entertain her, for she found the days "deathly long."

"Would you like to come home, Nil, and sing for *my* mother? She's lost all her songs!"

He had a way of saying yes without a word, placing his little hands in mine as if to tell me: You know very well I'd go to the world's end with you. And it went straight to my heart.

On the way I explained to him that my mother was much older than his, and that it was hard at her age to get back her lost confidence. I still don't know what possessed me to get into explanations of that kind with a child of six and a half. But he listened, deadly serious, trying with all his might to fathom what I expected of him.

When my mother, who had just had a nap, opened her eyes and saw beside her this manikin in his wide braces, she must have thought he was one of the poor kids I had so often brought home so that she could make them a coat or alter one to their size. She said a little bitterly, but more in sadness, I think, at no longer being able to help:

"What's this? You know I can't sew anymore, except little things I can do by hand."

"No, no, it's not that. It's a surprise. Listen."

I made a sign to Nil. He planted himself in front of my mother as if to resist a strong wind, and launched into the happy song of the cherry tree. His body swayed, his eyes sparkled, a smile came to his lips, his little hand rose up to point, far beyond this sickroom, to what? A highway? A plain? Some open landscape, anyway, that he made you want to see.

When he had finished he looked at my mother, who said not a word, hiding her gaze from him. He suggested:

"D'you want to hear another one of my songs?"

My mother, as if from a distance, nodded her head, without showing her face, which stayed hidden behind her hand.

Nil sang another song, and this time my mother held her head high, watching the smiling child; and with his help she too was away, taking flight far above life, on the wings of a dream.

That evening she asked me to bring her a strong kitchen chair with a high back and help her stand up behind it, using it as a support.

I suggested that the chair could slip and pull her forward, so she had me lay a heavy dictionary on it.

With this strange "walker" of her own invention my mother resumed her exercises. Weeks passed and I could see no change. I was growing completely discouraged. My mother too, no doubt, for she seemed to have given up. What I didn't know was that, having realized she was on the point of succeeding, she had decided to go on with her exercises in secret so as to give me a surprise. A surprise it was! I was in the blackest despondency that evening when I heard her shout from her room:

"I'm walking! I can walk!"

I ran to her. My mother, pushing the chair in front of her, was progressing with tiny mechanical steps, like those of a wind-up doll, and she kept up her cry of triumph:

"I can walk! I can walk!"

Of course I don't claim that Nil performed a miracle. But perhaps he gave a little puff at just the right time to the flickering faith of my mother.

However that may be, this experiment gave me the urge to try another.

The previous year I had gone along with one of my colleagues and a group of her pupils who were putting on a little play for the old people in a home in our town.

Of all the prisons that human beings forge for themselves or are forced to suffer, not one, even today, seems as intolerable as the one in which we are confined by age. I had sworn never again to set foot in that home; it had upset me so. Maybe during the year I had made some progress in compassion, for here I was thinking of taking Nil there. He seemed the only one likely to be able to comfort the old people I had seen immured in the institution.

I spoke to the principal who thought for a long time and then said the idea had its good points . . . very good points, but first I'd have to get permission from the mother.

I set about writing a letter to Nil's mother, in which I said something to the effect that the songs she had brought from the

Ukraine and passed on to her son seemed to be beneficial to the people here, as perhaps they had been to her own people . . . helping them to live. . . . And would she please lend me Nil for an evening that might go on rather late?

I read it to Nil, asking him to get it firmly into his head because he would have to read it at home and give an exact translation to his mother. He listened attentively and as soon as I had finished asked if I'd like him to repeat it word for word, just to be sure that he had memorized it. I said that wouldn't be necessary, that I had faith in his memory.

Next day Nil brought me the reply on a piece of paper cut out from a brown paper bag. It was in telegraphic style:

"We lend Nil to the old people."

It was signed in letters that looked like embroidery:

Paraskovia Galaida.

"What a beautiful name your mother has!" I said to Nil, trying to read it properly.

And on hearing my odd pronunciation, he burst out laughing in my face.

The old people's home had its own little auditorium, with a platform two steps high lit by a row of weak footlights which isolated it from the audience.

Caught in a beam of golden light, Nil was charming to see with his straw-coloured hair and the Ukrainian blouse with its embroidered collar, which his mother had made him wear. For my own part I missed a little seeing my manikin with the wide braces. On his face with its high cheekbones you could already see the joy he felt at the idea of singing. From my hiding place, where if need be I could prompt him as to what to do, I could see the audience as well as the stage, and it was among them, you might have thought, that the real drama was being played—that of life saying its last word.

In the first row was an old man afflicted with a convulsive palsy, like an apple tree that someone had shaken, still trembling long after its last fruit had fallen. Somewhere someone was breathing with a whistling sound like wind caught inside a hollow tree. Another old man tried to keep up with his lungs in a race with death. Near the middle of the room was one, half paralyzed, whose living eyes in his inert face had an unbearable lucidity. There was a poor woman, swollen to an enormous mass of flesh. And no doubt there were those who were still unscathed, if that happy chance consisted here of simply being worn, wrinkled, shrunken and eroded by some process of unimaginable ferocity. When is old age at its most atrocious: when you are in it, like these people in the home?—or seen from afar, through the eyes of tender youth that could wish for death at the sight?

Then, in that day's end, the clear, radiant voice of Nil rose as if from the shining morning of life. He sang of the flowering cherry tree, of the girls in love dancing their round on the plain, of the expectations of youthful hearts. With a gesture that was charmingly at ease he would raise his hand and point to a distant road to be followed . . . or a far horizon which, from his shining eyes, you imagined must be luminous. At one moment his lips parted in a smile that was so contagious it leapt over the footlights and appeared in all its fresh sweetness on the aged faces. He sang about Petrushka's adventure, and how he was caught by his own trickery. He sang a song that I had never heard, a gentle, melancholy song about the Dnieper River running on and on, bearing laughter and sighs, hopes and regrets, down toward the sea, until at the end everything melts into the eternal waves.

I didn't know the old people; they had changed so. In the dark evening of their lives this ray of morning had broken through to them. The palsied man succeeded in holding still a moment so as to hear more clearly. The eye of the paralytic no longer wandered, searching, calling for help, but turned and fixed upon Nil so as to see him as well as possible. The man who had been chasing his own breathing seemed to be holding his breath with his two hands clasped across his chest in a marvellous respite from his affliction. They all looked happy now, hanging on the next notes from Nil. And the tragic spectacle of the audience ended in a kind of parody, with old men excited as children, some on the verge of laughter, others of tears, because they were rediscovering so vividly in themselves the traces of what was lost.

Then I said to myself that this was, after all, too cruel, and I would never again bring Nil here to sing and reawaken hope.

How the renown of my little healer of the ills of life began to spread, I have no idea, but soon I was getting requests from all sides.

One day, through the high glass door-panel, the principal made a sign that he wanted to talk to me.

"This time," he said, "it's a psychiatric hospital that's asking for our little Ukrainian lark. This is a serious question, and we must think it over."

Yes, it was serious, but once again, and as if it were beyond my own will, my decision had been made. If Paraskovia Galaida gave her permission I would go with Nil to see the "madmen," as people called them then.

She agreed, with no trouble. I wonder now if she even worried about where we went. She seemed to have as much confidence in me as Nil did.

In the mental hospital also there was a little auditorium with a low platform, but without any bank of footlights or spots to separate this side from that. Everything was bathed in the same dull, uniform light. If the world of the aged in the home had made me think of tragedy's last act, here I had the impression of an epilogue mimed by shadows that had already passed on to a kind of death.

The patients were seated in docile ranks, most of them apathetic, their eyes bleak, twiddling their thumbs or biting at their lips.

Nil made his entrance on the narrow platform of the stage. There was a rustle of surprise in the audience. A few patients even grew excited at this marvellous apparition—a child, here! One of them, over-agitated, pointed his finger at him in a kind of joyous bewilderment, as if asking others to confirm what his eyes were seeing.

Nil took up his position, his feet apart, a lock of hair hanging over his forehead, his hands on his hips, for he was going to start with "Kalinka" which he had just learned from his mother. He caught its develish rhythm with fiery charm.

From the very first notes there was a silence such as you would feel when the forest hushes to hear a birdsong somewhere on a distant branch.

Nil was swaying, filled with an irresistible liveliness, sometimes tracing a gentle curve with his hand, sometimes passionately clapping both hands together. The patients followed his movements in ecstasy. And always this silence, as if in adoration.

"Kalinka" ended. Nil explained in a few words, as I had taught him, the meaning of the next song. He did this with complete ease, no more nervous than if he had been in class among his companions. Then he launched into his music again as if he would never grow tired of singing.

Now the patients were breathing together audibly, like a single, unhappy monster moving in the shadows, dreaming of its own release.

Nil went from one song to another, one sad, the next one gay. He no more saw the madmen than he had seen the aged, the sick, the sorrowful, with their torments of body and soul. He sang of the sweet, lost land of his mother which she had given him to keep, its prairies, its trees, a lone horseman crossing the distant plain. He ended with that gesture of his hand that I never tired of, pointing to a happy road, far away at the end of this world, and tapping the floor with his heel.

At once I was sure the patients were going to eat him alive. The nearest ones tried to reach him when he came down from the little platform. Those in the back pushed at the front ranks, trying to touch him too. A woman patient caught him by the arm and held him for a moment to her breast. Another pulled him away from her and kissed him. They all wanted to take possession of the wonder child, to take him alive, to prevent him at all costs from leaving them.

Nil, who had, without recognizing it, eased so much sadness, took fright at the terrible happiness he had unleashed. His eyes, filled with terror, called to me for help. A guard gently extricated him from the embrace of a sobbing patient:

"Dear child, little nightingale, stay here, stay here with us!"

Toward the back of the room another claimed possession of him, weeping:

"This is my little boy that they stole. Long ago. Give him back. Give me back my life."

He was all trembling when I got him in my arms.

"There, there, it's all finished! You made them too happy, that's all. Too happy!"

We had left the taxi, walking the rest of the way to Nil's house. He seemed to have forgotten the troublesome scene in the hospital, and his first care was to guide me, for as soon as we left the sidewalk I had no idea where I was going.

It was early May. It had rained hard for several days and the fields across which Nil was leading me were a sea of mud, with occasional clumps of low, thorny bushes that caught at my clothing. I could only guess at this strange landscape, for there were no street-lamps here. Not even what you could call a road. Just a vague path where trodden mud made the footing a little more firm than elsewhere. The path wound from one cabin to the next, and the feeble light from windows helped us somewhat. But Nil seemed not to need the light, for he jumped surefootedly from one fairly dry spot to the next. Then we stood on the edge of a stretch of soft mud that gave off water like a sponge. To cross it there was a walk of planks thrown zig-zag here and there. The gaps were always longer than a single step. Nil would leap across and turn around to give me his hand, encouraging me to spring. He was delighted to bring me to his home; there was not a hint of suspicion in this happy child that I might pity him for living in this zone of the disinherited. It was true that beneath that soaring sky filled with stars, these cabins with their backs to the city, looking out over the free prairie vastness, formed a strangely fascinating shantytown.

From time to time, a fetid smell wafted toward us in waves, spoiling the fresh spring air. I asked Nil where it came from, and at first he didn't know what I was talking about, I suppose because the smell was so familiar to him. Then he pointed behind us to a long, dark mass that blocked the horizon.

"The slaughterhouse," he said. "It must be the slaughterhouse that stinks."

Now we had crossed the muddy sea and I was fated that night to go from one surprise to the next, for the unpleasant smell suddenly gave way to the good, simple one of wet earth. Then the perfume of a flower reached me. We were coming close to Nil's house, and this was the powerful odour of a hyacinth in its pot outside near the door, struggling with a force almost equal to the last waves from the abattoir. Another few paces and the hyacinth had won. At the same time, from a nearby pond came a triumphant chorus of hylas.

Paraskovia Galaida must have been on the lookout for us. She came at a run out of their cabin which was itself, no doubt, made of old bits of plank and waste boards. In the light of a crescent moon filtering through the clouds it seemed to me amazingly pale, as clean and pleasant as if it had just been whitewashed. It stood in a fenced enclosure. A gate opened inward. So far as I could judge, it was made of nothing less than the foot of an iron bedstead mounted on hinges in the post. They squeaked as Paraskovia Galaida opened the gate and welcomed us into the perfumed dooryard. The strange light revealed that everything in the place was scrupulously clean.

Paraskovia took my hands and backed toward the house. In front was a rough wooden bench. She made me sit down between Nil and herself. At once the cat of the place left the shadows and leapt to the back of the bench, where he made his narrow bed, content to be one of us, his head between our shoulders, purring.

With Nil's help, I tried to express to Paraskovia Galaida something of the joy her small son's singing had brought to so many people; and she, with his help, tried to thank me for I wasn't quite sure what. Soon we had given up trying to pour out our feelings by means of words, listening instead to the night.

Then it seemed to me I caught a sign from Paraskovia Galaida to Nil. Her eyes closed, she gave him a starting note just as he gave it at school. A delicate musical throat vibration sounded. Their voices began together, one a little hesitant at first but quickly convinced by the stronger of the two. Then they flew upward, harmonizing as they rose in a strangely lovely song, one of life as it is lived and life as it is dreamed.

Under that immense sky it took your heart and turned it round and turned it over, as a hand might do, before leaving it an instant, with due gentleness, to the freedom of the air.

Translated by Alan Brown

Gabrielle Roy / 103

Things in the Silence

Harold Marshall

My Lord's Hill in Barbados was far from the white, monotonous flatness of the Saskatchewan prairieland in the middle of winter. But Arthur Chesterfield Waldron thought of it now as he listened abstractly to the grinding revolutions of the train, muted in the snow.

He sat in the small cubicle and listened. He had heard it all before. Many times. For thirty years he had watched the same uninteresting countryside in the winter, concealed and sterile under its white, frigid blanket. It seemed unfriendly to him in its frosty greatness and he felt he was an alien in it.

It had been this way from the very beginning. On his very first trip. He had been homesick at the time and the drab, stark loneliness had made him afraid. It had seemed like a nightmare and only the rocking sway of the carriage had made him realize it was real and not a dream.

He looked outside now and saw the cold. He knew the silence would only be disturbed by the muted sound of the train. He caught quick glimpses of the barrenness in the moving, white kaleidoscope of the window as the train hurtled into the face of the weak, late-rising sun on the muffled rhythm of its turning wheels.

They went past gaunt grain elevators, erect and disconsolate in the cold, waiting for spring and summer and fall to fulfill their destiny. He saw plumes of blue smoke and condensing heat rising from chimneys and flues in shuttered houses, some with strings of colored lights framing their doors, adding colour to their sameness . . . And then, he had passed them. They were captured and released in fragments of reflected light from the snow. Quick frames of moving landscape from the window of his cubicle.

Then the train slowed and stopped and waited for time to pass.

There was nothing to see except a blue dome of sky above the blanket of whiteness, and crystals of snow catching the light and breaking it into fragments. There was nothing to hear but the silence above the sounds of the motionless train.

The blurred images lingering at the bottom of his consciousness now came into sharp focus. He saw things and heard noises which had always been familiar to him.

He heard the tiny clang of the church bell he had known as a child, tinkling cracked, staccato echoes from its short, wooden steeple. He heard voices which stayed apart in dialect, then warped together in unison of worship. There were tenors of supplication and sopranos of piety in the early breaking of a Christmas morning fresh with dew and in the heat of a noon sun.

It all came to him now. Like darkness. Like sleep. Brief involuntary visions of the past that lurked in the quiet recesses of his mind waiting to invade his consciousness. But it was a world which was real to him, even after all the years of his absence. It was a place of sight and smell and sound. Even now, he could feel its dimension. It was rounded and full. Not flat and white and wearisome.

There was the scent of the sea. Pungent and tangy. And the sweaty smell of people dressed in pants stiff as boards and jackets which hung in creases. And flowery dresses which drooped and flared.

There was something about the way the sun shone from directly overhead, warming the wind, that made him feel the close affinity which had sustained him through the years. But it wasn't only the sun and the wind, and the warm rain which would sting his face. It was the sharp shadows which fell in silence, and the colors which invaded his mind and dyed his soul with bold, indelible tinctures. Vast and imponderable. The rich cadence of song and laughter, rising and falling, then gurgling into silence in the darkness of the night. But it was a different kind of silence from the one he heard now. It wasn't sterile and indifferent. It was slumbering. Immersed in langourous solitude. It stretched out into the distance in serenity.

Then time was slipping backwards into silence, into stillness, allowing the faraway images of the past to seem almost real. Purple flashes of memory punctuated by a soft darkness of the mind.

His body stiffened imperceptibly as he saw other things. Things that were not soft and cool like the velvet of the nights. He thought of the hysterical effort of life itself, but he discarded it as soon as it intruded on him.

Then he saw her. Her face was pale and languid and there were circles under her eyes. She was dressed in pink and she had long, blonde hair. She held the doll possessively and she surveyed him in grave silence. She drew her breath in, involuntarily and bit at her bottom lip and for an instant her deep blue eyes were downcast.

"Hello, little girl," he said softly with the friendly timbre which came readily to him.

She said nothing. She kept looking at him without reservation, with seriousness and concentration, and with big eyes which could grow huge.

"What's your name?" he asked, but the little girl ignored him and turned her attention to her doll, then she returns his gaze through her lowered lashes. Her face is soft and innocent in its quietness.

"You want to come and talk to me?" he asks, leaning towards her. She drew back. Startled. And he thought there was something exquisite about her fragile mask.

She shook her head, then she turned and left him and he was all alone again, feeling vaguely disappointed, and irritated at the motionless train. Then he felt a spasm of movement and it lurched forward slowly but it didn't gather speed, and there was something agonizing about the way it went, tortuous and intricate in a labyrinth of time along the numbing cold steel of the tracks. Then the motion of its wheels became faster and once more he caught the white landscape in rectangular shapes of never-ending flatness. There was no dimension. Neither in time nor space. It was just a monotonous oneness, to him.

He closed his eyes and saw a coral beach awash with frothy water from a surging tide. Coming and going with a curious deliberation. Restless and virile. Full of life. Responsive. Not lying flat on its back frigid and cold, like some woman, waiting for time to challenge it. It was the incredibly moving experiences of his early life which he now remembered and it sustained him.

His head lolled gently from side to side as he dozed off, dreaming short dreams as fragments of memory. Of things that mattered and things that didn't. Hearing the private debate of his mind in the echoes of his thoughts. Experiencing his minority and feeling the sadness of it in the fountain of his life, the energy of which had been expended while he moved on wheels, back and forth, forever, it seemed. Rocking and swaying. Subservient and polite. Attentive to others. Waiting to do their bidding.

In a shimmer of memory he saw the slant of white sails dirtied by time and the wind, catching a sharp shaft of sunlight cutting through a grey patch of cloud as the fishing boat cleaved its grotesque way through fussy rollers.

He heard quick snatches of unintelligible sounds reaching across the water before they were caught up by the jealous wind and lost forever.

He heard music coming in chords from the wheels as they rolled through the percussion of their circumference. A monotonous metronome without the descant lilt of a high-pitched steel drum.

It was the rhythm of the turning wheels that reminded him of the syncopations of long-forgotten melodies. Ribald and happy. Satirical and pungent. Bodies rocking and swaying in abandoned time. Lithe and twisting. Double-jointed and bent backwards in limbo. Performing in art what his fathers had done in forced abduction. Muscles raised and shone with sweat and activity. Not flat and flabby from the sedentary life. Eyes that flashed sensuously with excitement. Not listless and dulled by boredom. It was almost as if youth was perennial.

He opened his eyes with a start and looked out the window, but he felt the claustrophobia of the white vastness closing in about him, and he shut his eyes again against the glare. He felt the train slowing again and it stopped once more.

He became conscious of the little girl again. She was regarding him with the same look of open curiosity and shyness. He returned her silent gaze, wordlessly.

"Why's the train stopping?" she asked suddenly, in her high pitched voice.

"I dunno. Probably the track's not clear up ahead," he said.

"How'd they know that?" she queried inquisitively, with the solemnity of the seven-year-old. It was then that he saw the precociousness in her face which had escaped him before. It was how her eyes searched his face that made him conscious of the way she looked. What he had taken for softness and innocence was a mask. There was no fragility about her. He could see that now as her mouth pursed in tightness and he wondered how he could have been mistaken the first time.

"How'd they know all that?" she insisted impatiently.

"They've got signals and lights and things."

"Is that so?"

She looked at her doll for a moment and brushed back a blonde, nylon curl from its painted face, with a serious gesture, then she returned her attention to him.

"What's your doll's name?" he asked.

She contemplated him for a moment as if trying to decide whether she wanted to give more to their relationship. Whether she wished to barter anything on his terms. Her eyes narrowed in suspicion, as if remembering a warning she had been given, then she relaxed, but still remained on her guard.

"I jus' call her Doll. She's on'y a doll y'know. Not a real, real person, so I don' call her by a person's name."

"I suppose you can't. Not really."

There was a moment of silence.

"And what's your name?" he asked.

She hesitated again before she answered and once more her eyes narrowed. There was a knowing reflection in the pools of light behind the slits of her eyes.

"Mary," she said crisply.

"That's a nice name," he said.

The look of suspicion remained and she did not speak immediately, as if she was trying to make up her mind about him. When she spoke there was a trace of uncertainty which she tried to hide, but failed to do.

"No. Not really," she said slowly, picking her words. "Mary's a very common kind of name."

It was as if she had rehearsed the phrase many times before in her mind. She chose then to speak of it in a chord of discontent which was flat and valueless. For the first time he noticed that she had a trace of a lisp in her voice.

"I think it's a nice name," he told her, without really meaning it.

She shrugged her shoulders with disinterest and looked at her doll, then she turned to him, frankly.

"You know other Marys?"

"Yes."

A note of aggression crept into her voice. "See what I mean? That's why I don't like it. Other people have it, too. I wanna name all my own. My very own . . . so no one else c'n have it. A real pretty name."

"Like what?" he asked patiently, continuing the conversation for no particular reason.

She hesitated, lost for a moment in thought. She bit on her bottom lip and rubbed her shoe against the back of her leg as she balanced herself against the door.

"I dunno," she said, baffled. "But it'd be a beautiful name all the same, an' n'body else could use it. It'd be mine. Wouldn' that be good?"

"Yes."

There was another long silence and she turned half-voluntarily to leave, then she changed her mind and stayed.

"I shouldn' be talkin' to you," she remarked matter of factly.

"No?"

"No."

"Why not?" he asked, feigning surprise.

"Cause mommy says I shouldn' never talk to strangers," she said, seriously, and looked at her doll for confirmation. "Specially men. Ol' men too."

"Oh."

"Yes. They interfere with little girls, you know."

"Is that so?"

"Bad things too, my mommy says. She tells me so alla time. It's kinda scary, isn' it?"

"Yes it is."

"Mommy's kinda mean though, and she doesn' all the time say the truth. She fibs to me sometimes. But I can't fib to her. She beats me if I do," she said confidentially. "She's strange, sometimes, and she an' Daddy used to fight a lot."

"That's too bad for a little girl," he said, feeling some mechanical sympathy for the little girl.

"Mommy doesn't like me to talk to n'body. Says I musn' 'sturb them. It's kinda lonely sometimes."

"I guess it must get that way," he said, beginning to feel the weight of the conversation. He imagined he felt the press of evil invading innocence in the girl's mind.

He felt the irritation return once more and as he thought about it he became aware that it had always been with him, secreting some kind of sadness which now surrounded him like a deep lagoon he was unable to fathom.

The years had passed so swiftly on the rolling wheels and his life had been a continuing series of kaleidoscopic visions which came and went without leaving a firm imprint on his mind. They were blurs in time.

And people who came and went. Migrating through his life while he did their bidding. Reciprocating their smiles without substance and leaving no warmth behind.

"Course, he wasn' my real daddy," the girl said intruding on his thoughts once more. "Mommy said my real daddy went away somewhere 'fore I was born. Seems like he isn' coming back. But I wish he would. Mommy says we're going home now, but I don' know where home is. We been movin' 'round a lot. An' I've had more'n one daddy, too. But I didn't like none of them. Only the one that went 'way 'fore I was born. I think he mus' be a nice man. Only my mommy won' talk 'bout him. She shushes me when I ask. You would think she would tell me, won' you?"

"Yes."

"Are you goin' home, too?"

He nodded his head slowly. "Yes, I'm going home."

"That's nice. You've got a nice home?"

He nodded his head again. "Well . . . yes . . . you could say I have a nice home."

She cocked her head in suspicion and her eyes narrowed. "You don' seem too sure."

"Yes, I'm sure."

"I see," she said and remained silent for a long time before she spoke again. "Why aren't you workin' like them?"

"Like who?"

She inclined her head towards the dining car ahead. "Those others, y'know. You look like them. That's wha' my mommy says. Says you people all look alike. She means in the dinin' car. 'Course I think she fibbin', 'cause I don' think you look alike. Everybody's different, don' you think?"

"Yes. Everybody's different," he said, then fumbled in his pocket and brought out a candy. "Here. Take this."

She looked at him skeptically and drew back momentarily. "Mommy says I shouldn' take sweets from n'body. But I guess you're differ'nt. You're old, too."

"Yes. I'm old."

"Where's your home?" she asked, but before he could reply they were interrupted by a sharp voice calling the girl's name.

Her face grew slack and her eyes widened in sudden terror before they clouded over and went blank. "Oh, oh . . . That's mommy. She's goin' be mad 'cause I 'scaped from her. But you wouldn't tell her I was 'sturbin' you, would you?"

"No," he said and discovered he was holding the candy limply in his hand.

He looked up and saw the face of the woman looking down at him. It was young, but there were lines about her eyes, and her mouth drooped giving her a look of disdain. Her hair was parted in the middle and it flowered in an orderly mass down to her shoulders in even blondeness. It was the kind of face which presumed a lot and the initial reaction was to dislike it. But a closer look could evoke some sympathy for it. There was a quality of hurt behind it which the careful makeup could not hide. She looked at him with a drawn expression as if she was burdened by the responsibility of the confrontation and an absent, courteous smile came to her lips.

Harold Marshall / 111

Under her white dress with the red trim, he knew her body would be hard and unyielding. He saw her long talons of fingers curl around the girl's shoulders. The look of stark fear which came to the girl's face had disappeared and in its place was a passive immobility.

"I'm sorry," the woman said. Her voice was low and husky, but he knew it was capable of pitching itself an octave higher in nagging or in anger. Now it was crisp and controlled, and he guessed the woman was somewhere around twenty-five.

He shrugged his shoulders.

"I've told her to keep quiet and not to go around disturbing people," the woman said.

"I wasn' 'sturbin' him," the little girl said, then turned to him for support. "Was I?"

He shook his head and gave a lipless smile. "She wasn' disturbing me. We was jus' talking," he said.

"See," the little girl replied, turning her head, with the note of quiet triumph in her voice. The earlier antagonism had now gone, replaced by one of bravado.

"Still, you disobeyed me. I told you to stay in the roomette," the woman said harshly, with her voice pitched higher than the throaty tone she had used just a moment before.

"Well, you went 'way with that man . . . you know, the one we met at dinner las' night," the little girl said in a forced voice that had a note of challenge in it.

"Never mind that. You disobeyed me . . . You know what happens when you disobey me?"

The little girl tried not to nod her head, but it bobbed up and down involuntarily like a puppet's.

"But I wasn' 'sturbin' him. He said so hisself. We was jus' talkin'. Says he's goin' home too," the little girl started to babble quickly. "I mean, we are goin' home . . . Our new home, aren't we?"

"Yes."

"Tha's what we was talkin' 'bout."

"Were, dear . . . That's what we *were* talking about . . . not was. Now come along," the woman said in a voice now hardened by admonition.

He found it difficult to keep up with the rapid changes in her personality.

"We've had lots o' new homes y'know," the little girl told him abruptly, not heeding her mother's tightening grip on her shoulder.

"Come along," the woman insisted more shrilly.

"But look, he isn' workin' like the others. He's jus' sittin' an' listenin' to things with his eyes shut. Aren't you?" the little girl said in final appeal to the woman.

He interrupted before the woman could reply. "She wasn' disturbing me at all. I was just sitting here looking outside. Haven't been able to do this too often in the last thirty years."

"You been on the train f' . . . thir . . . thirty years?" the little girl asked, glad for the opportunity to try for a reprieve from the woman.

"Yes."

"Musta met lotsa people."

"Yes."

"That'd be neat . . . But I guess it musta been kinda lonely, too," the little girl said, sobering.

"Yes," he said impulsively.

"But why aren't you workin' like the others . . . You playin' hooky or somethin'?"

He smiled briefly and shook his head. "No, this is my last trip, so my friends told me to take it easy. Be a passenger for once. They'd wait on me."

"Come along now," the woman said insistently. "The man doesn't want to be disturbed any longer. He wants to sit here and think about things in silence."

"But . . . I . . ." the little girl protested.

"You disobeyed me . . . I told you to stay in the compartment . . . You know you're not to talk to strangers . . . Come along . . . And you'll stay in the compartment, this time."

There was no mistaking the manner of the voice this time. It carried the threat of pain and hurt with it, and the little girl who had heard the tone before, surrendered in defeat. The pout to her mouth lost its petulance and it trembled as quick tears filled her eyes.

She allowed herself to be propelled by her mother. She went without a word, holding her doll carelessly at her side. It was no longer important to her. It didn't share her confidences and her decisions.

The man became conscious of the train moving again. He was disturbed by the woman, and the irritation and discomfort returned to him once more. They remained at the base of his consciousness and snared his thoughts.

He thought of his life and the seasons of spring and summer and fall and winter as quick snatches of time on the wheels of a train. Waving colour and tall, gaunt trees. Everything running together in quick glimpses of days turning to years, coming and going before he was aware of them.

He closed his eyes once more and felt the agony of thinking of things in the silence. The train had gathered speed, rolling along effortlessly, devouring frigid miles. In a few days he would know the warmth of his youth once more. He had to escape and go back to where he did not have to experience his minority and his subservience. But even as he thought about it, he felt the guilt of his reason. He had left his home in the first place because he had felt restricted in it. There were other things to be done. More sights to be seen. Other ways to live, away from the solitary clang of a cheap church bell and people burdened by their own way of life.

It all came back to him now . . . Like darkness . . . Like sleep. The brief involuntary visions of the past. . . .

And that is how they found him later . . . slumped forward and lolling against the window of the cubicle he was in, with his sightless eyes looking at a small church framed in the snow next to the train, in the town where they had stopped.

He hadn't seen it, of course. The last thing he thought he saw was the soft, silken brown arrows of the sugar cane waving on the wind . . . beckoning . . . beckoning. . .

A Real Live Death

Katie Funk Wiebe

Death came in bunches that year, like grapes on a vine. First, there was the death of our grandmother, but it never seemed like a death, for it was only on paper. A letter from Russia, edged in black, to Mother and Dad, stated what had happened and how it had happened. And what she had said to her children before she died—about getting the milking done, and where the rope was to tie the cow. It was a death for Mother, for it was her mother, but it wasn't really a death for the rest of us, for it took nothing from our lives, even as our grandmother's life had added nothing to them. We had never known her.

Then there was the death of the father of Dorothy, my friend in school in fifth grade, and that wasn't really a death either, for one day her older sister found him hanging by a rope in the old barn by the slough. And he was dead with his tongue sticking out. She had run screaming from the place for someone to help her cut him down, and she only about seventeen. And the next day everyone was talking about it in school before the bell rang and during recess, but Dorothy wasn't there, so she didn't hear us. And then after a while, she came back to school and life went on as before, only she didn't have a father.

One day I attended a real funeral—with a coffin, a body, a few flowers, a sermon and mourners, real ones. The local United Church minister had died—an old man who always wore a grey wool worsted suit—to match his grey beard and hair, I thought. Maybe even his insides were grey—he looked so old to me. He walked all stooped over, as if his backbone had gotten tired. Yet he spoke to me with a kind, gentle voice, as if he were stroking a cat. My parents liked him and his preaching. Now he was dead.

I walked around the grey coffin lined with shiny shirred

material and set upon chairs at the front of the church and looked in. An old man who didn't look like the man I had known lay in the box, his eyes closed, his wrinkled hands clasped over his chest as if in silent prayer, like he sometimes held them when he prayed in church. Although the adults around me looked sad and teary, I felt nothing. I looked for the wart on the side of his face that moved when he talked. It was still there. This death and the dying of Mother's mother as it had been explained in that long black-edged letter didn't match. Which was real death? What was dying? What happened before it happened? After? I didn't know.

One spring day Dad told us over our macaroni and sausage that a woman and her husband from the country church had been driving to town. Stories always got told like this, from the beginning. The fabric cover of the buggy had torn loose and its wild flapping had terrified the horse. The animal had jerked forward, pitching the woman over backwards onto the dirt road. Her neck had been broken. The funeral would be Sunday.

Dad took Annie and me to the funeral with him to the Russian church, about seven miles in the country. Frieda, Mother and the others stayed home. Annie and I were used to sitting quietly through long services we didn't understand. We had attended plenty of services that were either all German or all Russian, but today the service did not resemble the usual high-spirited gathering of the Russian services. The strong, sonorant female voices in the choir that usually carried the entire congregation along in jubilant hymns, sang softly, mournfully without even trying. I watched openly as a woman nearby wept in loud gasps, rubbing her eyes vigorously with a handkerchief borrowed from her husband's pocket. A man in a dark Sunday suit and white shirt, face darkened by the sun to the clear line where he wore his cap, sat with two small solemn boys, each scrubbed shiny clean, near the front, all rigid like the statue in the Memorial Park. No one whispered across the aisle as they usually did. The preacher's voice sounded grim, though I could understand only the odd word.

At the graveside—a crude oblong hole gouged deeply out of the virgin prairie—the coffin was opened for the last time. It was the custom. The woman in the church and some others cried in louder even more violent gasps, clutching each other. The man in the dark Sunday suit stood dumbly, staring into space across the grave. Someone had taken the children away. Other men in unaccustomed stiff suitcoats, marked by black crepe armbands, stood near the mounds of dirt by the hole, ropes in hands, ready to do the men's work at the funeral. In the background, a few children played by the cars and buggies, their high shrieks piercing the self-imposed silence.

Annie and I edged close to Dad, who stood near the dark cavernous hole. Curiosity overcame me. I wanted to see a dead person. This dead person. I bent over the hole, over the coffin, with its missing lid, for a good look—and nearly tumbled in. Below me, in the semi-darkness which shrouded the body, I saw my mother lying quietly, eyes closed. Same oval face. Same auburn-red hair, parted and pulled back. Same pale complexion. Same well-defined lips.

Mother! My mother?

My heart thudded and twisted as if it wanted to leap out of its prison. My stomach churned. I felt my body shudder under the assault of this recognition.

Why hadn't Dad told us we were going to Mother's funeral? Was this the way it was done? We had seen her alive about an hour ago at home, sitting in the rocking chair by the dining-room window reading the *Zionsbote**. She hadn't been feeling well, as I remembered.

Dad didn't look particularly sad as he peered into the hole with me, although he looked solemn. But then I had never seen him crying for any reason. Fathers didn't cry. Only mothers and children cried. I wanted to shout, to scream, to force someone to explain to me what was happening before the men lowered the lid and nailed it shut. Mother—my mother! I needed my mother. I wasn't big like my mother who could get along in this country without her mother. I hadn't outgrown her—not yet.

No one listened to my pounding heart, and I had no courage to cry out. The men in the dark suits and crepe armbands lowered the lid, then one man jumped nimbly into the grave and nailed it shut. The others helped him clamber back out. Then I heard the

Zionsbote: the name of a newspaper

dull thumps of shovelfulls of soil hitting the lid, soil which probably had never been disturbed before, except for Indians riding or walking over it. The mourners and sightseers, restrained yet relieved, turned and left. Annie and I followed Dad to the car, parked on the far side of the church.

Dad guided the car over the rutty dirt roads back to town, all three of us sitting in the narrow front seat. I sat rigid, cold, clutching my insides to keep from crying. Dad drove into the driveway of our yard as he usually did, and Annie and I crawled out before he put the car away in the garage. He closed the garage doors and locked them, then he turned to close the yard gate. There were patterns to our family life—doors were locked and gates were closed at all times. Some gates and doors were used a lot and some were used only a little. Our front door with its small strip of stained glass symbolized a life that might some day come to our family in this new country. We used that door very little, though it led to the parlor where the couch, the piano, the Victrola and the large fern reigned in joint solitary splendor. In winter the door was covered with heavy corrugated cardboard to keep out the icy drafts, and couldn't be opened at all. The back door handled the family and even the guest traffic. It led to Mother, the kitchen and warmth. But we had been away, and now it was time to close the gate and open the kitchen door. I hesitated to enter.

I swung the door quickly. There stood Mother, as usual, in her blue checked dress and white apron, bending over the kitchen stove, cooking something for supper in the blue enamel pot.

*"Wie ging es?"** she asked, glancing up from the pot she was stirring. It smelled like cocoa. We often had cocoa on Sunday evenings.

I looked at her, wanting to run to her, grab her, hold her, but I stayed in the small entryway where we kept the wood, the snow barrels, and the washing machine and outdoor clothes, took off my coat with deliberate movements, looking at Mother sideways. Mother was not dead, not in that box they had buried in the ground. That woman had been someone else's mother. I still had

"Wie ging es?": "How was it?"

my own. But some day she would die. Some day I might die, and they would lay me in a box and cover me with dirt. Death terrified me, but not as much as the fear of being buried alive. What if they buried me in a coffin before I was so dead I would never come alive again?

Lying beside my sister in the darkness of the night, I heard the clock strike ten, then eleven—and the story of the two young men in one of the German villages in the Ukraine who had died of typhus came back in many forms. In Russia when a person died, family members laid the body out on boards in the *Sommastoav*, washed it, then swabbed it with alcohol to preserve it until the relatives from neighboring villages showed up for the funeral. On the day of the funeral of the young men, the men who came to take the bodies to the church noticed beads of perspiration on the forehead of one of the bodies. They listened for a heartbeat but could find none. They placed a feather before his nostrils, but it stayed motionless. They argued back and forth what to do. What if he were alive and they buried him? They tried to rouse him, but it was useless. Finally they buried him with the other one, convinced he was more dead than alive.

The thought made me burrow deep into the hollow spot in the mattress of our white iron bed. I imagined the young man waking in the darkness of his narrow resting place and hearing the dirt being thrown onto the lid. Plunk! Plunk! Another clod! Buried alive! His weak shouts had nowhere to go in the small dark space. I could feel his heart racing as fast as my own as the realization hit him. I nearly smothered myself in the tunnel I burrowed for myself in the covers smelling thickly of sleep and human bodies.

And then strangely, I forgot about death.

For many years, each morning before we ate Mother usually read us stories from a German Bible storybook. I liked the Old Testament stories better than the New Testament ones. I didn't like the ones about Jesus being betrayed by Peter and Judas, then whipped by some other men, and crucified on the cross. I tried hard not to listen when Mother got to that section, which was usually before Easter. As she read, I thought my own thoughts about the play we were practicing in school or whom I would ask to play jacks or knife with me at recess. When I looked at the pictures by myself, I usually skipped the whole section about the crucifixion of Christ. I knew what was on those pages—the thief twisted in pain, the sad women kneeling at the foot of the cross where Jesus hung, his crown of thorns puncturing his brow, and blood and water spurting from his side. That death didn't make sense.

Because Easter usually came before the roads to our own German church across the river opened up in spring, we often attended services at the country Russian church. The Russians were friendly, generous people. On this special day they brought the symbols of the risen Christ with them to the service—big mushroom-shaped loaves of decorated *Paska* resting in baskets lined with colourfully embroidered napkins. When the people met on Easter Sunday, they greeted each other with special words—not "How are you?" or "Good morning" but with *"Christoss Voskress!"* (Christ is risen) to which the one being greeted responded, *"Voistinno Voskress"* (has risen indeed). Occasionally the women would exchange *pysanky*, eggs painted in batik fashion with multi-colored design, as a symbol of the new life.

I couldn't say the Russian words, but the happy chorus of deep and high voices in the small crowded entry, intermingled with human and sometimes barn smells, lifted the gloom of the previous days. I wished I could speak Russian so I could say the greeting to someone also. But always I was glad we could forget the terrible stories of Jesus on the cross for another year. When I was bothered about going to hell, and about the world ending suddenly on December 31, I stood in the clothes closet where Mother's nightgown hung limp but secure and said, "Come into my heart, Lord Jesus; Come into my heart, Lord Jesus," and hoped he had by the time I was finished.

If my parents at times clung to Old Country customs, or at least enjoyed the *Paska* and colored Easter eggs, they found some of the new Canadian ones hard to accept. They had grown up in a country where the poor had actually begged door to door for food or starved. Therefore, they had no understanding of the custom of trick or treating at Halloween. The first years we children asked to go out with our friends, Mother's answer was a firm "no" and Dad's even firmer. Go out begging? Unthinkable!

No child of his would beg for candy from his customers and friends. He would bring us some candy from the store. We accepted the unpleasant ultimatum for several years, though bug-eyed with jealousy when our school chums came to the classroom the next morning burdened with candy kisses, gum, and apples, while we cradled our little handful of suckers in one palm.

Every Halloween I came to Mother and Dad with the same question. I wanted to dress up like a ghost and go trick or treating. It wasn't begging, not the Russian kind where a boy or girl in tatters walked from door to door with soulful eyes, pleading for *Khleb** to keep from starving. This was Canada, not Russia. This was fun, a kind of game. No one minded us children coming to their door for treats. Didn't mother give cookies to the children who came to our door? Didn't Dad give gum and suckers to the children who came to the store? Couldn't I go, just once?

One year after first talking it over with Dad in the little upstairs bedroom, Mother agreed to let me go with my friend Mona for "a little while." I found an old sheet, cut some holes in it for eyes, and joined Mona and the other girls under the corner lightpost, a paper shopping bag under my arm. At last. I had made the break. I was one of the gang hollering "Trick or treat" at door after door. Up one street, down another we went. We collected a weighty bag of candy, gum, apples and cookies. The butcher gave us each a wiener. The druggist handed out samples of toothpaste.

My "little while" was nearly used up when we knocked at a small white house, dimly lit, on a side street. I was shivering from the cold already and knew it was time to quit, but we wanted to finish off a few last houses before we went home to show off our loot to younger brothers and sisters. I banged on the door of this small house with new-found bravado—I was doing it like the others—a real Canadian—no longer an immigrant—and shouted "trick or treat!" We never actually soaped anyone's windows if the people didn't give us treats, but this was what the bigger children always said, so we said it too. "Trick or treat!" we shrieked as we waited for someone to answer our knock.

*Khleb: bread (in Russian)

A greying, thinnish woman with deep lines in her forehead, dressed in a limp gingham housedress, opened the door to say brusquely, "There're no treats here tonight! A man's dying in here," and swung the door shut in my face.

My feet refused to move. Dying? How often had she said those words that evening? A man was dying behind that wooden door of the house with the low porch and the broken step we had walked up. Was it her husband? Was he lying on the bed or sitting? What did people do when they knew they were dying? Did they talk about milking stools and ropes or about Halloween treats? Mona and I turned and went home, never saying a word. I never went trick or treating again.

And then one spring, death moved close again in another way. Next door to us lived an elderly couple named Zbitnoffs. I never figured out what Mr. Zbitnoff did for a living, anymore than I ever figured out what many people in our small community did for a living who didn't go to work on Main Street in one of the businesses there like the grocery store, hardware, shoemaker shop, law office, drugstore, bank, cafe, or poolroom. I think he may have been a retired farmer. This congenial couple spoke too little English for me to understand their conversation with Mother, who spoke Russian well.

Mrs. Zbitnoff had a flourishing garden of vegetables with lots more cabbage, dill, and cucumbers than we grew. We children ate the raspberries from their canes that grew over our side of the wooden fence. Our houses, built close together, looked almost like twins. If we had had windows on their side, I could have touched their wall with a long reach through a window—at least using a short stick. The long run alongside the house on our side of the fence, closed off at one end by a rain barrel and a pile of wood, made a wonderful place to hide in the early evening when we children played Run my Good Sheep Run. Mrs. Zbitnoff often knew we were hiding there when we crouched next to the galvanized iron rain barrel as she worked in her garden, but she never told on us, only smiled her quiet gentle smile while her eyes got lost in the crinkles of her skin.

One day Mrs. Zbitnoff told Mother that her daughter Glycera was coming home from her missionary work in North Africa sick with tuberculosis, that terrible disease. TB meant first isolation, then surgery, then a slow death. The doctors in the East (meaning Toronto—always Toronto) had done the surgery, removing a lung and some ribs. Now she was coming home to die. Mrs. Zbitnoff's eyes glistened unusually bright as she talked to Mother, who later relayed the story to us.

Death was coming closer to me and our family. Next door. So close I could touch the tree, the rain barrel, the house, that would shelter it. My skin prickled at the thought.

We met Miss Z. several days later resting on her bed in the small front bedroom off the living room. She didn't mind us children staring at her and at the dozens of bottles and containers lined up on the small table—or even at her clothes lying on the patchwork quilt on her narrow bed. I examined everything carefully, especially trying to get a good look at Miss Z. This dark-haired, dark-eyed woman with the thinned out face and caved-in back and shoulder looked sick in her body, I decided, but her eyes looked like living and like a person who liked living. Which seemed strange. She joked and laughed and then spat into her paper sputum cups, which her mother burned almost immediately in the crackling flame of the kitchen stove. Sputum. I almost liked the sound of the word. In Blaine Lake lots of men spat, and the little globs, sometimes stained a deep tobacco brown, looked disgusting as they withered on the sidewalk on Main Street beside the dog turds. I watched carefully where I put my feet when I walked in front of the poolroom. But hers wasn't spit. It was sputum and she burned it in the stove.

Signs of dying were all over her body, I agreed to myself, if you looked hard enough. Paper-thin skin stretched over her high cheekbones. Her legs and arms were really skiny—like chopsticks. She had a strange, slow way of moving her body when she wanted to get up. Her clothes hung loosely, like a hundred-pound flour sack trying to cover only fifty pounds of the stuff.

The signs of death were there. But they had missed her eyes. They sparkled, as if daring death to overtake her. But then, maybe, eyes were the last to die, and some day I would walk over to her house, and her eyes would look like the rest of her or like the eyes of the minister in the coffin several years ago. I decided to watch her eyes. Then I'd find out about death.

We girls visited her often in that small front bedroom of the nextdoor house. Miss Z. assured us there was no danger of catching TB. We should come as often as we liked. The sputum cup was an extra precaution because she had been a nurse.

As she lay in bed she told us stories about working in a hospital for natives in Africa, always with a chuckle or the desire to amuse. Another day she showed us how deeply corroded the underside of her wristwatch had become because of perspiring heavily in the tropics. We stood and marveled at the power of human sweat. In cold Saskatchewan we hardly knew what sweat was, even in summer. She told us about the last trip home on the ship and how the ship's officers had wanted to carry her off ship to shore on a stretcher. She had refused. "As long as I can walk, I will." Sometimes we heard stories about growing up on a farm in Blaine Lake in the early pioneer days and of nurse's training in the city when duty hours were long and strenuous. She brought a new dimension into our lives of a life of possibility beyond the borders of our small town. That her life had ended in TB didn't make the previous years less worthwhile.

Then one day the sparkling eyes looked sad. We were paging through Eaton's mail order catalogue together, ooh-ing and ah-ing over the gorgeous lace-trimmed wedding dresses with long trains and beaded veils cascading down the brides' back in billows of white airy foam. "I shouldn't be looking at wedding dresses," she commented to no one in particular. "I should be looking at funeral clothes." She spat the remark out like the men downtown spat their chewing tobacco.

So it was coming after all. And for a long time I didn't want to go next door anymore.

Shortly after Miss Z. returned to Blaine Lake, her father built a screened-in porch on the upstairs verandah. She wanted to sleep there in the open air, he told my mother. The doctors said it might help. He would humor her.

Each evening through the short summer and late into fall when the snow was already falling gently on the dried grass and the air was getting crisp so that my nose tingled when I walked to school, she had her mother wrap her snugly in wool comforters with hot water bottles and heated bedstones and roll her cot onto the porch for the night.

Early, very early in spring she started sleeping out there again. As I lay in my bed with Annie just a few feet from Miss Zbitnoff on the open porch, but separated now by only one wall and one screen, I thought about her. Glycera. A different name. Not like my plain one. A romantic name. I let it roll off my tongue. There she was alone on that verandah—always the last to see the fireflies flitting in the night air, the first to check out the Big Dipper and to see the brilliant northern lights scramble through the heavens to find the best place to glimmer. In spring she was the first to hear the rain dripping from the eaves, the first to smell the fresh breezes, the first to see the sun rising in the East, the first to hear the meadowlark greet the day. She was dying close to life, I decided. A rather nice way to go.

Glycera wore mules. I had seen the word in a storybook, so I knew what they were. Black satin ones, and a cotton dress that buttoned down the front to accommodate her weakened shoulder and arm muscles where the lung and bones had been cut out. As the months wore on, occasionally she walked to our house in her mules and cotton dress, entering through the kitchen door, sometimes going as far as the dining room to visit with Mother and drink a cup of tea. I decided she always carried her sputum cup with her, so that if death overtook her at an unguarded moment, she could cough its essence into the paper container and give it to someone to burn. I watched carefully for the day to come—and yet once again the eyes sparkled.

One Saturday Mother sent me to Zbitnoffs with some freshly baked crumbcake. I carried the plate carefully so as not to lose any of the buttery-crisp crumbs. Miss Zbitnoff was lying on her bed, dressed in a flowered navy silk dress—one without buttons marching down the front. The mules had been exchanged for solid black oxfords—low and comfortable. A new brown coat with a wolf-fur collar lay on her suitcases beside her. I looked so hard, I stumbled into the doorway and almost lost the cake.

She took the plate from me with a wide grin. Her mother smiled her usual crinkly smile, her dark eyes happy. Then Glycera reached down. Her eyes hugged me first. She stretched her arms out and drew me close. My hands felt the bones stick out and the hollow places gape as my arms closed around her cut-up body.

"I'm going to Toronto to visit some friends—say thanks to your mother for the cake," she whispered. "I'll see you in the fall. You helped me get well by visiting me."

I ran out the door and back home, not stopping to miss the cracks in the sidewalk as I usually did. My heart was singing. Glycera wasn't dying. She was going to live. She had stared into the darkness each night with those dark brown eyes and refused to let the darkness fill them. She had looked out, beyond the verandah screens and seen life. I had looked into the darkness of the hole at the church graveyard that day when the woman was buried and seen death—and been afraid.

Life was a gift, not a hostile force that tried to kill us off, one by one. Grandmother Janzen in Russia had died lying on her thin mattress. She had struggled for life and to stay with those who had to milk the cows, but death had come. Yet there was a rhythm to life that included both the limits of human finitude to suffer and the potential of the human spirit to strike back. Glycera had looked up night after night and found strength to die, and now she was going to live.

"Christoss Voskress," I shouted as I ran to tell Mother the good news. My plate was empty, yet Glycera had just given me a whole mountain of colored Easter eggs. And Easter was still two weeks away. I would listen to the Easter story this year. I understood.

"Voistinno Voskress! Voistinno Voskress!" shrilled a meadow-lark on a fencepost.

Vaivém

Laura Bulger

An icy wind sweeps across the prairie. *We have become resigned.
It has been like this since we arrived.* Today, it slashes like
sharpened steel. Twenty four degrees below zero and still dropping. Centigrade, of course. Now, they begin to think in Centigrade; the population is still confused by the conversion. Distances can no longer be measured; the metric system threatens the
general well-being. *A few days ago, a plane had to make a forced
landing: the pilot had made a mistake with the conversions. He
noticed he was short of gasoline way up there, so they say.* The streets
are deserted; shiny polished extensions under a bright sun, which
fails to melt the icy layers. Many folk often end up stretched out
on the ground. *Some time ago . . . I slipped on my ass and saw stars!
It was near my friend's store. No one even bothered to help me get up.
Who cares? Each one for himself!* The only difference between the
foot path and the track for the cars is that it looks darker and
thinner. Vehicles of all sizes travel it—automobiles, trucks,
coaches, wagons, big cars, small cars, fumes, pollution. No one
ventures on foot. It has always been like this since the snow. It is
hot inside the stores. The Jingle Bells remind us it's Christmas.
*This is our area. We are honest, hard-working people, everybody
knows that, even the politicians, when they come here and talk to us.
That's the truth, we are honest, hard-working people. When those
guys at the factory wanted to go on strike, we all gathered, Zé Vieira,
Seixas, Medeiros and I, and decided we were going back to work.
Those thugs want to live on insurance and welfare. Then, they say
there is no work. We can always find work, even for low wages. We
are honest and hard-working people, and that's a fact.* They come
here in the hope of a better life. Fortunes to be made in a short

while. They had heard . . . they were told . . . but they were not sure. *There is everything here; it's not like in my country, shrunk and empty, now that people are gone. Those who stay don't want to work, they don't want to go through all this, as we do.* "We", heroes of the sea surrounded by the vastness of the steppe and by a river of dubious memory: RED RIVER. They might have been compelled by centuries of atavistic longings, a taste for adventure, illusion, hopelessness, greed, survival. *I arrived here penniless, no work, no family, no friends. I didn't even speak the language, but I managed. Let everyone else do the same!* Compassion is dead. And the others? Some were even sponsored. *My elder brother came before, alone. Then, it was my turn; I found a job right away in the mines.* The dream of a far away country is fading and, instead, a nostalgia, not always of pleasant memories, begins creeping into their souls. Perhaps, no one there will prepare a feast for the prodigal son, nor will there be a fanfare in the village. He may have to stay put. *I'm tired. I have worked hard. Sometimes, I think of going back, but Ana likes it here. She is used to it. She makes a little money, has her own friends and now that her children are grown up, she thinks of going back to school.* Some arrived after a long journey through other foreign lands, homes built and rebuilt, dreams shattered and hopes yet to be realized; children born along the way, of different nationalities, whom the parents will never come to know. The tenacity of those early times has been weakened and tempered. *We bought a piece of land over there to build a little house, just for us; the children want to stay here.* The fatigue does not erase memories. They recall the day they left as if it were yesterday. In their fantasy they create heroes, heroes of the steppe determined by the logic of their emotions. *I am tired, you know. I would like to go back one day but . . . a grandson was born to us.* There is faith in continuity. His face lights up with a sudden hope which carries him back to his beginnings. *We want our children to know our history, theirs as well. They should feel pride in their origins. I say ORIGINS. Language, history, culture. Yes, our culture is very important. But . . . my son only speaks English. He is a real Canadian. He was born here after I had gone to the mines.* Joe, Mary and

Fern were born here too. They only speak English. No participation, no complaints either; they just try to follow parents, teachers, the Constitution. *That's where the rights of citizens are defined*. Everything is clear for those who want to read it, rather, for those who can understand it. They are Canadians by law. They are Canadians by the jeans they wear, the French fries, the junk food they eat . . . never to be served at home! In other words, a subculture which is the basis of homogeneity. *It's fundamental to study these children, to do further research with more scientific guidelines on these questions of identification, on individuals whose identities remain . . . unidentifiable*. This is the opinion of sociologists, psychologists, psychiatrists, educators, guidance counsellors, social workers and all those who offer their lives for the public good. It is necessary to catalogue and reach conclusions. Though for some it doesn't matter, for the others the paternal influence is still strong. *And that's how it should be! After all, it's for our own good. This society is rotten* . . . Others say: *I avoid the gatherings of the club on Sundays. Men play billiards and talk about things which are of no interest. It is boring!* They go on trying to understand. *Do people live like this in Portugal? Are young people more liberated? It's different in Brazil, so say my cousins, who live there*. It's so far away and the distance makes things less important. The weather forecast is threatening; strong winds sweep across the prairies. *This Summer I was there for two months. My house is not yet ready. You know, that sonofabitch fooled me. He didn't even use the tiles I had chosen. He has done nothing! Everything has changed, you know. Here, we only live to work while, there, they do nothing; all they want is the good life. Gozar a vida!** The bitter criticism hiding the fading hopes. The anguished doubts of what might have been . . . *My children like it here and she . . . she doesn't want to go back. She is used to it*. Blinding snow, wind, the violence of winter wreaking

---

**Gozar a vida!: this Portuguese expression means "to enjoy life"— in context, an emphatic exclamation of disgust against those who only want to live "the good life."*

vengeance on those fierce plains. *I like to go there for holidays. The place I come from is beautiful but . . . it's difficult now, with my grandson. What a hellava life! Always coming and going, from here to there, there to here, um vaivém . . .* The sky darkens over the plains. Probably tomorrow the sun will shine again over this icy land.

I got used to it, you know.

Winnipeg, 1983.

POETRY

*Then the time of exile began,
the endless search for justifi-
cation, the aimless nostalgia,
the most painful, the most
heartbreaking questions, those
of the heart which asks itself
'Where can I feel at home?'*

ALBERT CAMUS, *THE REBEL*

I am a Canadian

Duke Redbird

I'm a lobster fisherman in Newfoundland
I'm a clambake in P.E.I.
I'm a picnic, I'm a banquet
I'm mother's homemade pie.
I'm a few drafts in a Legion hall in Fredericton
I'm a kite-flyer in a field in Moncton
I'm a nap on the porch after a hard day's work is done.
I'm a snowball fight in Truro, Nova Scotia
I'm small kids playing jacks and skipping rope
I'm a mother who lost a son in the last great war
And I'm a bride with a brand new ring
And a chest of hope
I'm an Easterner
I'm a Westerner
I'm from the North
And I'm from the South
I've swam in two big oceans
And I've loved them both
I'm a clown in Quebec during carnival
I'm a mass in the Cathedral of St. Paul
I'm a hockey game in the Forum
I'm Rocket Richard and Jean Beliveau
I'm a coach for little league Expos
I'm a baby-sitter for sleep-defying rascals
I'm a canoe trip down the Ottawa
I'm a holiday on the Trent
I'm a mortgage, I'm a loan
I'm last week's unpaid rent
I'm Yorkville after dark

I'm a walk in the park
I'm Winnipeg gold-eye
I'm a hand-made trout fly
I'm a wheat-field and a sunset
Under a prairie sky
I'm Sir John A. Macdonald
I'm Alexander Graham Bell
I'm a pow-wow dancer
And I'm Louis Riel
I'm the Calgary Stampede
I'm a feathered Sarcee
I'm Edmonton at night
I'm a bar-room fight
I'm a rigger, I'm a cat
I'm a ten-gallon hat
And an unnamed mountain in the interior of B.C.
I'm a maple tree and a totem pole
I'm sunshine showers
And fresh-cut flowers
I'm a ferry boat ride to the Island
I'm the Yukon
I'm the North-West Territories
I'm the Arctic Ocean and the Beaufort Sea
I'm the prairies, I'm the Great Lakes,
I'm the Rockies, I'm the Laurentians,
I am French
I am English
And I am Métis
But more than this
Above all this
I am a Canadian and proud to be free.

Select Samaritan

Robert Finch

We think we might adopt two children and
The problem is to know which kind we want.
Not Canadians. Refugees. But they can't
Be Jewish. A couple of Spaniards would be grand
If they were fair. My husband hates dark hair.
Afraid they are mostly dark in any case.
Germans would do, we don't care about race,
Except Chinese, must draw the line somewhere.

So would you let us know soon as you could
What sort's available? We have a car
And would be glad to come and look them over
Whatever time you say. Poles might be good,
Of the right type. Fussy? Perhaps we are
But any kids we take will be in clover.

The Immigrants

Margaret Atwood

They are allowed to inherit
the sidewalks involved as palmlines, bricks
exhausted and soft, the deep
lawnsmells, orchards whorled
to the land's contours, the inflected weather

only to be told they are too poor
to keep it up, or someone
has noticed and wants to kill them; or the towns
pass laws which declare them obsolete.

I see them coming
up from the hold smelling of vomit,
infested, emaciated, their skins grey
with travel; as they step on shore

the old countries recede, become
perfect, thumbnail castles preserved
like gallstones in a glass bottle, the
towns dwindle upon the hillsides
in a light paperweight-clear.

They carry their carpetbags and trunks
with clothes, dishes, the family pictures;
they think they will make an order
like the old one, sow miniature orchards,
carve children and flocks out of wood

but always they are too poor, the sky
is flat, the green fruit shrivels
in the prairie sun, wood is for burning;
and if they go back, the towns

in time have crumbled, their tongues
stumble among awkward teeth, their ears
are filled with the sound of breaking glass.
I wish I could forget them
and so forget myself:

my mind is a wide pink map
across which move year after year
arrows and dotted lines, further and further,
people in railway cars

their heads stuck out of the windows
at stations, drinking milk or singing,
their features hidden with beards or shawls
day and night riding across an ocean of unknown
land to an unknown land.

Provincial

Miriam Waddington

My childhood
was full of people
with Russian accents
who came from
Humble Saskatchewan
or who lived in Regina
and sometimes
visited Winnipeg
to bring regards
from their frozen
snowqueen city.

In those days
all the streetcars
in the world slept
in the Elmwood
car-barns and the
Indian moundbuilders
were still wigwammed
across the river
with the birds
who sang in the bushes
of St. Vital.

Since then I have
visited Paris
Moscow London
and Mexico City
I saw golden roofs
onion domes and the
most marvellous
canals, I saw people
sunning themselves
in Luxembourg Gardens
and on a London parkbench
I sat beside a man
who wore navy blue socks
and navy blue shoes
to match.

All kinds of miracles:
but I would not trade
any of them for the
empty spaces, the
snowblurred geography
of my childhood.

Great-Aunt Rebecca

Elizabeth Brewster

I remember my mother's Aunt Rebecca
Who remembered very well Confederation
And what a time of mourning it was.
She remembered the days before the railway.
And how when the first train came through
Everybody got on and visited it,
Scraping off their shoes first
So as not to dirty the carriage.
She remembered the remoteness, the long walks between
     neighbours.
Her own mother had died young, in childbirth,
But she had lived till her eighties,
Had borne eleven children,
Managed to raise nine of them,
In spite of scarlet fever.
She had clothed them with the work of her own fingers,
Wool from her own sheep, spun at home,
Woven at home, sewed at home
Without benefit of machine.
She had fed them with pancakes and salt pork
And cakes sweetened with maple sugar.
She had taught them one by one to memorize
'The chief end of man is to know God',
And she had also taught them to make porridge
And the right way of lighting a wood fire,
Had told the boys to be kind and courageous
And the girls never to raise their voices
Or argue with their husbands.

I remember her as an old woman,
Rheumatic, with folded hands,
In a rocking chair in a corner of the living room,
Bullied (for her own good) by one of her daughters.
She marveled a little, gently and politely,
At radios, cars, telephones;
But really they were not as present to her
As the world of her prime, the farmhouse
In the midst of woods, the hayfields
Where her husband and the boys swung their scythes
Through the burning afternoon, until she called for supper.

For me also, the visiting child, she made that world more real
Than the present could be. I too
Wished to be a pioneer,
To walk on snowshoes through remote pastures,
To live away from settlements an independent life
With a few loved people only; to be like Aunt Rebecca,
Soft as silk and tough as that thin wire
They use for snaring rabbits.

Grandfather

George Bowering

Grandfather
        Jabez Harry Bowering
strode across the Canadian prairie
hacking down trees
                    and building churches
delivering personal baptist sermons in them
leading Holy holy holy lord god almighty songs in them
red haired man squared off in the pulpit
reading Saul on the road to Damascus at them

Left home
        big walled Bristol town
at age eight
        to make a living
buried his stubby fingers in root snarled earth
for a suit of clothes and seven hundred gruelly meals a year
taking an anabaptist cane across the back every day
for four years till he was whipped out of England

Twelve years old
        and across the ocean alone
to apocalyptic Canada
            Ontario of bone bending child labor
six years on the road to Damascus till his eyes were blinded
with the blast of Christ and he wandered west
to Brandon among wheat kings and heathen Saturday nights
young red haired Bristol boy shoveling coal
in the basement of Brandon college five in the morning

Then built his first wooden church and married
a sick girl who bore two live children and died
leaving several pitiful letters and the Manitoba night

He moved west with another wife and built children and
　　churches
Saskatchewan Alberta British Columbia Holy holy holy
lord god almighty
　　　　　　　　struck his labored bones with pain
and left him a postmaster prodding grandchildren with
　　crutches
another dead wife and a glass bowl of photographs
and holy books unopened save the bible by the bed

Till he died the day before his eighty fifth birthday
in a Catholic hospital of sheets white as his hair

equal opportunity

Jim Wong-Chu

in early canada
when railways were highways

each stop brought new opportunities

there was a rule

> the chinese could only ride
> the last two cars
> of the trains

that is

until a train derailed
killing all those
in front

(the chinese erected an altar and thanked buddha)

a new rule was made
> the chinese must ride
> the front two cars
> of the trains

that is

until another accident
claimed everyone
in the back

(the chinese erected an altar and thanked buddha)

after much debate
common sense prevailed

the chinese are now allowed
to sit anywhere
on any train

inspection of a house paid in full

Jim Wong-Chu

I could not hide
my curiosity at your pride
in paying cash in full

perhaps it was
because you arrived
in canada
young and penniless

while working at our restaurant
you came up with the strangest notion
that some day
when you own your own place
you could get away
with substituting ink
for coffee

(cheap profitable imitation)

those wild hopeful impossibilities
made yours a rocky one man road
up the golden mountain

yet you made it

and today
looking me squarely in the eye
you tell me you have arrived
your family at your side

my last words
are

BEWARE THE TAXMAN

Autobiographical

Abraham Klein

Out of the ghetto streets where a Jewboy
Dreamed pavement into pleasant Bible-land,
Out of the Yiddish slums where childhood met
The friendly beard, the loutish Sabbath-goy,
Or followed, proud, the Torah-escorting band,
Out of the jargoning city I regret,
Rise memories, like sparrows rising from
The gutter-scattered oats,
Like sadness sweet of synagogal hum,
Like Hebrew violins
Sobbing delight upon their Eastern notes.

Again they ring their little bells, those doors
Deemed by the tender-year'd, magnificent:
Old Ashkenazi's cellar, sharp with spice;
The widows' double-parloured candy-stores
And nuggets sweet bought for one sweaty cent;
The warm fresh-smelling bakery, its pies,
Its cakes, its navel'd bellies of black bread;
The lintels candy-poled
Of barber-shop, bright-bottled, green, blue, red;
And fruit-stall piled, exotic,
And the big synagogue door, with letters of gold.

Again my kindergarten home is full—
Saturday night—with kin and compatriot:
My brothers playing Russian card-games; my
Mirroring sisters looking beautiful,
Humming the evening's imminent fox-trot;

My uncle Mayer, of blessed memory,
Still murmuring maariv, counting holy words;
And the two strangers, come
Fiery from Volhynia's murderous hordes—
The cards and humming stop.
And I too swear revenge for that pogrom.

Occasions dear: the four-legged aleph named
And angel pennies dropping on my book;
The rabbi patting a coming scholar-head;
My mother, blessing candles, Sabbath-flamed,
Queenly in her Warsovian perruque;
My father pickabacking me to bed
To tell tall tales about the Baal Shem Tov—
Letting me curl his beard.
Oh memory of unsurpassing love,
Love leading a brave child
Through childhood's ogred corridors, unfear'd!

The week in the country at my brother's—(May
He own fat cattle in the fields of heaven!)
Its picking of strawberries from grassy ditch,
Its odour of dogrose and of yellowing hay—
Dusty, adventurous, sunny days, all seven!—
Still follow me, still warm me, still are rich
With the cow-tinkling peace of pastureland.
The meadow'd memory
Is sodded with its clover, and is spanned
By that same pillow'd sky
A boy on his back one day watched enviously.

And paved again the street: the shouting boys,
Oblivious of mothers on the stoops,
Playing the robust robbers and police,
The corncob battle—all high-spirited noise
Competitive among the lot-drawn groups.
Another day, of shaken apple trees

In the rich suburbs, and a furious dog,
And guilty boys in flight;
Hazlenut games, and games in the synagogue—
The burrs, the Haman rattle,
The Torah dance on Simchas Torah night.

Immortal days of the picture calendar
Dear to me always with the virgin joy
Of the first flowering of senses five,
Discovering birds, or textures, or a star,
Or tastes sweet, sour, acid, those that cloy;
And perfumes. Never was I more alive.
All days thereafter are a dying off,
A wandering away
From home and the familiar. The years doff
Their innocence.
No other day is ever like that day.

I am no old man fatuously intent
On memoirs, but in memory I seek
The strength and vividness of nonage days,
Not tranquil recollection of event.
It is a fabled city that I seek;
It stands in Space's vapours and Time's haze;
Thence comes my sadness in remembered joy
Constrictive of the throat;
Thence do I hear, as heard by a Jewboy,
The Hebrew violins,
Delighting in the sobbed Oriental note.

Curriculum Vitae IV

Walter Bauer

He had said No
when very many said Yes.
For this No he had to give up his profession.
For this No they had smashed his teeth.
For this No they had deported him to a camp.
He had endured
because he was waiting for the dawn
of a human world and for judgement.
Did it come? Does dawn ever come?
Does judgement ever come?
The others came back,
made their nests, strutted about,
proved their innocence,
enjoyed patronage everywhere.
He could fight no longer;
he saw truth lacerated and torn apart;
he felt himself betrayed by time
which always betrays.
So he left—for this land of the maple leaf.
He wanted to forget—but can one ever forget?
He liked it here, the country was big
and its youth made him fresh again.
But at night he looked back in sorrow:
What are they doing over there? I have left my friends.
Friends, what are you doing?—
Then he was alone.
Then he felt those unforgotten blows again
and the expectation again of a dawn
which never came.

Translated by Henry Beissel

What Do I Remember of the Evacuation?

Joy Kogawa

What do I remember of the evacuation?
I remember my father telling Tim and me
About the mountains and the train
And the excitement of going on a trip.
What do I remember of the evacuation?
I remember my mother wrapping
A blanket around me and my
Pretending to fall asleep so she would be happy
Though I was so excited I couldn't sleep
(I hear there were people herded
Into the Hastings Park like cattle.
Families were made to move in two hours
Abandoning everything, leaving pets
And possessions at gun point.
I hear families were broken up
Men were forced to work. I heard
It whispered late at night
That there was suffering) and
I missed my dolls.
What do I remember of the evacuation?
I remember Miss Foster and Miss Tucker
Who still live in Vancouver
And who did what they could
And loved the children and who gave me
A puzzle to play with on the train.
And I remember the mountains and I was
Six years old and I swear I saw a giant

Gulliver of Gulliver's Travels scanning the horizon
And when I told my mother she believed it too
And I remember how careful my parents were
Not to bruise us with bitterness

And I remember the puzzle of Lorraine Life
Who said "Don't insult me" when I
Proudly wrote my name in Japanese
And Tim flew the Union Jack
When the war was over but Lorraine
And her friends spat on us anyway
And I prayed to the God who loves
All the children in his sight
That I might be white.

Immigrant

Madeline Coopsammy

I see her every day
Crossing the parking lot at four,
A black anomaly within a land of snow,

A lonely and misplaced woman
Desperately squeezing from the land
Its celluloid comforts.

Caribbean temper chilled
By guarded hostile looks
That stop the blood more than the blizzards and the frosts
Of barren prairie winters,
She often wonders *why*.

Not slave, neither *ayah** nor domestic
But now as pedagogue she comes,
Wistfully seeking a better life.

To Canada, land of silver dreams,
Refuge of slave, reject and persecuted,
But when the dross of mass-produced catalogue-bought trifles
Has worn,
And when the shiny metallic coach
Has spluttered and groaned its last
Somewhere upon a lonely highway
Its guts congealed by biting cold,
And when the sun petulantly hides its head,

Then insane jungle rhythms reverberate from
The gaudy Hilton perched crazily upon the
Belmont Hills.*
And amidst the fevered tingle of rum punches
Carnival spectres arise from
Decaying baronial mansions around the
Queen's Park Savannah
And return to haunt her.

*ayah: a nurse or maid, usually native to India.
*Belmont Hills: in Port-of-Spain, Trinidad.

Guest Worker Blues

Charles Roach

Long Summer days in South Ontario
I'm working hard like hell
They call me a guest worker
But I don't live in no hotel
Long summer days in South Ontario
The land is strong they say

So if you good enough to work
You should be good enough to stay
My country sold me into neo-slavery
Took me from Port-of-Spain
Put me on a jet plane
But see oh! see my plight
They said it was a boon
But it's a blight

This is the hard life
Of a guest worker
Here in Canada

They say that Canada
is a land with plenty dough
So I leave my wife and child
For Ontario
Now without friends and family
The bosses exploiting me

This is the hard life
Of a guest worker
Here in Canada

Conditions on this plantation
Are the same as before emancipation
But they take taxes from your pay
Unemployment dues, OHIP and pension
But you get no benefits
When they dump you an' say "That's it!"

This is the hard life
Of a guest worker
Here in Canada

In the land of Opportunity
The true north strong and free
You get no attention
When you complain of oppression
They'll say shut up and don't complain
Or we'll deport you on the next plane

This is the hard life
Of a guest worker
Here in Canada.

I Fight Back

Lillian Allen

ITT ALCAN KAISER
Canadian Imperial Bank of Commerce
These are privileged names in my Country
But I AM ILLEGAL HERE

My Children Scream
My Grandmother is dying

I came to Canada
And Found the Doors
Of Opportunities Well Guarded

I Scrub Floors
Serve Backra's Meals on Time
Spend two days working in one
And Twelve Days a Week

Here I Am in Canada
Bringing Up Someone Else's Child
While someone Else and Me in Absentee
Bring Up My Own

AND I FIGHT BACK

And Constantly they ask,
"Oh Beautiful Tropical Beach
With Coconut Tree and Rum,
Why did you Leave There
Why on Earth did you Come?"

AND I SAY:
  For the Same Reasons
  Your Mothers Came

  I FIGHT BACK

  They label me
  Immigrant, Law-breaker, illegal
  Ah No, Not Mother, Not Worker, Not Fighter

I FIGHT BACK
Like my Sisters Before Me
I FIGHT BACK
I FIGHT BACK

Winter '84

Krisantha Sri Bhaggiyadatta

I tell the corner store owner
"pretty cold out there"
he says
"ain't what it used to be"
"oh," i say, "why is that"
innocently
tensing
wondering if coloured immigration
has affected the seasons. . . .
"they've been fooling around
with the weather,"
he says
(his wife nods)
"ever since they sent a man
to the moon
it hasn't been right"

"oh," i say,
breathing out
intrigued
"yeah, i know what you mean"

in the valley of the towers
of king & bay
the base of the toronto-dominion, royal bank
first canadian place, royal trust, bank of nova scotia:

secretaries, clerks (1, 2, & 3) lunching with junior
    junior
management, mail boys scurrying, senior management
striding
in close huddle, new immigrants & tourists breathing in
vast
scenery:

music by Latin Fever, a band with a Cuban leader
and white
musicians in black suits playing "Manhattan skyline."
One woman
on the bandstand in low cleavaged formal wear red
corsage tapping
high heel shoes singing "songs from all over the
world: South America, US & Italy!" and "a song you
haven't
heard in a long time, 'You Light Up My Life.'" Low
applause.

midst the dull & gleam of high rise filing cabinets, one
tree
islands of earth encased by concrete squares, people
munching
fast food, between the 10-storey layers of parked cars: i
glimpse

the nondescript Strathcona Hotel where they lock
    migrant
workers
prior to deportation; where some kill themselves
    trying to
escape
or not wanting to go back. . . .

Cultura Canadese

Joseph Pivato

pick and shovel
        in a ditch
        calloused hands
        hard hats
boots planted in sewage
is the clay mud of Ontario fertile?

        la bella vita in America
pasta lancia
primo unico
mamma bravo
chin radio*

telejournale
"doferin e san cler"
        where are we now?
        the snow falls
        the wind is cold
where is our history in this land?
do the indian spirits understand italian?
have they heard of da Vinci or Verdi
or even Columbus?

        speak english only
not italian not even french
is this a paese*
or a geographical hypothesis?

*chin radio: the call letters of a Toronto radio station
    featuring multicultural programming.
*paese: a community of like-minded citizens.

Lucia's Monologue

Mary Di Michele

So much of my life has been wasted feeling guilty
about disappointing my father and mother.
It makes me doubt myself.
It's impossible to live my life that way.
I know they've made their sacrifices,
they tell me often enough,
how they gave up their lives,
and now they need to live their lives through me.
If I give it to them, it won't make them young again.
it'll only make me fail along with them,
fail to discover a different, if mutant, possibility,
succeed only in perpetuating a species of despair.

Most of the time I can't even talk to my father.
I talk to mother and she tells him what she thinks
he can stand to hear.
She's always been the mediator of our quarrels.
He's always been the man and the judge.
And what I've come to understand about justice
in this world isn't pretty,
how often it's just an excuse to be mean or angry
or to hoard property,
a justice that washes away
the hands of the judge.

Nobody disputes the rights of pigeons to fly
on the blue crest of the air across the territory
of a garden, nobody can dispute that repetition
is the structure of despair and our common lives

and that the disease takes a turn for the worse
when we stop talking to each other.

I've stopped looking for my father in other men.
I've stopped living with the blond child that he loved
too well.
Now I'm looking for the man with the hands of a musician,
with hands that can make wood sing,
with the bare, splintered hands of a carpenter.
I want no auto mechanics with hands blind with
grease
and the joints of a machine.
I want no engineers in my life,
no architects of cages.
I want to be with the welders of bridges
and the rivers whose needs inspired them.

I learned to be a woman in the arms of a man.
I didn't learn it from ads for lipstick
or watching myself in the mirror.
I learned more about love from watching my mother
wait on my father hand and foot
than from scorching novels on the best seller lists.
I didn't think I could be Anna Karenina or Camille.
I didn't think I could be Madame Bovary or Joan of Arc.
I didn't think that there was a myth I could wear
like a cloak of invisibility
to disguise my lack of self knowledge.

The sky is wearing his snow boots already.
I have to settle things with my father before the year is
dead.
It's about time we tried talking
person to person.

More than a tired man, my father is a such a lonely,
disappointed man.
He has learned through many years of keeping his mouth
shut
to say nothing,
but he still keeps thinking about
everything.

"If I had the language like you," he says to me,
"I would write poems too about what I think.
You younger generation aren't interested in history.
If you want people to listen to you
you got to tell them something new,
you got to know something about history to do that.
I'm a worker and I didn't go to school,
but I would have liked to be an educated man,
to think great thoughts, to write them,
and to have someone listen.
You younger generation don't care about anything in the
past,
about your parents,
the sacrifices they made for you,
you say: 'What did you do that for,
we didn't ask you!'
right,
is that right?
These are good poems you have here Lucia,
but what you think about Italy!
'a country of dark men full of violence and laughter,
a country that drives its women to dumb despair.'

That's not nice what you say,
you think it's very different here?
You got to tell the truth when you write,
like the bible. I'm your father, Lucia,
remember, I know you."

The truth is not nice,
the truth is that his life is almost over
and we don't have a common language any more.
He has lost a tooth in the middle of his upper plate,
the gap makes him seem boyish and very vulnerable.
It also makes me ashamed.

It's only when he's tired like this that he can
slip off his reserve, the roman stoicism,
the lips buttoned up against pain
and words of love.

I have his face, his eyes, his hands,
his anxious desire to know everything,
to think, to write everything,
his anxious desire to be heard,
and we love each other and say nothing,
we love each other in that country
we couldn't live in.

In My Backyard

Celestino De Iuliis

I own a house now.
My father sowed his seeds
in his backyard,
and reaped the lettuce and tomatoes.
He had known who he was when
his hands formed the cheese
drawn from the milk of his flock.
Having come here, he was less sure
and worked in factories or construction sites.
He made his own wine and slaughtered still
the Easter Lamb for us
(and for himself too, there's no denying).
He loved what was his own with little show
and fewer words.
The language never yielded to him, strong as he was.
I wrote the numbers out on a sheet
so he could write his cheques,
pay his bills . . .
My youth was spent in shame of him.
My tiny face would blush, my eyes avert
on parents' night when he would timid come
to ask in broken syntax after me.
In my backyard
I have my grass and flowers
and buy my produce at Dominion.
My eyes avert in shame now
that I ever was that boy.

ESSAYS & ARTICLES

No one will go home tonight.
The night gets cooler.
They build up the fire.
No one goes home.
And then the sun.

BARBARA SAPERGIA, *FOREIGNERS*

History's Racial Barriers

John Barber

T he Canadian West was almost empty in 1896 when Clifford Sifton, interior minister in Prime Minister Wilfrid Laurier's cabinet, began his ambitious program to populate the Prairies with pioneer farmers. But a shortage of English-speaking immigrants forced Sifton to recruit candidates from central Europe. It was a radical policy for its time, and he defended it by extolling the virtues of "a stalwart peasant in a sheepskin coat, born on the soil, whose forebears have been farmers for 10 generations, with a stout wife and a half-dozen children." But the immigrants who subsequently poured into the country were referred to as "the scum of Europe" by many established Canadians. In 1899 Toronto's daily *Mail and Empire* called the developing West "a sort of anthropological garden" populated by "the waifs and strays of Europe, the lost tribes of mankind, and freaks of creation."

Racism

The *Mail's* jaunty racism was a typical reaction to Canada's first attempt at multiculturalism. And during the next half-century of immigration, that attitude hardened. In 1922, writing in *Maclean's*, Sifton himself complained that the stalwart peasants had been overtaken by foreign "wasters and criminals, ne'er-do-wells and scalawags," and "the off-scourings and dregs of society." Virulent opposition to the newcomers united the most disparate elements of Canadian society, from the Anglican Church to the Trades and Labor Congress. The Ku Klux Klan in Canada grew quickly during the 1920s, especially in Saskatchewan, because of its hatred of what one Klansman called "men who tighten their bellyband for breakfast, eat spaghetti and hotdog and rye bread for lunch and suck in limburger cheese for supper." In 1919 J.W. Dafoe, the otherwise liberal-minded journalist, captured mainstream opinion when he proposed "to clean the aliens out of the community and ship them back to Europe, which vomited them forth a decade ago."

But English Canada's xenophobia was no match for the countervailing economic imperatives. Canada's rapidly expanding railways, mines and lumber camps required a large supply of cheap and malleable workers. And for a time, according to Donald Avery, author of *Dangerous Foreigners*, "the railways became the outstanding spokesmen for an open-door immigration policy." Their success in influencing government reached a peak with the Railway Agreement of 1925, which gave them virtual control of the administration of immigration. Public opposition, coupled with the advent of the Depression, brought it to an end five years later.

The Ukrainians, Poles, Finns and Hungarians who answered the call of the railway lived hard, often miserable lives. But compared with aspiring Asian immigrants, they were privileged. Fear of the "Yellow Peril" led to regulations that all but barred their entry; the remaining trickle was stanched in 1923 by the Chinese Immigration Act. The task of blocking East Indian immigration was more complex because Indians, in theory at least, could claim special rights as citizens of the British Empire. The 400 Sikhs who appeared in Vancouver harbor in 1914 aboard the freighter Komagata Maru sparked a fierce debate, but ultimately they were forced by one half of Canada's new two-ship navy to turn around and sail away.

Jews and blacks fared no better; most were denied admission to the country by Section 38 of the old Immigration Act, which allowed the cabinet to turn away "immigrants belonging to any nationality or race deemed unsuitable."

Intense
The tide of public opinion only began to turn in the 1930s, as reports of the plight of European Jews began to reach North America. Even then, despite repeated petitions and intense lobbies, Ottawa remained adamantly opposed to accepting Jewish

refugees from Nazi Germany. Between 1933 and 1945, the United States accepted more than 200,000 Jewish refugees. Tiny Bolivia embraced almost 15,000. The Canadian figure: fewer than 5,000. It was only after the war, when the full horror of Nazi crimes was exposed, that Canada began to dismantle the racial barriers to immigration. At the same time, the admission of displaced persons from Eastern Europe ushered in a new policy that has since welcomed refugees from almost every continent to Canadian shores. That humanitarian tradition is a source of pride for many Canadians. But it is a recent innovation, one that even now has yet to garner the support that Canadians voiced for its frankly racist predecessor.

Opening the Doors

Ken MacQueen

They waited for years, living on hope in quarters smaller than the single room they now occupy in Winnipeg's Balmoral Hotel. At age 29, Bun Thoeun had spent seven years in a refugee camp in Thailand after fleeing the Communists in Kampuchea. Waiting for a visa, he married Hok Seam and fathered two sons. Two weeks ago they arrived in Winnipeg. First they will learn English, then they will find jobs. But they will never again worry about being sent back to Kampuchea.

Five years ago Vietnamese-born Thien Chi Tran's home was also a refugee camp in Thailand. Now, he plays second violin in the Calgary Civic Symphony. He fishes and camps, and this fall Thien, 30, began a qualifying year at the University of Calgary. He became a Canadian citizen in June, and this summer he married Sandra Taylor, a teacher specializing in English as a second language. "The first time I felt I belonged here," he recalled, "is when Calgary made the Stanley Cup finals."

The history—and the future—of Canada consists of millions of such stories. Canada is a nation of immigrants. Its trees were felled, its rails laid, its prairies cleared and its cities built by successive generations of misfits and refugees. In the suspicious view of the ruling majority, they often spoke the wrong language, wore the wrong clothing or worshipped the wrong God. But while they were exploited and isolated, they were also allowed in by the hundreds of thousands—the necessary raw material for the nation.

Controlled

Now, after a decade of blocking out a troubled world with some of the lowest immigration levels in its history, Canada is again reopening its borders. Defying chronic unemployment and spotty economic growth, the government is planning to risk a significant increase in immigration in a bold attempt to stimulate the economy and counteract a dramatically declining birthrate and an aging population. "Immigrants create jobs and expand markets and demand," said Gerry Weiner, appointed minister of state for immigration on June 30. "My vision is to open the doors—but, of course, in a controlled fashion."

It has exhilarated some Canadians—and unsettled many more—that there has never been a genuine blueprint for the country or the making of a Canadian. Instead, Bun Thoeun in Winnipeg and Thien Chi Tran in Calgary have contributed to the perpetual evolution of Canada. The process never rests, even long enough for a clean, sharp definition of nationhood to emerge. The changes can only be noted in passing: new words in the vocabulary, new faces in the neighborhood, new languages on the buses, new foods in restaurants and stores. The ground shifts incrementally as each new wave of immigration beats on the shore.

Vision
The process has changed not only the nation's demography but its sense of itself. The Canada of the First and Second World Wars—when author Hugh MacLennan wrote precisely of the nation's two solitudes, French and English—is now faded and indistinct, like a footprint on the beach. As for the future, the Conservatives seem prepared to gamble that a significant component still rests offshore.

The nation's immigration policy has often seemed as incoherent as it has been controversial. In 1974 Ottawa's most extensive study of the subject concluded that one could search Canada's history in vain for any public consensus or consistent policy. What amazes many in the field of immigration, as the debate begins anew, is not the absence of a guiding vision but the fact that Canada has survived so well without one.

Early next month Weiner will table a report in Parliament establishing immigration levels for 1987. The report is expected to call for a "moderate, controlled increase" in immigration. Without such an increase—given the current low birthrate—

Canada's population will go into a decline by the year 2021. And according to a 1984 Statistics Canada study, static birth rates mean that 275,000 immigrants a year—three times the current level—would be needed by the end of the century to keep the national population growing by just one per cent.

It is doubtful that Ottawa has yet committed itself to tripling immigration as that report implied it should, but already there has been a marked shift in policy. In 1985 the new Conservative government allowed just 84,273 immigrants into the country— the lowest intake in 23 years. This year the door eased open; between 105,000 and 115,000 workers, families and refugees are expected. And if federal ambitions are realized, the level will climb to 125,000 immigrants next year, with an eventual annual target of 200,000. Still, no major leap is likely before 1988, when the government receives the findings of a major demographic study assessing the impact of declining birthrates and an aging population.

Backlash

The government's caution seems well founded. Even during the flood of European immigration after the Second World War, the annual level rarely reached 200,000 people. Now, with 1.2 million Canadians unemployed, even a moderate increase in immigration is fraught with risk. The arrival of only 155 Sri Lankan refugees— found floating in lifeboats off the coast of Newfoundland last August—generated an intense national debate after Ottawa ruled that they could live and work in Canada until their claims for refugee status were processed. Both Weiner and senior Employment and Immigration Minister Benoit Bouchard weathered a withering backlash after it was discovered that the Sri Lankans had not sailed from India as they claimed, but from West Germany.

Fear

Weiner, whose Montreal-area riding of Dollard includes a large immigrant population, blamed much of the reaction on misunderstanding. The Tamils, he said, would not jump the line ahead of those seeking to enter the country as immigrants. "All of the Sri Lankans who came this summer are working," Weiner said.

"There were jobs available that were not being filled by Canadians." Nor will the incident sway the government's commitment to a more open border, said Weiner, himself the grandson of Eastern European immigrants. But it does underline Ottawa's need to sell the public on the benefits of a more culturally diverse nation. Racism is not an inherent Canadian trait, he insisted, but "there is always a fear of the unknown."

Before a national debate on immigration policy can begin, however, the Mulroney government must resolve divisions within its own caucus. MP Barry Turner (Ottawa-Carleton) contends that there is broad public support for increasing immigration levels in order to avert economic stagnation. Said Turner: "Without immigration, there will be fewer workers, less revenue to government, less new business." Across the spectrum, Alex Kindy (Calgary East) argues for maintaining current immigration levels until unemployment drops and the economy can absorb more workers. After the Sri Lankan affair, Kindy asked his constituents for their views on immigration. Of the 1,500 who responded, 65 per cent wanted immigration levels reduced and only seven per cent favored admitting more Canadians. Kindy, a Ukrainian who immigrated in 1949 at age 19, said that today's immigrants "are not always as productive" as those of his generation.

Echoes

The debate outside the capital echoes the one on Parliament Hill. "It's strange how so many immigrant groups don't want any more immigrants coming," says Wilson Head, president of the Toronto-based Urban Alliance on Race Relations. "They're glad to be here, but now they want us to close the doors." But for those seeking work, the notion of more competition is especially unsettling. Asked Marcel D'Amour, 41, currently unemployed and living in Quebec City, "There aren't enough jobs. Where will they work?" In the end, argues Desmond Morton, a historian at the University of Toronto, immigration is not a question of philanthropy. "We can't solve the poverty of the Third World by bringing it here," Morton said.

Historically, Canadians have viewed each successive wave of immigration with suspicion, but the newcomers' stories form the history of Canada. Each has walked the same difficult path: years of sacrifice, exploitation in the labor market and isolation in ghettos; years of struggle to reunite their families; children of first-generation immigrants being pushed to succeed in their Canadian schools, yet chastised for straying from the culture of their parents. Finally, when a sufficient price has been exacted, outsiders are accepted.

Resented

In the mid-1800s it was the Irish who flooded into Canada, dirt-poor, clannish, resented for the way they came to monopolize many jobs in Eastern Canada. Now, Brian Mulroney, a fourth-generation Canadian of Irish ancestry, is the Prime Minister. In the 1930s, as Gerry Weiner was growing up in the hardscrabble Jewish neighborhood of Montreal's St. Urbain Street, Canada rejected as undesirable thousands of Jews seeking asylum from Hitler's Germany. "And now there is a Jew welcoming people to this country," said Weiner. "We've come a long way."

But for thousands of the most recent generation of arrivals, the battle for economic survival, let alone social acceptance, is still being waged. At age 36, almost eight years after he arrived in Quebec City from Chile, Miguel Cerda is still stung by what he calls his "powerlessness" in Canadian society. An auto mechanic who was jailed and tortured for working against Chile's right-wing military dictatorship, Cerda has been denied work in his trade in Quebec because he lacks a provincially regulated "competence card." Last week, after years of low-paying odd jobs, Cerda, his wife, Miriam, and their two daughters were preparing to move to Toronto, where he has found work as a painter. "Moving is not a question of taste," he said. "It's to make a better future for our children."

Marathon

On Toronto's busy Bathurst Street, Yon-Mook Lee and his wife, Chung-Ja, put in marathon 14-hour days behind the counter of their Stop'N'Go convenience store. Yon-Mook, who earned a degree in chemical engineering from a Korean university, brought his family to Canada in 1974. He blamed his imperfect English for limiting his opportunities, but said, "Nobody forced me to come to Canada." Both he and Chung-Ja place their hope in the future of their children, Jean, 15, and Kenny, 14. Said Yon-Mook: "Our responsibility as parents is to make sure they go to university, to force them to learn even if they don't always want to."

Gift shop owner Parkash Singh, 35, arrived in 1974. Although she and her 39-year-old husband, Narinder (Paul) Singh, are among just 40 Sikh families now living in Halifax, she said, "I've always been accepted by the people." During a recent visit to India she found that her two Canadian-born children "couldn't cope. They didn't like it." Their future rests in Canada, she said. "My son wants to be an engineer or a doctor. My daughter wants to be a doctor too. Why not?"

Core

At the core of any successful increase in immigration is a question that many new arrivals feel has yet to be answered. Can a predominantly white society ever fully accept a Chilean, a Korean or a Sikh? History has not always been kind to Canada's visible minorities, from the economically oppressed blacks of Halifax to the Japanese of British Columbia, who were herded into internment camps during the Second World War. But because Canada long pursued a virtual whites-only immigration policy, the issue is only now being addressed.

In fact, it was not until 1967, when policy changes eliminated discrimination by race or nationality for all classes of immigrants, that the face of Canada began to change significantly. In the 1980s, for the first time, Asia replaced Britain and Europe as the principal source of new immigrants. Last year Asia accounted for almost 41 per cent of all new arrivals, with Latin America and the Caribbean growing to more than 18 per cent.

Despite the shift, Statistics Canada calculates the visible ethnic minority at no more than eight per cent of the population. Proportionately, that figure is "a teeny drop in the bucket," said Gertrude Neuwirth, head of a refugee resource centre at Ottawa's Carleton University. Philosophically, however, it is a fundamental realignment. Said Neuwirth, an Austrian who came to Canada in 1967: "The change is absolutely enormous and very impressive."

But even advocates of increased immigration have noted danger signals. The 1985 Royal Commission on the Economy noted that the increasing number of non-European immigrants is "one of the most potentially explosive sources of political conflict." Although the commission supported a gradual increase in immigration, it said that the government would have to work hard to sell its concept of a harmonious multiracial society. "It would be imprudent to ignore early signals indicating the possibilities of racial strife in the years ahead," the commission concluded.

Omen

One clear omen is a dramatic and consistent drop in public support for immigration since the Second World War, as measured by a series of Gallup polls. In 1945, 65 per cent of Canadians polled said that they wanted a larger population. Four decades later only 14 per cent favored increasing the immigrant pool, while 38 per cent backed the status quo. Refugees fare even worse. A Gallup survey last month said that 72 per cent of Canadians feel that the nation is doing more than its share to help the estimated 12 million refugees worldwide. And 58 per cent wanted cuts in refugee levels.

In fact, although Ottawa has been plagued by a backlog of residents awaiting validation of their claims as refugees, humanitarian and refugee programs do not account for the largest group of new arrivals. In 1985, 19,740 people arrived under that broad category. Reacting to the backlog—and concerns that thousands entered the country with illegitimate claims—the government pledged in its speech from the throne last week to simplify the process, assisting genuine refugees and discouraging abuse of Canada's humanitarian tradition.

The uncontrolled surge of refugee claimants who arrive from the world's trouble spots, often with no money and few job skills, prompted a federal task force earlier this year to recommend a "positive" selection program. Many refugees would never meet Canada's immigrant selection standards, said the joint government-private sector panel headed by former deputy prime minister Erik Nielsen. Refugees, it concluded, are "increasingly inappropriate for our technological society."

For now, family reunification, a program allowing established immigrants to sponsor members of their immediate families, remains the core of immigration policy. Last year 38,501 people entered under that category. But if Ottawa hopes to sell the public on the economic benefits of more immigrants, it is likely to place even greater emphasis on recruiting entrepreneurs and independent workers, whose job skills fill a need in the Canadian market.

Blunder

The government is also moving cautiously to increase the number of independent immigrants, a category of skilled workers that was almost eliminated during the recession of the early 1980s. Indeed, the 1982 decision to block independent immigrants unless they had jobs guaranteed before their arrival is regarded by Conservative MP James Hawkes (Calgary West) as one of the biggest single blunders in modern immigration policy. Hawkes, the influential chairman of the Commons committee on immigration, said that Canada's policy has been too concerned with short-term labor trends, while lacking any vision about what the nation needs and what it can become. "We have to make it easier for people to come into the country who are needed by the country," he said.

In recent months Hawkes's all-party committee has added its voice to the call for more immigration, recommending that the Canadian population reach 30 million by the turn of the century, an increase of almost five million. What Canada needs are people motivated to come to Canada, says Hawkes, people with a "pioneering predisposition."

Across the country, new pioneers are already in place. Hoa Ta, his wife, May, and their three children (Hang, 9, Lan, 7, and Tuan, 5) live in a snug, well-furnished trailer in the northern Alberta community of Fairview, their home for almost seven years. The couple, both 34, fled North Vietnam in 1979, surviving a one-month voyage to Hong Kong in a motorless boat. They spent six months in a refugee camp. "I applied for Canada, Germany and the United States," Hoa recalled. "Canada picked me, so that's why I'm here."

Three days after his arrival in Fairview, Hoa went to work as a railcar maintenance worker, a job he still holds. "Here, we have a good Canadian life," said Hoa, "good fellow workers. No trouble." Simply said—but no different from the aspirations of millions of Canadians, those who fear immigrants and those who welcome them.

Ancestors—The Genetic Source

David Suzuki

—Prologue—

My grandparents emigrated from Japan to this country at the turn of the century. Like so many immigrants, they left their homeland reluctantly. But they came from a poverty so profound that they were prepared to take the risk and deal with the terrifying unknown of a totally alien culture and language. Their children, my parents, were born in Vancouver over seventy-five years ago. They were Canadians by birth. By culture, they were genuine hybrids, fluently bilingual but fiercely loyal to the only country they had ever known—Canada.

On December 7, 1941, an event took place that had nothing to do with me or my family and yet which had devastating consequences for all of us—Japan bombed Pearl Harbor in a surprise attack. With that event began one of the shoddiest chapters in the tortuous history of democracy in North America. More than twenty thousand people, mostly Canadians by birth, were uprooted, their tenuous foothold on the West Coast destroyed, and their lives shattered to an extent still far from fully assessed. Their only crime was the possession of a common genetic heritage with the enemy.

Although I have little recollection of that time, Pearl Harbor was the single most important event shaping my life; years later in reassessing my life during a personal trauma, I realized that virtually every one of my emotional problems went right back to it.

Throughout the entire ordeal of those war years, my parents acted with a dignity, courage and loyalty that this young country did not deserve. Today, my mother is dead, never having known the symbolic acknowledgement that a wrong was committed against her. But if there is anything worthwhile to be salvaged from those years, it is that her story and my father's, through me, will not be forgotten and will serve as a legacy to all Canadians, a reminder of the difficulty of living up to the ideals of democracy. The stories of how my parents and their parents fared in Canada are both a tribute to their strength of character and a record of the enormous changes that have occurred in this country. Whatever I am has been profoundly shaped by these two facts.

My genes can be traced in a direct line to Japan. I am a pure-blooded member of the Japanese race. And whenever I go there, I am always astonished to see the power of that biological connection. In subways in Tokyo, I catch familiar glimpses of the eyes, hairline or smile of my Japanese relatives. Yet when those same people open their mouths to communicate, the vast cultural gulf that separates them from me becomes obvious: English is my language, Shakespeare is my literature, British history is what I learned and Beethoven is my music.

For those who believe that in people, just as in animals, genes are the primary determinant of behaviour, a look at second- and third-generation immigrants to Canada gives powerful evidence to the contrary. The overriding influence is environmental. We make a great mistake by associating the inheritance of physical characteristics with far more complex traits of human personality and behaviour.

Each time I visit Japan, I am reminded of how Canadian I am and how little the racial connection matters. I first visited Japan in 1968 to attend the International Congress of Genetics in Tokyo. For the first time in my life, I was surrounded by people who all looked like me. While sitting in a train and looking at the reflections in the window, I found that it was hard to pick out my own image in the crowd. I had grown up in a Caucasian society in which I was a minority member. My whole sense of self had developed with that perspective of looking different. All my life I had wanted large eyes and brown hair so I could be like everyone else. Yet on that train, where I did fit in, I didn't like it.

On this first visit to Japan I had asked my grandparents to contact relatives and let them know I was coming. I was the first in the Suzuki clan in Canada to visit them. The closest relative on my father's side was my grandmother's younger brother, and we arranged to meet in a seaside resort near his home. He came to my hotel room with two of his daughters. None of them spoke any English, while my Japanese was so primitive as to be useless. In typical Japanese fashion, they showered me with gifts, the most important being a package of what looked like wood carved in the shape of bananas! I had no idea what it was. (Later I learned the package contained dried tuna fish from which slivers are shaved off to flavour soup. This is considered a highly prized gift.) We sat in stiff silence and embarrassment, each of us struggling to dredge up a common word or two to break the quiet. It was excruciating! My great uncle later wrote my grandmother to tell her how painful it had been to sit with her grandson and yet be unable to communicate a word.

To people in Japan, all non-Japanese—black, white or yellow—are *gaijin* or foreigners. While *gaijin* is not derogatory, I find that its use is harsh because I sense doors clanging shut on me when I'm called one. The Japanese do have a hell of a time with me because I look like them and can say in perfect Japanese, "I'm a foreigner and I can't speak Japanese." Their reactions are usually complete incomprehension followed by a sputtering, "What do you mean? You're speaking Japanese." And finally a pejorative, "Oh, a *gaijin*!"

Once when my wife, Tara, who is English, and I went to Japan, we asked a man at the travel bureau at the airport to book a *ryokan*—a traditional Japanese inn—for us in Tokyo. He found one and booked it for *"Suzuki-san"* and off we went. When we arrived at the inn and I entered the foyer, the owner was confused by my terrible Japanese. When Tara entered, the shock was obvious in his face. Because of my name, they had expected a "real" Japanese. Instead, I was a *gaijin* and the owner told us he wouldn't take us. I was furious and we stomped off to a phone booth where I called the agent at the airport. He was astonished and came all the way into town to plead our case with the innkeeper. But the innkeeper stood firm and denied us a room. Apparently he had accepted *gaijin* in the past with terrible consequences.

As an example of the problem, Japanese always take their shoes off when entering a *ryokan* because the straw mats (*tatami*) are quickly frayed. To a Japanese, clomping into a room with shoes on would be comparable to someone entering our homes and spitting on the floor. Similarly, the *ofuro*, or traditional tub, has hot clean water that all bathers use. So one must first enter the bathroom, wash carefully and rinse off *before* entering the tub. Time in the *ofuro* is for relaxing and soaking. Again, Westerners who lather up in the tub are committing a terrible desecration.

To many Canadians today, the word "Jap" seems like a natural abbreviation for Japanese. Certainly for newspaper headlines it would seem to make sense. So people are often shocked to see me bristle when they have used the word Jap innocently. To Japanese-Canadians, Jap or Nip (from *"Nippon"*) were epithets used generously during the pre-war and war years. They conjure up all of the hatred and bigotry of those times. While a person using the term today may be unaware of its past use, every Japanese-Canadian remembers.

The thin thread of Japanese culture that does link me to Japan was spun out of the poverty and desperation of my ancestors. My grandparents came to a Canadian province openly hostile to their strange appearance and different ways. There were severe restrictions on how much and where they could buy property. Their children, who were born and raised in Canada, couldn't vote until 1948 and encountered many barriers to professional training and property ownership. Asians, regardless of birthplace, were third-class citizens. That is the reality of the Japanese-Canadian experience and the historical cultural legacy that came down to the third and fourth generations—to me and my children.

The first Japanese immigrants came to Canada to make their fortunes so they could return to Japan as people of wealth. The vast majority was uneducated and impoverished. But in the century spanning my grandparents' births and the present, Japan has leapt from an agrarian society to a technological and economic giant.

Now, the Japanese I meet in Japan or as recent immigrants to Canada come with far different cultural roots. Present-day Japanese are highly educated, upper-middle class and proud of their heritage. In Canada they encounter respect, envy and curiosity in sharp contrast to the hostility and bigotry met by my grandparents.

Japanese immigrants to North America have names that signify the number of generations in the new land (or just as significantly, that count the generational distance *away* from Japan). My grandparents are *Issei*, meaning the first generation in Canada. Most *Issei* never learned more than a rudimentary knowledge of English. *Nisei*, like my parents, are the second generation here and the first native-born group. While growing up they first spoke Japanese in the home and then learned English from playmates and teachers. Before the Second World War, many *Issei* sent their children to be educated in Japan. When they returned to Canada, they were called *Kika-nisei* (or *Kibei* in the United States). Most have remained bilingual, but many of the younger *Nisei* now speak Japanese with difficulty because English is their native tongue. My sisters and I are *Sansei* (third generation); our children are *Yonsei*. These generations, and especially *Yonsei*, are growing up in homes where English is the only spoken language, so they are far more likely to speak school-taught French as their second language than Japanese.

Most *Sansei*, like me, do not speak Japanese. To us, the *Issei* are mysteries. They came from a cultural tradition that is a hundred years old. Unlike people in present-day Japan, the *Issei* clung tightly to the culture they remembered and froze that culture into a static museum piece like a relic of the past. Not being able to speak each other's language, *Issei* and *Sansei* were cut off from each other. My parents dutifully visited my grandparents and we children would be trotted out to be lectured at or displayed. These visits were excruciating, because we children didn't understand the old culture, and didn't have the slightest interest—we were Canadians.

My father's mother died in 1978 at the age of ninety-one. She was the last of the *Issei* in our family. The final months of her life, after a left-hemisphere stroke, were spent in that terrible twilight—crippled, still aware, but unable to communicate. She lived the terminal months of her life, comprehending but mute, in a ward with Caucasian strangers. For over thirty years I had listened to her psychologically blackmailing my father by warning him of her imminent death. Yet in the end, she hung on long after there was reason to. When she died, I was astonished at my own reaction, a great sense of sadness and regret at the cleavage of my last link with the source of my genes. I had never been able to ask what made her and others of her generation come to Canada, what they felt when they arrived, what their hopes and dreams had been, and whether it was worth it. And I wanted to thank her, to show her that I was grateful that, through them, I was born a Canadian.

On Racial Origins

Pierre Berton

My friend, Ray Silver, who is known in some quarters as "Lucky Silver" because during the war he survived three air crashes and a train wreck and was once hurled six hundred feet over a mountain into a different country, is having an argument with the Vital Statistics people.

It all began when, after the birth of his fourth baby, Lucky Silver got a government form asking him to name the racial origin of the parents.

Well, this made him both angry and confused. His maternal grandparents were born in the United States, his paternal grandfolk in the U.S.S.R. His maternal great-grandparents came from Alsace-Lorraine, which is either German or French, depending on the date. His paternal great-grandparents were from Poland. His wife's paternal line is Irish, but her maternal line is English and Cornish, and in addition there's a fair amount of Semitic strain in Silver from one side of the Urals or the other.

So, when Silver got this form asking him to state his new baby's racial origin he blew a gasket and wrote the following wonderful letter to the Deputy Registrar-General of the Government of Ontario:

DEAR MR. WALLACE: I am today in receipt of form 68(4)13-1691 over your signature requesting certain information in connection with the registration of a birth. Your records will show that I promptly complied with the provision of basic and pertinent data concerning the birth of our fourth child. However, I decline to state—or attempt to state—the racial origin of either my wife or myself. My reasons for so declining to comply are several, and are stated below:

I am aware that under the Vital Statistics Act you have the authority to prosecute and that I may be jailed, or fined, etc. Notwithstanding this threat to liberty of my person and property, let me state at the outset that I categorically refuse to provide any information whatsoever concerning "racial origin" of myself or any member of my family, at this or any future time. . . .

My peculiar reluctance to comply with a statement of racial origin on my own behalf or that of my family is influenced by:

1. The basis of your department for definition of such a term as "race" is absurdly unscientific and impossible to properly answer.

2. Racial statistics, so called, have proven to be of little or doubtful significance and value to sociologists.

3. So-called racial data has too frequently been the material on which undemocratic procedures and philosophical bases for discrimination have been developed. The Rosenberg-Hegel philosophy of Nazi Germany, the racist policies of Strydom in South Africa, and the "mongrelization" theories of Southern Americans were all based on so-called racial distinction. I suggest—and am prepared to contest the conviction—that there is no place for such distinctions in the province of Ontario.

4. While I can trace one of my ancestors back to the person of a Russian prince who fought Gengis Khan, I have neither the time nor interest to pursue my other forebears back to a basic racial source. I am sure my wife would probably have as much difficulty in determining her origins.

I and my wife are native-born Canadians; my parents were both native-born Canadians.

This may not satisfy your department, but I am sure it satisfies the purpose of any sociological pursuits which the Government of Ontario might reasonably be expected to pursue.

What Ray Silver is saying is that he is a mammal, and that is as far as he is prepared to go, and that anybody who takes up time trying to trace his racial origin through his father's father's father's father would be better employed making party pies out of old toothbrush handles.

For this system, which insists that your "racial origin" is determined by the country your father comes from, makes no sense at all.

If your father comes from Armenia they put you down as an Armenian in origin, even if *his* father was a Zulu. Yet, if your father comes from Canada, you are not allowed to put your racial origin down as Canadian because, they tell you patiently, the word "Canadian" doesn't identify you by race. And that's quite right; but neither does the world "English", for most Englishmen are a mixture of Celtic, Roman, Saxon, Danish, and Norman.

I feel keenly about this because it so happens that my family has been on this side of the Atlantic since the year 1681. Before that they came from France and from Germany and from England and from God knows where.

What, then, is my racial origin? I say it is Canadian, if we are going to use terms loosely. But why use terms like "racial origin" at all when they are so inexact?

The statistics that these forms reveal are, quite obviously, misleading and dishonest. After eleven generations am I still a Frenchman, rather than a North American? Are my children, who are half-Scottish, to be listed as French because three hundred years ago one of my ancestors was Huguenot?

The Ontario government quite rightly no longer allows any employer to inquire about his prospective employees' racial background since, under the Fair Employment Practices Code, such information is held to be irrelevant.

It is not only irrelevant, it is meaningless. And it is more than meaningless: it is dangerous since its official acceptance contrives to prop up the silly arguments of the racial purists.

There is no such thing as racial purity, of course, and in this great melting pot of a country we ought long since to have stopped pretending on our official forms that there is.

PS There has been no official reply to Lucky Silver's letter. Perhaps up at Queen's Park they are hoping that if everybody forgets about it, the nasty problem will go away.

'I'm not racist but . . .'

Neil Bissoondath

Someone recently said that racism is as Canadian as maple syrup. I have no argument with that. History provides us with ample proof. But, for proper perspective, let us remember that it is also as American as apple pie, as French as croissants, as Jamaican as ackee, as Indian as aloo, as Chinese as chow mein, as . . . Well, there's an entire menu to be written. This is not by way of excusing it. Murder and rape, too, are international, multicultural, as innate to the darker side of the human experience. But we must be careful that the inevitable rage evoked does not blind us to the larger context.

The word "racism" is a discomforting one: It is so vulnerable to manipulation. We can, if we so wish, apply it to any incident involving people of different color. And therein lies the danger. During the heat of altercation, we seize, as terms of abuse, on whatever is most obvious about the other person. It is, often, a question of unfortunate convenience. A woman, because of her sex, easily becomes a female dog or an intimate part of her anatomy. A large person might be dubbed "a stupid ox," a small person "a little" whatever. And so a black might become "a nigger," a white "a honky," an Asian "a paki," a Chinese "a chink," an Italian "a wop," and French-Canadian "a frog."

There is nothing pleasant about these terms; they assault every decent sensibility. Even so, I once met someone who, in a stunning surge of naiveté, used them as simple descriptives and not as terms of racial abuse. She was horrified to learn the truth. While this may have been an extreme case, the point is that the use of such patently abusive words may not always indicate racial or cultural distaste. They may indicate ignorance or stupidity or insensitivity, but pure racial hatred—such as the Nazis held for

Jews, or the Ku Klux Klan for blacks—is a thankfully rare commodity.

Ignorance, not the wilful kind but that which comes from lack of experience, is often indicated by that wonderful phrase, "I'm not racist but . . ." I think of the mover, a friendly man, who said, "I'm not racist, but the Chinese are the worst drivers on the road." He was convinced this was so because the shape of their eyes, as far as he could surmise, denied them peripheral vision.

Or the oil company executive, an equally warm and friendly man, who, looking for an apartment in Toronto, rejected buildings with East Indian tenants not because of their race—he was telling me this, after all—but because he was given to understand that cockroaches were symbols of good luck in their culture and that, when they moved into a new home, friends came by with gift-wrapped roaches.

Neither of these men thought of himself as racist, and I believe they were not, deep down. (The oil company executive made it clear he would not hesitate to have me as a neighbor; my East Indian descent was of no consequence to him, my horror of cockroaches was.) Yet their comments, so innocently delivered, would open them to the accusation, justifiably so if this were all one knew about them. But it is a charge which would undoubtedly be wounding to them. It is difficult to recognize one's own misconceptions.

2 True racism is based, more often than not, on wilful ignorance, and an acceptance of—and comfort with—stereotype. We like to think, in this country, that our multicultural mosaic will help nudge us into a greater openness. But multiculturalism as we know it indulges in stereotype, depends on it for a dash of color and the flash of dance. It fails to address the most basic questions people have about each other: Do those men doing the Dragon Dance really all belong to secret criminal societies? Do those women dressed in saris really coddle cockroaches for luck? Do those people in dreadlocks all smoke marijuana and live on welfare? Such questions do not seem to be the concern of the government's multicultural programs, superficial and exhibitionistic as they have become.

So the struggle against stereotype, the basis of all racism, becomes a purely personal one. We must beware of the impressions we create. A friend of mine once commented that, from talking to West Indians, she has the impression that their one great cultural contribution to the world is the oft-repeated boast that "We (unlike everyone else) know how to party."

There are dangers, too, in community response. We must be wary of the self-appointed activists who seem to pop up in the media at every given opportunity spouting the rhetoric of retribution, mining distress for personal, political and professional gain. We must be skeptical about those who depend on conflict for their sense of self, the non-whites who need to feel themselves victims of racism, the whites who need to feel themselves purveyors of it. And we must be sure that, in addressing the problem, we do not end up creating it. Does the *Miss Black Canada Beauty Contest* still exist? I hope not. Not only do I find beauty contests offensive, but a racially segregated one even more so. What would the public reaction be, I wonder, if every year CTV broadcast the *Miss White Canada Beauty Pageant*? We give community-service awards only to blacks: Would we be comfortable with such awards only for whites? In Quebec, there are The Association of Black Nurses, The Association of Black Artists, The Congress of Black Jurists. Play tit for tat: The Associations of White Nurses, White Artists, White Jurists: visions of apartheid. Let us be frank, racism for one is racism for others.

Finally, and perhaps most important, let us beware of abusing the word itself.

A Black View of Canada

Mary Janigan

In Gwen Robinson's yellowing photographs, the blacks pose self-consciously for the camera, prosperous and proud. There is James (Gunsmith) Jones, the son of a slave, who moved to Chatham, Ontario, in 1849 and who won prizes for his firearms at a Montreal exhibition in 1860. There is Jones's daughter, Sophia, solemn and self-possessed, who went to Michigan to study medicine. There are the members of the Chatham Knights Templar, a 19th-century Masonic society of black community leaders, who stand in a row, shoulders thrown back beneath capes, the plumes of their hats floating in the breeze.

But as Robinson, 53, thumbs those photographs, she also sees reminders of the brutal discrimination of the past—and the subtle racism of the present. "We blacks have been largely eliminated from the history books," declared the Chatham hairdresser and amateur local historian. Added her husband John, 59, a postal clerk: "Blacks have been left out of the Canadian mosaic."

Racism

That conviction was echoed by many black Canadians across the nation last week as, along with American blacks, they struggled to assess how far they have come—and how much farther they have to go. As the United States prepared to celebrate a new national holiday named after America's pre-eminent modern black leader, the late Dr. Martin Luther King Jr., many Canadian blacks told *Maclean's* that overt discrimination is lessening. Many added that they drew comfort from the fact that black communities in 1986 face challenges and opportunities that seemed impossible only a generation ago. But many also stressed that subtle discrimination—in schools, housing and the job markets—confines thousands to the role of second-class citizens. "This country has changed dramatically—Canada is doing quite well on civil rights," said Windsor, Ontario, New Democrat Howard McCurdy, the nation's only black MP. "But there is still not a single black in this country who has not been subjected to racism."

Their tales of pride and of prejudice also underlined the fact that blacks in Canada are united only by their colour—and by their desire for the new generation to achieve success. Indeed, the current black community is one of the least cohesive of Canada's minority groups. And unlike its American counterpart, it still lacks political strength and a firm political agenda. Some blacks, including Gwen Robinson, trace their Canadian roots back into the mid-19th century. Others, including Lincoln Alexander, Ontario's new lieutenant-governor, are the children of more recent immigrants from the Caribbean. "The only thing we have in common is that we are black," Alexander told *Maclean's*. Added McCurdy: "We are talking about different cultures, different backgrounds."

Complaints

One measure of those differences is that Statistics Canada does not know the number of black Canadians—because the category "Black" was not listed in the 1981 census. That survey did indicate that there are about 240 000 blacks in several categories: 31 000 Haitians, 160 000 of other Caribbean origin, and 48 000 African and Canadian-born blacks. But government officials admit that large numbers of Canadian-born blacks—especially those in Metropolitan Toronto and Nova Scotia—were simply overlooked if they did not write the word "Black" on the census form. This year's scheduled census corrects that omission by adding the category "Black" under a question about ethnic origin. But until that census is tabulated there are only rough estimates of the size of Canada's three largest black communities: 30 000 in Nova Scotia, the vast majority Canadian-born; 115 000 in Montreal, including 35 000 Haitians, 35 000 West Indians, and 40 000 Canadian-born; and at least 70 000 in Toronto, the majority from the West Indies.

The three communities feature different ethnic and cultural strains but share disturbing complaints of discrimination. The most accurate reflection of that discontent appeared last summer when pollster Martin Goldfarb interviewed 200 Toronto blacks about their experiences in Canada. Although 76 per cent said they were "very satisfied" with opportunities for their children in Canada, roughly 65 per cent declared that they have less opportunity than other Canadians to obtain senior positions in business or to win election to political office. And almost as many blacks felt that prejudice is increasing as believed that it is decreasing.

Indeed, Toronto's Urban Alliance on Race Relations and the Social Planning Council of Metro Toronto released a study last year disclosing that white job applicants receive three offers for every one obtained by blacks. A follow-up survey showed that only nine per cent of 199 Toronto employers in firms with more than 50 employees believed firmly in racial equality. Fully 28 per cent said that nonwhites lack the ability to compete, 13 per cent viewed them as threatening and seven per cent expressed "outright contempt" for them.

Drinking

Many blacks told *Maclean's* that they feel—and fight—racism in every facet of their lives. In Nova Scotia last week the provincial court referred to the judicial council a dispute over comments about blacks by Digby provincial court judge John Nichols. The remarks followed a four-day trial last October when an all-white jury acquitted a 29-year-old white, Jeff Mullen, on a second-degree murder charge for the shooting of Graham Jarvis, a 32-year-old black. Last month Nichols, the presiding judge at Mullen's preliminary hearing, told *The Toronto Star* that he would not have sent the case to trial if he had known all the facts. Said Nichols: "You know what happens when those black guys start drinking."

Blacks also say that discrimination spills into the educational system. Iona Crawley, the program director at a senior citizens' home in Windsor, N.S., is a single parent who has raised four children—a vocational school graduate and three university graduates. But she notes that there are no black high school teachers or guidance counsellors in Halifax. And for his part, Halifax lawyer H.A.J. (Gus) Wedderburn credits his career to the role models and motivation in his native Jamaica. Declared Wedderburn: "If I had been born here, I doubt if I would be a lawyer today."

Even students who do not perceive overt discrimination cite examples of racial stereotyping. Guyana-born June Ann Nobrega, 19, says that her Toronto teachers have always pushed her to go further than the Grade 12 academic course in which she is enrolled. But black males, she conceded, are encouraged to devote more time to sports than to academic work. "I remember another thing that seemed strange to me," Nobrega told *Maclean's*. "They put me straight into the choir—no auditions like the other kids. I wondered how they knew that I could sing."

Stereotyping often pursues blacks into the job market. Gwen Lord, 50, is the black principal of Montreal's Northmount high school, a school with a 55-per-cent black population. Frequently—and candidly—she tells her students about the problems of discrimination. "I tell them that they are going to be treated differently than other people," she explained. "Traditionally, we are the last hired and the first released." Montreal's Tommy Kane, 22, has a four-year athletic scholarship in football to Syracuse University in New York. After he graduates, Kane intends to remain in the United States. Employment opportunities for blacks, he says, are better. "All my [Montreal black] friends are doing is getting older," he said. "For them, time is just passing. I try to encourage them, but they just see a straight tunnel to nowhere."

Slavery
Indeed, the history of blacks in Canada is an extraordinary chronicle of dashed hopes and brave spirits. The first recorded black resident of Canada was a six-year-old slave from Madagascar, Olivier LeJeune, who arrived on a British ship in New France in 1628. LeJeune was a rarity, since the law of France officially forbade slavery. But in 1689 King Louis XIV permitted his New France colonists to hold slaves as field hands and household servants. By 1749 the British were using black slaves to build Halifax. And after their conquest of Québec in 1760 the British hastily assured the residents that they could keep their slaves. During the American Revolution the British offered to free any

slaves who would join their forces. When the war ended in 1783 many of those blacks fled or were transported to Canada: about 10 per cent of Nova Scotia's 30 000 United Empire Loyalists were black. And many of the 10 000 Loyalists who settled in Central Canada held black slaves. The slavery system was gradually phased out as first the British and then the Americans after the Civil War abolished it, but the social stigmas that attached to it linger even now.

Southern Ontario's history is rich with their sagas. Among them: Dresden's Rev. Josiah Henson, the model for Harriet Beecher Stowe's powerful antislavery novel, *Uncle Tom's Cabin;* American abolitionist John Brown, who planned in Chatham to overthrow the governments of the slaveholding states and was hanged for treason in 1859 after leading an attack on the U.S. federal armoury at Harpers Ferry in West Virginia; and Harriet Tubman, the underground railroad's organizing genius, who funnelled hundreds of escaped slaves into St. Catharines.

In the wake of the U.S. Civil War and Abraham Lincoln's 1863 Emancipation Proclamation, many blacks returned to the United States. The result was a net loss of black citizens until the start of the First World War. The 1921 census showed about 18 300 blacks in Canada, a population that remained stable for the next 30 years. That pattern changed with the first surges in migration from the West Indies. Between 1950 and the mid 1960s Canada's black population doubled to about 40 000 with approximately 90 per cent of the new arrivals from the Caribbean. Since then about 10 000 West Indian immigrants have arrived each year. And the number of African immigrants has occasionally reached an annual high of 5000. Most of the new immigrants possess educational and professional skills surpassing those of the Canadian-born blacks. And those gaps have added to the strains between communities.

Other experts say that what blacks need are better schools, a co-ordinated job strategy and more support for black business ventures. Halifax physician Anthony Sebastian came to Canada from St. Kitts in 1968 and is still astonished by the passivity of Canadian-born blacks. He says blacks must push harder to get an education and into local politics. "Blacks are their own worst enemies here," Sebastian told *Maclean's*. And in a speech last fall Rick Joseph, executive director of Nova Scotia's Black United Front, cautioned, "If we do not move quickly, we will see our grandchildren trying to fare well on welfare."

Strength

That sense of urgency is tempered by the knowledge that the black community has come a long way in a short time. Thirty-four years ago Chatham's Robinson could not eat in the dining room of a local hotel—even though her place in the community could be traced back to her great-great-grandfather, Abraham Shadd. Toronto senior public school principal Wilson Brooks, 61, recounts that when he applied for a department store job 30 years ago, "I was told to my face that they did not want blacks waiting on their customers." Now, racists are more subtle, and blacks are more determined. Ontario Housing Minister Alvin Curling, who came to Canada in 1965 from Jamaica, told a black audience last month to seek—and find—unity. "When one man pulls, he has only the strength of one," Curling said. "But when two pull together, they have much more than the strength of two. And when all of us, hundreds of thousands of black people, pull together, our strength shall be a strength beyond any human measure." That lyrical prayer is the challenge—and could be the salvation—for Canadian blacks.

Growing Up Greek

Helen Lucas

One of my earliest recollections, when I was about three, is of standing outside our home and wondering what I had done that was so wrong. Why would I go to hell? I wondered if God would take into consideration the fact that I was so little. This sense of having done something wrong—of being wrong—is an impression that has remained with me over the years.

My parents emigrated from a village in Greece, forced by poverty to come to Canada. My two sisters and I grew up in Saskatoon, then a city of 50 000, but our lives revolved around the Greek community of sixty people. Since families from the same village banded together, out of the sixty we were about twenty. Another ten relatives lived in Regina, so these thirty people were the ones that mattered in our lives.

We were raised to respect and slightly fear our elders—fear in the sense that we were taught never give them a reason to talk about us. Of course we were model children—submissive, scholastic, music-lessoned, clean-scrubbed, quiet, with our thick, centre-parted hair in long, lush braids. During national Greek holidays we would don Greek costumes and recite patriotic poetry about a war with the Turks which, of course, we had won.

Everyone was struggling. The effects of the Depression were still around. I wore my cousin Jack's hand-me-downs. I remember wondering what the front slit in the underwear was for. Mother would spend a day washing and drying the clothes. Then she'd spend a day mending. New mending went patiently over previous mending. Yet as little as we had, we'd periodically fill a flour sack with clothing to send to our even poorer relatives in Greece. Supposedly when you are young you are not aware of being poor, but because of our strong ties with impoverished relatives "over there," we were constantly reminded that our roots were poverty.

Letters arrived regularly, addressed in awkward English handwriting, and inside were the onion-thin pages filled with the complicated Greek scribbles only my mother could decipher. Once in a while came the envelope edged in black, preparing us for the news inside. I hated looking at the photographs of everyone grouped around the open coffin of the dead relative. Why did they send such photographs? "So you can see how good he looked when he died," I was told. Black was the colour of death, old women, and priests.

I was caught in the drama I made of the world in which I lived, the world from which I came, and the world in which I wanted to be.

To this day, if you ask me where I come from, I cannot answer precisely. Part of me is from the Canadian prairies where I was born and raised, and part is from Greece, where I have never been. At home I spoke Greek and lived a Greek life. At school I was Canadian but even there the Greek values kept interfering. I could work with my Canadian friends but I could not play with them or behave like them. I kept mostly to myself.

Now I can look back and understand my parents' need to cling to the values of the country they had left behind. Change is frightening and slow. They could not manage to accept, in those early years, even a part of the new without fearing it would be at the expense of what they already believed in.

What was the world I wanted to be in? Next door lived the Evans family. Mrs. Evans was elegant, refined, glamorous, gracious, and soft-spoken. Sunday mornings she put on a riding habit and went off to her horses. She even had a maid. I absolutely worshipped her and wanted to be a lady like her.

But she was English, I was Greek. I came to the conclusion, probably again around three, that anyone not English was second-best. Then and there began my bountiful inferiority complex.

My parents must have felt this too. They came to someone else's country. Did they feel second-best? The message we children got was that we would have a better station in life than they did. Their dream was that we would definitely be first-class citizens. Our entrance to this better world would be through an education. "No one can ever take an education away from you," my father frequently said. It never mattered that we were girls; we were expected to go to university. Marriage would come later. Besides, the education guaranteed a better husband.

After a year of university I ended up in Toronto studying at an art college. It was a natural progression. Being by myself much of the time had given me a chance to develop my imagination. I found enjoyment in making images on paper. This child who felt so insignificant could actually receive attention, even admiration, by bringing a drawing to her teacher.

There were many reasons I became an artist. As a loner I could still work alone; no one else need be involved. I was timid with people. Alone I could do exactly what I wanted with no one to judge me. I was no longer caught between two sets of values; in fact, the conflicts of my youth became subject matter for my studio. The past was working for me. It didn't matter that I had no role models, for this way I had no predetermined boundaries to maintain. Boundaries had been a way of life. I also enjoyed my exclusiveness. I was in unexplored territory; it was exciting, it was freedom.

How has my mother responded? She is pleased and proud of what I do, although she doesn't completely understand it. If I'm a painter, why won't I paint like Leonardo da Vinci? While I was teaching painting it was more comfortable for her to think of me as a teacher. I keep sending home newspaper clippings about me or my work but I don't get the "bravo" I seek. If I were to call and say, "Mother, I'm off to Oslo to accept the Nobel Prize," she'd probably say, "Careful, don't speak to any strangers while you're away."

My values confuse her just as her values once confused me. We will never totally understand each other because we have lived such different lives. That is why the total approval I seek can never come. It could only happen if both of us had similar experiences in related lifestyles. Yet she is unbelievably supportive and whole-heartedly respects my need to paint. More than anyone she has been there to help me with problems that have prevented me from painting.

A friend of mine, on meeting Mother, felt we were not one but two generations apart. That may be so. Yet when I get angry about Greek women kept in black, or the archaic values of the church, or about passivity being death, I remember that my widowed mother wears blue, that she has some of the same lack of tolerance for the church that I have, and that she leads an exceptionally active life.

When I telephone and we talk about something we both understand—a recipe, or how to plant a lily, or whatever—we are again mother and daughter, and there is for a little while no distance between us.

Jewish Christmas

Fredelle Bruser Maynard

Christmas, when I was young, was the season of bitterness. Lights beckoned and tinsel shone, store windows glowed with mysterious promise, but I knew the brilliance was not for me. Being Jewish, I had long grown accustomed to isolation and difference. Difference was in my bones and blood, and in the pattern of my separate life. My parents were conspicuously unlike other children's parents in our predominantly Norwegian community. Where my schoolmates were surrounded by blond giants appropriate to a village called Birch Hills, my family suggested still the Russian plains from which they had emigrated years before. My handsome father was a big man, but big without any suggestion of physical strength or agility; one could not imagine him at the wheel of a tractor. In a town that was all wheat and cattle, he seemed the one man wholly devoted to urban pursuits: he operated a general store. Instead of the native costume— overalls and mackinaws—he wore city suits and pearl-grey spats. In winter he was splendid in a plushy chinchilla coat with velvet collar, his black curly hair an extension of the high Astrakhan hat which he had brought from the Ukraine. I was proud of his good looks, and yet uneasy about their distinctly oriental flavor.

My mother's difference was of another sort. Her beauty was not so much foreign as timeless. My friends had slender young Scandinavian mothers, light of foot and blue of eye; my mother was short and heavyset, but with a face of classic proportions. Years later I found her in the portraits of Ingres and Corot—face a delicate oval, brown velvet eyes, brown silk hair centrally parted and drawn back in a lustrous coil—but in those days I saw only that she too was different. As for my grandparents, they were utterly unlike the benevolent, apple-cheeked characters who presided over happy families in my favorite stories. (Evidently all those happy families were gentile.) My grandmother had no fringed shawl, no steel-rimmed glasses. (She read, if at all, with the help of a magnifying glass from Woolworth's.) Ignorant, apparently, of her natural role as gentle occupant of the rocking chair, she was ignorant too of the world outside her apartment in remote Winnipeg. She had brought Odessa with her, and—on my rare visits—she smiled lovingly, uncomprehendingly, across an ocean of time and space. Even more unreal was my grandfather, a black cap and a long beard bent over the Talmud. I felt for him a kind of amused tenderness, but I was glad that my schoolmates could not see him.

At home we spoke another language—Yiddish or Russian—and ate rich foods whose spicy odors bore no resemblance to the neighbors' cooking. We did not go to church or belong to clubs or, it seemed, take any meaningful part in the life of the town. Our social roots went, not down into the foreign soil on which fate had deposited us, but outwards, in delicate, sensitive connections, to other Jewish families in other lonely prairie towns. Sundays, they congregated around our table, these strangers who were brothers; I saw that they too ate knishes and spoke with faintly foreign voices, but I could not feel for them or for their silent swarthy children the kinship I knew I owed to all those who had been, like us, both chosen and abandoned.

All year I walked in the shadow of difference; but at Christmas above all, I tasted it sour on my tongue. There was no room at the tree. "You have Hanukkah," my father reminded me. "That is *our* holiday." I knew the story, of course—how, over two thousand years ago, my people had triumphed over the enemies of their faith, and how a single jar of holy oil had miraculously burned eight days and nights in the temple of the Lord. I thought of my father lighting each night another candle in the *menorah*, my mother and I beside him as he recited the ancient prayer: "Blessed art Thou, O Lord our God, ruler of the universe, who has sanctified us by thy commandments and commanded us to kindle the light of Hanukkah." Yes, we had our miracle too. But how could it stand against the glamor of Christmas? What was *gelt*, the traditional gift coins, to a sled packed with surprises?

What was Judas Maccabaeus the liberator compared with the Christ child in the manger? To my sense of exclusion was added a sense of shame. "You *killed* Christ!" said the boys on the playground. "*You* killed him!" I knew none of the facts behind this awful accusation, but I was afraid to ask. I was even afraid to raise my voice in the chorus of "Come All Ye Faithful" lest I be struck down for my unfaithfulness by my own God, the wrathful Jehovah. With all the passion of my child's heart I longed for a younger, more compassionate deity with flowing robe and silken hair. Reluctant conscript to a doomed army, I longed to change sides. I longed for Christmas.

Although my father was in all things else the soul of indulgence, in this one matter he stood firm as Moses. "You cannot have a tree, *herzele*. You shouldn't even want to sing the carols. You are a Jew." I turned the words over in my mind and on my tongue. What was it, to be a Jew in Birch Hills, Saskatchewan? Though my father spoke of Jewishness as a special distinction, as far as I could see it was an inheritance without a kingdom, a check on a bank that had failed. Being Jewish was mostly not doing things other people did—not eating pork, not going to Sunday school, not entering, even playfully, into childhood romances, because the only boys around were *goyishe* boys. I remember, when I was five or six, falling in love with Edward Prince of Wales. Of the many arguments with which Mama might have dampened my ardor, she chose surely the most extraordinary. "You can't marry him. He isn't Jewish." And of course, finally, definitely, most crushing of all, being Jewish meant not celebrating Christ's birth. My parents allowed me to attend Christmas parties, but they made it clear that I must receive no gifts. How I envied the white and gold Norwegians! Their Lutheran church was not glamorous, but it was less frighteningly strange than the synagogue I had visited in Winnipeg, and in the Lutheran church, each December, joy came upon the midnight clear.

It was the Lutheran church and its annual concert which brought me closest to Christmas. Here there was always a tree, a jolly Santa Claus, and a program of songs and recitations. As the town's most accomplished elocutionist, I was regularly invited to perform. Usually my offering was comic or purely secular—

Santa's Mistake, The Night Before Christmas, a scene from *A Christmas Carol*. But I had also memorized for such occasions a sweetly pious narrative about the housewife who, blindly absorbed in cleaning her house for the Lord's arrival, turns away a beggar and finds she has rebuffed the Savior himself. Oddly enough, my recital of this vitally un-Jewish material gave my parents no pain. My father, indeed, kept in his safe-deposit box along with other valuables a letter in which the Lutheran minister spoke gratefully of my last Christmas performance. "Through her great gift, your little Freidele has led many to Jesus." Though Papa seemed untroubled by considerations of whether this was a proper role for a Jewish child, reciting *The Visit* made me profoundly uneasy. And I suppose it was this feeling, combined with a natural disinclination to stand unbidden at the feast, which led me, the year I was seven, to rebel. ⎯

We were baking in the steamy kitchen, my mother and I—or rather she was baking while I watched, fascinated as always, the miracle of the strudel. First, the warm ball of dough, no larger than my mother's hand. Slap, punch, bang—again and again she lifted the dough and smacked it down on the board. Then came the moment I loved. Over the kitchen table, obliterating its patterned oilcloth, came a damask cloth; and over this in turn a cloud of flour. Beside it stood my mother, her hair bound in muslin, her hands and arms powdered with flour. She paused a moment. Then, like a dancer about to execute a particularly difficult pirouette, she tossed the dough high in the air, catching it with a little stretching motion and tossing again until the ball was ball no longer but an almost transparent rectangle. The strudel was as large as the tablecloth now. *"Unter Freidele's vigele Ligt eyn groys veys tsigele,"* she sang. "Under Freidele's little bed A white goat lays his silken head." *Tsigele iz geforen handlen Rozinkes mit mandlen. . . ."* For some reason that song, with its gay fantastic images of the white goat shopping for raisins and almonds, always made me sad. But then my father swung open the storm door and stood, stamping and jingling his galoshes buckles, on the icy mat.

"Boris, look how you track in the snow!"

Already flakes and stars were turning into muddy puddles. Still booted and icy-cheeked he swept us up—a kiss on the back of Mama's neck, the only spot not dedicated to strudel, and a hug for me.

"You know what? I have just now seen the preacher. Reverend Pederson, he wants you should recite at the Christmas concert."

I bent over the bowl of almonds and snapped the nutcracker.

"I should tell him it's all right, you'll speak a piece?"

No answer.

"Sweetheart— dear one—you'll do it?"

Suddenly the words burst out. "No, Papa! I don't want to!"

My father was astonished. "But why not? What is it with you?"

"I hate those concerts!" All at once my grievances swarmed up in an angry cloud. "I never have any fun! And everybody else gets presents and Santa Claus never calls out 'Freidele Bruser'! They all know I'm Jewish!"

Papa was incredulous. "But, little daughter, always you've had a good time! Presents! What presents? A bag of candy, an orange? Tell me, is there a child in town with such toys as you have? What should you want with Santa Claus?"

It was true. My friends had tin tea sets and dolls with sawdust bodies and crude Celluloid smiles. I had an Eaton Beauty with real hair and delicate jointed body, two French dolls with rosy bisque faces and—new this last Hanukkah—Rachel, my baby doll. She was the marvel of the town: exquisite china head, overlarge and shaped like a real infant's, tiny wrinkled hands, legs convincingly bowed. I had a lace and taffeta doll bassinet, a handmade cradle, a full set of rattan doll furniture, a teddy bear from Germany and real porcelain dishes from England. What *did* I want with Santa Claus? I didn't know, I burst into tears.

Papa was frantic now. What was fame and the applause of the Lutherans compared to his child's tears? Still bundled in his overcoat he knelt on the kitchen floor and hugged me to him, rocking and crooning. "Don't cry, my child, don't cry. You don't want to go, you don't have to. I tell them you have a sore throat, you can't come."

"Boris, wait. Listen to me." For the first time since my outburst, Mama spoke. She laid down the rolling pin, draped the strudel dough delicately over the table, and wiped her hands on her apron. "What kind of a fuss? You go or you don't go, it's not such a big thing. But so close to Christmas you shouldn't let them down. The one time we sit with them in the church and such joy you give them. Freidele, look at me. . . ." I snuffed loudly and obeyed, not without some satisfaction in the thought of the pathetic picture I made. "Go this one time, for my sake. You'll see, it won't be so bad. And if you don't like it—pffff, no more! All right? Now, come help with the raisins."

On the night of the concert we gathered in the kitchen again, this time for the ritual of the bath. Papa set up the big tin tub on chairs next to the black iron stove. Then, while he heated pails of water and sloshed them into the tub, Mama set out my clothes. Everything about this moment contrived to make me feel pampered, special. I was lifted in and out of the steamy water, patted dry with thick towels, powdered from neck to toes with Mama's best scented talcum. Then came my "reciting outfit." My friends in Birch Hills had party dresses mail-ordered from Eaton's— crackly taffeta or shiny rayon satin weighted with lace or flounces, and worn with long white stockings drawn up over long woolen underwear. My dress was Mama's own composition, a poem in palest peach crepe de chine created from remnants of her bridal trousseau. Simple and flounceless, it fell from my shoulders in a myriad of tiny pleats no wider than my thumbnail; on the low-slung sash hung a cluster of silk rosebuds. Regulation drop-seat underwear being unthinkable under such a costume, Mama had devised a snug little apricot chemise which made me, in a world of wool, feel excitingly naked.

When at last I stood on the church dais, the Christmas tree glittering and shimmering behind me, it was with the familiar feeling of strangeness. I looked out over the audience-congregation, grateful for the myopia that made faces indistinguishable, and began:

A letter came on Christmas morn
In which the Lord did say
"Behold my star shines in the east
And I shall come today.
Make bright thy hearth. . . ."

The words tripped on without thought or effort. I knew by heart every nuance and gesture, down to the modest curtsey and the properly solemn pace with which I returned to my seat. There I huddled into the lining of Papa's coat, hardly hearing the "Beautiful, beautiful!" which accompanied his hug. For this was the dreaded moment. All around me, children twitched and whispered. Santa had come.

"Olaf Swenson!" Olaf tripped over a row of booted feet, leapt down the aisle and embraced an enormous package. "Ellen Njaa! Fern Dahl! Peter Bjorkstrom!" There was a regular procession now, all jubilant. Everywhere in the hall children laughed, shouted, rejoiced with their friends. "What'd you get?" "Look at mine!" In the seat next to me, Gunnar Olsen ripped through layers of tissue: "I got it! I got it!" His little sister wrestled with the contents of a red net stocking. A tin whistle rolled to my feet and I turned away, ignoring her breathless efforts to retrieve it.

And then—suddenly, incredibly, the miracle came. "Freidele Bruser!" For me, too, the star had shone. I looked up at my mother. A mistake surely. But she smiled and urged me to my feet. "Go on, look, he calls you!" It was true, Santa was actually coming to meet me. My gift, I saw, was not wrapped—and it could be no mistake. It was a doll, a doll just like Rachel, but dressed in christening gown and cap. "Oh Mama, look! He's brought me a doll! A twin for Rachel! She's just the right size for Rachel's clothes. I can take them both for walks in the carriage. They can have matching outfits. . . ." I was in an ecstasy of plans.

Mama did not seem to be listening. She lifted the hem of the gown. "How do you like her dress? Look, see the petticoat?"

"They're beautiful!" I hugged the doll rapturously. "Oh Mama, I *love* her! I'm going to call her Ingrid. Ingrid and Rachel. . . ."

During the long walk home Mama was strangely quiet. Usually I held my parents' hands and swung between them. But now I stepped carefully, clutching Ingrid.

"You had a good time, yes?" Papa's breath frosted the night.

"Mmmmmmm." I rubbed my warm cheek against Ingrid's cold one. "It was just like a real Christmas. I got the best present of anybody. Look, Papa—did you see Ingrid's funny little cross face? It's just like Rachel's. I can't wait to get her home and see them side by side in the crib."

In the front hall, I shook the snow from Ingrid's lace bonnet. "A hot cup cocoa maybe?" Papa was already taking the milk from the icebox. "No, no, I want to get the twins ready for bed!" I broke from my mother's embrace. The stairs seemed longer than usual. In my arms Ingrid was cold and still, a snow princess. I could dress her in Rachel's flannel gown, that would be the thing. . . . The dolls and animals watched glassy-eyed as I knelt by the cradle. It rocked at my touch, oddly light. I flung back the blankets. Empty. Of course.

Sitting on the cold floor, the doll heavy in my lap, I wept for Christmas. Nothing had changed then, after all. For Jews there was no Santa Claus; I understood that. But my parents. . . . *Why* had they dressed Rachel?

From the kitchen below came the mingled aromas of hot chocolate and buttery popcorn. My mother called softly. "Let them call," I said to Ingrid-Rachel. "I don't care!" The face of the Christmas doll was round and blank under her cap; her dress was wet with my tears. Brushing them away, I heard my father enter the room. He made no move to touch me or lift me up. I turned and saw his face tender and sad like that of a Chagall violinist. "Mama worked every night on the clothes," he said. "Yesterday even, knitting booties."

Stiff-fingered, trembling, I plucked at the sleeve of the christening gown. It was indeed a miracle—a wisp of batiste but as richly overlaid with embroidery as a coronation robe. For the first time I examined Rachel's new clothes—the lace insets and lace overlays, the French knots and scalloped edges, the rows of hemstitching through which tiny ribbons ran like fairy silk. The petticoat was tucked and pleated. Even the little diaper showed an edge of hand crochet. There were booties and mittens and a ravishing cap.

"Freidele, dear one, my heart," my father whispered. "We did not think. We could not know. Mama dressed Rachel in the new clothes, you should be happy with the others. We so much love you."

Outside my window, where the Christmas snow lay deep and

crisp and even, I heard the shouts of neighbors returning from the concert. "Joy to the world!" they sang,

Let earth receive her King!
Let every heart prepare Him room
And heaven and nature sing . . .

It seemed to me, at that moment, that I too was a part of the song. I wrapped Rachel warmly in her shawl and took my father's hand.

Final dance on racism's grave?

David Suzuki

I walked into my favorite bar a couple of months ago and was hailed by a friend who is a regular there.

As I ambled over, I could see that he was involved in an argument with someone I didn't recognize. You could tell it had been heated by the way people in a circle around them were hushed and kept looking over surreptitiously. As I approached, the stranger wheeled on me and demanded, "What do you people want?"

Looking back on that moment, I am amazed at the brain's demand for understanding. I hadn't heard a word of their argument and this question was totally incomprehensible, yet immediately my brain began to try to make sense out of it.

Faster than you can read this line, my mind had decided that since my friend also worked at the CBC, the issue must have been the recent budget cuts.

"Look," I waded in, "there should have been an increase, not a cut." "No, David," my friend interjected. "That's not what it's about." Instead of helping, that threw me back into confusion and now my brain began a search down various alleys trying to make sense out of "you people."

My friend used to live in B.C., could they be discussing the province's economy? Or was it all of us people who had gone to university? Perhaps it had to do with everyone who works out at the Y. Gradually, my dim wits began to realize that he had lumped my friend and me together because while we are both Canadians by birth, he is of East Indian extraction and I am Japanese. He meant all of us "colored" Canadians. What an irony when this guy turned out to have emigrated here from Central Europe when he was a child!

Being an articulate academic, I turned on the full heat of my scorn and persuasively told him to "(expletive deleted) off" and walked away. I showed him not to tangle with someone who has a way with words.

My point in relating this story, in addition to reflecting on how the brain functions to make sense of the world around, is to share an experience that every member of a visible minority has had in Canada.

These days, our media are full of stories of racial incidents. But you know, I think we've got it all wrong. Sure, there is a lot of bigotry here—show me a country where there isn't. But don't let anyone tell you it's worse now than it was.

Every day when I take the bus to work, we pass Jesse Ketchum School (it could be any other school in Toronto) and it fills me with delight to watch youngsters of every color playing, fighting, hugging—in short doing what youngsters do but with total unawareness of visible differences.

I see in Toronto today a mix of races that would have been impossible to foresee when I was a kid. Back then, most countries of origin of visible minorities were allowed to send 100 immigrants a year in Canada.

This country is a bold experiment. Modern Canada is grounded on the historic rivalries between those of French and English extraction and the paternalistic oppression of the original inhabitants.

There have been a lot of horror stories and mistakes and there will be more, but surely we have learned from past errors and as we become aware of our often unconscious biases, we do change.

I think Canadians (and I'm one of the guilty ones) are too self critical—we judge ourselves very harshly. But we shouldn't forget the plusses. My eldest daughter, a fourth generation Canadian but genetically pure Japanese, never gave a thought to the fact that her husband is a Caucasian from Chile, yet in my parent's day, interracial marriage was unthinkable.

My parents, although born in Canada, could not vote until 1948, had to face a quota system in the universities and could not buy property like everyone else. Shortly after the war, my family moved to a town in southern Ontario called Leamington where kids would boast that "No black had ever stayed there beyond sunset."

My point here is not to decry past injustices, but to indicate that many are simply not acceptable today. Yes there is still a lot of bigotry and we must always fight it when we see it, but I believe for every discriminatory episode, there are dozens of acts of generosity, friendship and assistance that cross racial barriers, but they never make the papers.

I was amazed and filled with pride at the response of Canadians to the Boat People and to the Ethiopians. It was generous and genuine. Our record of assistance to the Third World, through agencies like CIDA and IDRC, is an example for the rest of the world.

And as we grope towards our ideal of equal opportunity and justice for all, we can look to those children in the schoolground with hope. I'm reminded of two episodes in parochial Leamington of the 1940s that give me faith in youngsters. One of my great chums went to a club once a week where he had lots of fun playing games. He wanted me to join too and I was delighted at the prospect.

So I tagged along with him but when I got there, the grown-ups made me sit outside the whole evening. My friend had wanted me to join the Sons Of England! The other experience involved another pal. We were playing together when my dad rode by on a bike.

I waved and hollered at him to the amazement of my friend. "How do you know him?" he asked. "That's my dad," I replied. "But he's a Chinaman!" he exclaimed.

Yes, kids are colorblind.

The Saga of the Fine-Toothed Comb

James H. Gray

Machray school where I was enrolled in 1913 was far from being a slum district school, yet its population was almost as cosmopolitan as any. Mountain Avenue was a sort of border-land between the congested new Canadian settlements to the south and the predominantly Anglo-Saxon district to the north. But the former was steadily expanding northward by sheer force of numbers. Thus many families that had moved out of the ghetto to more comfortable quarters often gave shelter to relatives or friends newly arrived from the old country. So there was a steady infusion of immigrant children into Machray school. My own experience illustrates the situation. My transfer from Norwood school was issued with the space for the name of the new school left blank. I took it to Strathcona school near Stella and Salter and was accommodated there for a couple of months. But so great was the crush of new immigrant pupils into Strathcona that I was shifted to Machray, which was somewhat closer to our home on Salter Street.

The Strathcona school year was a towerless Babel and during my short attendance I often felt completely out of place because I spoke no language but English. It was different, and a lot more comfortable, at Machray, where English predominated. Both schools, however, wrestled with the problem of beginning children who came into class without a word of English to their names. By this time the teachers had worked out a rough-and-ready system of handling the problem.

They would seat the children who could speak some English next to those who could speak none so that work could proceed with one translating for the other. Within a matter of weeks, even days sometimes, the children caught on so quickly that translation could be dispensed with. Once compulsory school attendance became law in 1916, however, it brought such an influx into the school system of pupils who could speak no English that this method would no longer work. There were rooms in Strathcona school, for example, where scarcely a child understood more than a dozen or so words of English. The teachers there solved their instructional dilemma by a combination of signs, sounds, and gestures. The day might begin with three words, "take out book", repeated slowly by the teacher several times. Then the class would repeat each word with pantomimic action. Then the sounds went onto the blackboard and letters were made in scribblers.

In the schoolyards the kids tended at first to cluster together in national groups and to use their native languages. That once led to an agitation by the super patriots that a regulation be enforced requiring only English to be spoken in the schoolyards. However, some sort of centrifugal force operated to spin the children out of their national groups into conglomerates. The most potent force was the playing of schoolyard games. A couple of Polish girls might have some qualms about inviting a Jewish girl into their skipping game. But rope-turners were always needed, so they handed her one end of the rope and she was in. With the boys, who tended more towards team sports, rounding up a couple of soccer teams or baseball teams required the participation of every boy in the room. Left to their own devices, the small fry tended to use their own languages at the games. But there were usually enough English-speaking children around to dominate the shouting. While all the other children learned English, the only foreign words we ever learned were the swear words.

Of all the immigrant groups the swear words of the Ukrainians were probably the most earthy. For years and years a Ukrainian bookstore on North Main Street exhibited a huge print in its window of a famous painting by a Russian master. It was entitled "The Cossacks' Reply to the Czar". It showed a group of rowdy Cossack soldiers gathered around a table at which one of their number was writing down insults dictated by the others. The soldiers were laughing uproariously at their epistle, which ran to several pages. A Ukrainian acquaintance once said that many of the insults were readable, upside down, in the original, but the print maker had opaqued the writing to make it indecipherable to the more prudish eyes of modern Ukrainians. When the small fry got angry at their games, which was frequently, most of them turned to their homey native oaths to express their displeasure. The English language was vastly inferior when it came to name-calling, so we all picked up their oaths and added them to our vocabulary.

Once, when we lived on Mountain Avenue, I had gotten into a row with a couple of Ukrainian kids who chased me home crying. When I reached the safety of my yard I turned and let fly a string of swear words I had accumulated. My mother heard the ruckus and came out to investigate just as a Ukrainian woman was passing.

"Missus," she said. "Missus know what boy say?"

My mother shook her head. "He say so bad words." She held her hand over her mouth. "Oh so bad words." Then she beckoned to my mother and whispered a rough translation of what I had said. My horrified mother caught me by the back of the neck and lathered me up the steps and into the house. All the time she was threatening to tell my father when he came home. She never did, largely, I suspect, because she couldn't bring herself to repeat the translation even in a whisper to my father. It was, as I later discovered, an all-encompassing, mouth-filling oath that ran the gamut from bestiality through incest to rape and was usually the last insult hurled before the fight started.

Every nationality delighted in the ancient game of teaching the *auslander* swear words for articles of common usage. In this game we came out far ahead because the foreign kids were much more eager to learn our language than we were to learn theirs. Eventually they learned the danger of asking any of us Anglo-Saxons, "Please, how do you say 'drink'?"

It was a common occurrence for a shy little immigrant child to raise her hand in school to ask to leave the room and use one of our four-letter words for something entirely different. That set off a storm of laughter which made the day for the Anglo-Saxons in the room. I have always suspected that the practice of identifying desired purposes by holding up one, two, or three fingers derived from such earthy language difficulties.

The language problem was by no means as acute at Machray school as it was at Norquay and Strathcona. If I had been in Grade Three or Four when I came to Winnipeg I might never have known it existed. By that time English was the language of communication among the various ethnic groupings. But I started school in Grade One, which was where all the new immigrants in the neighbourhood started regardless of age unless they could speak English. Naturally, as quickly as they picked up the language they moved into the appropriate peer group. But in the beginning our Grade One at Machray struggled with the same problems that occurred in Strathcona and the other melting-pot schools.

Winnipeg, no less than Canada itself, owes its existence in large measure to Sir Clifford Sifton's immigration policies. No Canadian history ignores this policy or fails to mention the hundreds of thousands of settlers who came to Canada as the direct result of it. But my generation knew nothing of Sifton or policies of immigration. We knew only the end result of his policy as it was personified by a funny-looking little immigrant boy standing by the edge of the Norquay schoolyard watching the rest of us play soccer, and wanting passionately to participate. Or as it was illustrated by a little immigrant girl in the beginners' class at Machray school, reaching up to scratch her head and triggering a class uproar.

"Anna," the teacher would call sharply, putting her work to one side and reaching into the middle drawer of her desk, "come up here, please."

There was always a short pause while the teacher zeroed in on which of the half-dozen Annas in the class she wanted. When that was sorted out the little girl would usually burst into tears before getting to her feet. Sometimes the teacher had to come and take her by the arm. There were even times when more physical force than a girl teacher could muster was needed to move the pupil out of her seat. Then the teacher would appeal to one of the other children to explain to the little girl in her own language what was involved and what had to be done. For some reason or other, it always seemed to take two other little girls, both talking at once in Ukrainian, Polish, German, or Yiddish, to quiet the object of the teacher's attention and get her to co-operate.

What was involved was a hair-combing with a fine-toothed comb, in search of lice in the hair of the pupil. The teacher knew from experience that when any pupil started scratching at a real insect it would not be long before half the room would be scratching away at imaginary itches. So Anna took her place beside the teacher's desk while the teacher ran her comb through the pupil's hair in long, slow strokes. At Machray school our teacher was Miss Horn, who kept a newspaper in a bottom drawer. This she spread out over the desk, and leaned the pupil's head over the centre of the sheet so that the lice that failed to adhere to the comb dropped onto the paper, to be squashed with an inkwell. When the combing was finished the pupil returned to her seat and the room went back to work. Our first brush with public school delousing at the beginning of the term was an exciting event and we all watched goggle-eyed. A girl in the front row near the teacher's desk squealed excitedly, "There it is, Miss Horn! There it is! I saw it drop on the paper, right there."

So there was a lot of neck-craning and some of us even left our seats. As the weeks passed the lice hunt eventually lost its zest and we ignored it and went on with whatever we were doing while the operation was being performed. Or perhaps the homes of the immigrant children became less infested, and less public combing was needed. Certainly a fine-toothed comb was standard equipment in all the North End homes, for lice were no less endemic in the overcrowded immigrant homes than they were in the schools.

The regular North End school teachers quickly learned to cope with the scratching problem. There were other problems that took longer. The worst thing that could happen to a little immigrant boy was to make a winter entry into the public school system and bump into a substitute teacher with unrealistic ideas about neatness. Our standard winter footwear was a pair of moccasins or shoepacks with two or three pairs of socks. Immigrant children, however, often wore knee-length heavy felt mukluks to which rubbers were permanently attached at the bottom. Some of them kept slippers in their pockets and in school they'd take off the mukluks and wear the slippers. But many of the newcomers had the tops of their mukluks stitched to the bottoms of their pant legs just below the knees. When these kids started clumping around the room, a new teacher would instruct them to go into the clothes lobby and take off their rubbers. Impossible. If the rubbers came off, so did the mukluks and so did the pants! Most regular teachers understood all this and learned to survive in rooms reeking with the smell of mukluks drying out. But every now and then a teacher from south Winnipeg would turn up. It would take the class half the morning to get her straightened out about the facts of daily life in the North End of Winnipeg.

Teachers were easily shaken down, but I have often wondered since what effect the first few months in Canadian schools had on the personalities of the immigrant children. It was hard enough for an Anglo-Saxon like me, who knew the language, to move only from one school to another. Each move always entailed a couple of split lips and bloody noses before I settled into my place in the schoolyard pecking order. How much more painful, terrifying even, it must have been for the newcomers to be pitchforked into such an environment, where the natives were unfriendly and the language was impossible. It must have been humiliating in the extreme for a shy and sensitive seven-year-old to be summoned forward, by a teacher she feared, to have her hair combed, often ungently, by a sharp-toothed instrument that dug at the scalp or got snagged on knots. And it must have been cold comfort to discover later that the combing ordeal was one that everyone in the room would undergo eventually, for such was the way of the migrant lice in the cloakrooms of the North End schools. But painful though the experiences were at the time, I doubt that they did much permanent harm to the psyches of the new Canadians. For one thing, they were a lot stronger and tougher physically than we were. For another, they had already come halfway round the world and survived a hundred shocks and surprises, not the least of which was an interminable ocean voyage followed by an interminable railway journey. Mere teachers they could take in their stride, and if not, they could work off their frustrations beating up the Anglo-Saxon kids in the neighbourhood. They did.

I have often wondered how much of the prejudice that developed in Winnipeg against the whole immigrant population germinated in what could be called the fine-toothed-comb syndrome. For many Anglo-Saxon families, it was the first intimate contact they had with the immigrant world, and to use my mother's word, a "disgusting" one it was. It was not that the average Anglo-Saxon was any more fastidious than the average Ukrainian or Jewish family. Nor did the immigrant kids have a monopoly on transporting lice to school. At this stage, however, the Anglo-Saxons were firmly established several rungs further up the economic ladder than the immigrants. Hence they were not hived off in enclaves crowded with lice-infested rooming houses in the older parts of the city. The English, Scottish, and Irish immigrants, moreover, were not driven to congregate together because they could not speak the language of the country. They were thus able to spread out a little more, in cottages clustering around the C.P.R. shops in Weston, for example. If they lived in North Winnipeg, however, there was no way in which they could isolate themselves from the lice if they had children in school.

Even in the best homes in North Winnipeg, as in the district's better schools, the scratching of a young head evoked an automatic response. Out came the fine-toothed comb. When the lice were extracted they were dispatched simply by squashing between thumb-nails or, for the more squeamish, by drowning in coal oil or by burning.

"There! That must be all of them," an impatient mother would sigh. "Now for goodness' sake stay away from those hunky kids because I am sick and tired of combing bugs out of your hair!"

Where parents harboured no original prejudices against the immigrants, the repetition of hair-combing incidents was well designed to create them. They were certainly prejudiced against lice; "hunky" kids and lice went together. The fact that there were immigrant families who were as finicky about bugs as they were probably never occurred to them. Their responses were as automatic as those of Pavlov's dogs. Scratching signified lice, which produced the fine-toothed comb and the combination spelled hunky.

It would, however, be unwise to blame too much of the prejudice on lice. Adult Winnipeg of the era was as race-proud, bigoted, and prejudice-driven as any city on earth. The Ukrainians, Poles, and Jews who had come to Canada to escape from the Czar's military conscription did not rush madly to join the Canadian army when war broke out. Indeed, the only big rush was by the recently arrived British immigrants, many of whom saw the war as a free ride home for a visit, as something that would be over long before it involved them. When that illusion was shattered, and recruiting fell off, the aliens became a target for everyone. If an Anglo-Saxon wanted a job that some immigrant had, he thought nothing of demanding it as his right and insisting that the immigrant be fired. When labour troubles developed, they were blamed on alien agitators. The deportation of aliens was demanded by newspapers, labour leaders, preachers, and politicians with varying degrees of intensity.

Winnipeg prejudice, moreover, was not something about which simple generalizations were possible. Within the prejudices of each of the general categories of people were a lot of subsidiary ones. My father, for example, thoroughly disliked all Englishmen. How much of this went back to his days in anti-British Buffalo, and how much was new growth from the fact that the English dominated the civil service in Manitoba, is problematic. Whenever he failed in an attempt for some sort of clerical job in the civil service, his explanation was always the same: "They gave it to a bloody Englishman!"

There may have been a shadow of substance to his reasoning. All the immigrant groups quickly developed mutual aid associations, formal or informal. Getting a start in the new world was hard enough for any of the newcomers. When one got a job, he naturally looked around for a job for his wife's brother or the cousin of a Liverpool, Manchester, or London neighbour. There were not only English, Irish, and Scottish fraternal societies running full blast, there were secret societies and trade unions in which they could work for mutual advancement. A circumspect immigrant from Glasgow could certainly improve his chances if he were a Royal Arch Mason of the Scottish Rite, a member of the

Sons of Scotland or the Knights of Pythias, a Knight Templar, and a supporter of the Dunfermline, Dundee, and Strathroy Association. Even the religious denominations tended to become mutual assistance societies, functioning to exclude those they disliked from gainful employment. It was curious how one catch-phrase was used by so many diverse groups: "Let one of them in and they'll take over the place."

The Presbyterians used it against the Catholics, the Catholics used it against the Jews. The Irish and English used it against the Scots and all the Anglo-Saxons used it against all the aliens.

But this was in the adult world. In ours, we also chose up sides racially and nationally, perhaps with the herd instinct operating in the interest of self-preservation. If a couple of Irish, English, Jewish, or Polish kids got into a fight with each other, the rest of us tended to stand back and let them go at it. We confined our participation to shouting encouragement to the one we favoured. But if a Jewish kid tangled with a Polish kid, it was not long before several other Jewish-Polish fights were going on, or two or three of one group would gang up on one of the other. We learned quickly, in the North End, always to make a quick nose count of the odds before letting the first fist fly. But in our vocal world, as distinct from our physical world, we tended to use all the labels without cluttering them with odious connotations. "Hunky" was a generic term that included all aliens of whatever national origin or religious persuasion. If we didn't know the name of a boy we were trying to identify we would refer to him as "the hunky kid who lives down the lane in that brown house".

Whether the process was helped by referring to him as a "hunky kid" never caused us any concern. It was a word we used when a better one did not come readily to mind. When we wanted to differentiate more sharply, we might refer to him as the "Polack kid", or the "Uke kid", or the "Jew kid". It was only when we got mad and started bandying insults that we used words that were intended to cut and slice—words like "bohunk" or "kike" or "wop"—and these usually were coupled with "dirty" for better effect. All these words, it should be emphasized, were words that got into our vocabulary in the schoolyards and were not consciously selected to define social attitudes. What the foreign kids called us we never really knew because, as I have said, they reached into the language underground of their own tongue for suitable epithets.

The plain truth was that many an Anglo-Saxon kid spent much of his life envying the foreign kids. The Jews, for example, always seemed to be getting off on special holidays of their own while we had to stay in school and work. Not only did the Ukrainian kids have our Christmas holidays, they had a week in January when they had Christmas all over again. Even the Catholics who were not foreigners got away with murder, in our judgment. They had saints' days and feast days which gave them extra time away from school. There was even a custom then of honouring St. Patrick's Day, St. George's Day, and Burns' Day with special entertainment in the schools. Except for Victoria Day, the only day Canadian kids had anything to celebrate was the First of July and that was a holiday anyway.

There was undoubtedly a great deal of anti-Semitism in the North End of Winnipeg, and some of the parental attitudes must have filtered down to the children. Certainly the Poles and the Jews kept their distance from each other and the Ukrainians brought with them when they came their prejudice against both. For us, however, "Jew" was just another generic word that often included the peddlers who were Italian or Greek. When we scrounged bottles and scrap metal it was to sell to "the Jew", who was anybody that came along buying junk. The word "Jew" was also a verb that was synonymous for "bargain vigorously". If we haggled successfully over something we would say, "I Jewed him down."

I was well on in school, indeed, before I discovered that the Jews did not celebrate Christmas like the rest of us. We were living in the Rozell Apartments on Clark Street by then. A Jewish family lived on the third floor and their boy Izzy was in my brother's room at school. On Christmas morning I was overjoyed with my present—a pair of C.C.M. Automobile D skates which were screwed to my summer boots. My brothers each got a sleigh and my father bought a table gramophone for my mother. It came with half a dozen records. Four of them were Christmas hymns; one was "Carry Me Back to Blighty" and the other was a comic recitation entitled "The Preacher and the Bear".

After we had taken turns winding the gramophone and had squeezed as much laughter as possible out of it, I wanted to try out my skates. So I went to see if Izzy wanted to go skating with me. He had also got some new skates and I brought him down to see our new gramophone and listen to "The Preacher and the Bear". He wanted to listen to our other records so I put them on one after the other. He liked "Hark! the Herald Angels Sing" and "Adeste, Fideles". He kept time with those by pretending he was playing the piano and whistling. We played them a couple of times. Then he asked my mother if he could borrow the two records to play on his gramophone and see if he could follow them on the piano. It didn't come off. He would get going nicely and then hit a couple of wrong keys while the gramophone music got away and he could never catch up. It never occurred to me then, or even much later, that his was the only kosher household in Winnipeg from which Christmas carols could be heard emanating that morning.

The enemies of time

H.S. Bhabra

First, some facts:

Fact One: I'm an Indian—East Indian as the jargon has it here—of a Punjabi Sikh family. It's a pretty obvious fact. This isn't a great tan frosting my epidermis. It is my epidermis. No one could confuse it for the Cornish Pasty complexion of the native Brit.

Fact Two: I grew up in England; arrived there as a babe-in-arms back in the '50s, when Received Standard Speech still ruled the roost, before it lost out to Cockney and Liverpudlian. Which is why I sound obviously—some would say ostentatiously—English.

Fact Three: I sometimes still get confused in Downtown Toronto. Fact Three began it all. I was on a streetcar, going in the wrong direction. But this is a friendly city. This is Toronto the Good. So I asked my fellow passengers, in (though I say it myself) a nicely judged tone of rueful stupidity, if this streetcar was taking me where I wanted to go.

It wasn't, as they began to explain to me, giving me more and yet more complicated instructions: get off this streetcar, take that one, that subway, that other streetcar . . . I'm not complaining. I've done the same myself in London and Paris. The obvious route to a resident has a tendency to sound, to a stranger, like going to Roncesvalles by way of Arkansas and Mars.

And that was when he broke in, in the kind of Northern Irish accent you can use to barb wire, cut glass or gralloch deer. "I'm getting off here," he said. "I can show you the way." He took me by the shoulder and plunged us down to the street.

I hadn't come across that kind of instinctive helpfulness to strangers since Cairo. Not that his swift directions helped much. I hadn't expected them to. What are maps for?

But then, as we were parting, a change came over him, and here I have to ask the phoneticians to forgive me as I try to convey the color and rhythms of our exchanges.

"Are ya-ew Onglish?" he asked suspiciously.

Facts One and Two flashed through my mind. "Well, British," I replied.

"Ya-ew sound Onglish."

Fact Two did a little dance inside my head, but never got the chance to show its steps.

"Ya-ew should get out of Arland," he told me, with just a touch of hostility. "Bloddy omperialosm."

Well, what could I say? That, like millions of other Britons, I did think Britain should get out of Northern Ireland, leaving it an autonomous country, to decide its own relationship with Eire? That I knew perfectly well the consequences of such an action would, on the Algerian model, be civil war in the Six Counties and five years of monstrous terrorism in England, Scotland and Wales? Or should Fact One assert itself? Should I say I'd take the blame for a lot, but not for imperialism? Should I point at my face and say, "after all, I used to be the British Empire?"

It seemed the quickest way out, and as usual it worked.

But I was thinking already of an evening, years ago, my first year at university one vacation, when my girlfriend telephoned from her parents' house in Hampshire to ask if I could get any news from Guildford, quite close to where we lived. Her sister was in Guildford, meeting her boyfriend in a pub, a pub we had just heard had been destroyed by an IRA bomb, with as yet unknown numbers of fatalities.

As it happened, sister and friend had left 10 minutes before the blast.

And I was thinking of corpses on the streets and in the hedgerows of the Punjab, or blown out of the air into the chilly waters off Ireland.

He had turned amicable again. "Stay here," he told me. "Ya-ew don't want to go back to Ongland. Canada's a lovely country."

Yes it is. Yes, it is.

But I was thinking of heritage cultures, of what comes packed in the bags some immigrants bring with them. Folk-costumes, folk-dances, folk-music, folk memories—of violence, of vengeance, of hell. I was thinking of how some people safe at last from the places where the world's wounds still fester will do anything they can to keep those wounds open. How they always will, until Canada has some active notion of itself, of Canadianness, to set beside its honorable commitment to heritage cultures.

An active notion? Why active? Will time not weave some magic? Will it not cancel the memories?

I fear not.

Because the majority of immigrants who want to see it happen have no set of concepts, no dense community support, arising out of this whole culture, to set against the age-old stories, the iterated axioms, of those who have no self if they forget, much less if they forgive.

Because the enemies of time hold one mighty hostage—the liberalism of this country; the very liberalism they do not choose to share.

Because, without some central conception of Canadianness, there are people to whom multiculturalism will always mean only uniculturalism, means not having to give up one whit of what they bring with them.

He was speaking now of poetry, the poetry of Ireland, a whole great and humiliated culture.

He repeated his instructions one last time, waving me on my way.

But I was thinking of the first line of the Irish poet Derek Mahon's great poem, A Disused Shed In County Wexford:

Even now there are places where a thought might grow.

$$\overline{\overline{\overline{}}}$$

The Dene Declaration

The Dene of the Northwest Territories

We the Dene of the N.W.T. insist on the right to be regarded by ourselves and the world as a nation.

Our struggle is for the recognition of the Dene Nation by the Government and people of Canada and the peoples and governments of the world.

As once Europe was the exclusive homeland of the European peoples, Africa the exclusive homeland of the African peoples, the New World, North and South America, was the exclusive homeland of the Aboriginal peoples of the New World, the Amerindian and the Inuit.

The New World, like other parts of the world, has suffered the experience of colonialism and imperialism. Other peoples have occupied the land—often with force—and foreign governments have imposed themselves on our people. Ancient civilizations and ways of life have been destroyed.

Colonialism and imperialism is now dead or dying. Recent years have witnessed the birth of new nations or rebirth of old nations out of the ashes of colonialism.

As Europe is the place where you will find European countries with European governments for European peoples, now also you will find in Africa and Asia the existence of African and Asian countries with African and Asian governments for the African and Asian peoples.

The African and Asian peoples—the peoples of the Third World—have fought for and won the right to self-determination, the right to the recognition as distinct peoples and the recognition of themselves as nations.

But in the New World the Native Peoples have not fared so well. Even in countries in South America where the Native

Peoples are the vast majority of the population there is not one country which has an Amerindian government for the Amerindian peoples.

Nowhere in the New World have the Native Peoples won the right to self-determination and the right to recognition by the world as a distinct people and as Nations.

While the Native people of Canada are a minority in their homeland, the Native People of the N.W.T., the Dene and the Inuit, are a majority of the population of the N.W.T.

The Dene find themselves as part of a country. That country is Canada. But the Government of Canada is not the government of the Dene. These governments were not the choice of the Dene, they were imposed upon the Dene.

What we the Dene are struggling for is the recognition of the Dene Nation by the governments and peoples of the world.

And while there are realities we are forced to submit to, such as the existence of a country called Canada, we insist on the right to self-determination as a distinct people and the recognition of the Dene Nation.

We the Dene are part of the Fourth World. And as the peoples and nations of the world have come to recognize the existence and rights of those peoples who make up the Third World the day must come and will come when the nations of the Fourth World will come to be recognized and respected. The challenge to the Dene and the world is to find the way for the recognition of the Dene Nation.

Our plea to the world is to help us in our struggle to find a place in the world community where we can exercise our right to self-determination as a distinct people and as a nation.

What we seek then is independence and self-determination within the country of Canada. That is what we mean when we call for a just land settlement for the Dene Nation.

We Must Have Dreams

John Amagoalik

We need the patience and understanding of our white brothers.

Will the Inuit disappear from the face of this earth? Will we become extinct? Will our culture, our language and our attachment to nature be remembered only in history books? These questions bring a great sadness to me. To realize that we Inuit are in the same category as the great whales, the bold eagle, the husky and the polar bear brings me great fear. To realize that our people can be classified as an endangered species is very disturbing. Is our culture like a wounded polar bear that has gone out to sea to die alone? What can be done? There does not seem to be one single answer to these questions.

It may be that the physical part of our culture has been eroded to the point where it can never return to its full potential. But the non-physical part of our culture—our attitude towards life, our respect for nature, our realization that others will follow who deserve the respect and concern of present generations—are deeply entrenched within ourselves. The presence of our ancestors within ourselves is very strong. The will to survive is there. This part of our culture will die a slow death, if it ever dies at all. If we are to survive as a race, we must have the understanding and patience of the dominant cultures of this country. We do not need the pity, the welfare, the paternalism and the colonialism which has been heaped upon us over the years.

We must teach our children their mother tongue. We must teach them what they are and where they came from. We must teach them the values which have guided our society over the thousands of years. We must teach them our philosophies which go back beyond the memory of man. We must keep the embers burning from the fires which used to burn in our villages so that we may gather around them again. It is this spirit we must keep alive so that it may guide us again in a new life in a changed world. Who is responsible for keeping this spirit alive? It is clearly the older people. We must have the leadership which they once provided us. They must realize this responsibility and accept it. If the older people will remember, the young must listen.

In a world which becomes more complicated with each passing year, we must rely on the simple, gentle ways of our people to guide us. In a world so full of greed, we must share. We must remember that, of all the things in this world, nothing belongs to us. Of what we take we must share.

A lot of people tell me that we must forget the past, and instead, look to the future. To me it would be a mistake to completely ignore the past because the past determines the present and the present determines what will be in the future. Sometimes it is necessary to look to the past to make decisions about the future. When I talk about the future and try to describe what I would like for my children, some people sometimes say to me that I am only dreaming. What is wrong with dreaming? Sometimes dreams come true, if only one is determined enough. What kind of world would we live in if people did not have dreams? If people did not strive for what they believe in? We must have dreams. We must have ideals. We must fight for things we believe in. We must believe in ourselves. But there are also realities we must face. We can only attempt to make the best of any given situation or circumstances. If we are not successful, we must not give up hope. We must tell ourselves that we can only try a little harder the next time.

Over the past few years, in my visits to Inuit communities, I have had many private conversations about what is happening to our people and what the future holds for us. I have become more and more concerned about the angry words which some of our people are starting to use. I cannot really blame them for their feelings. Their feelings towards the white man are easy to under-stand. It is very easy to blame the white man for the predicament we find ourselves in today. But anger and hate are not the answers. We need the patience and understanding of our white brothers. If we are to expect that from them, we must offer the same in return. The Inuit, by nature, are not violent people. This is one of our virtues which we must not lose.

It disturbs me a great deal to hear about native organizations squabbling with other native organizations. If we are to achieve anything, we must not fight among ourselves. We can agree to disagree, but we must sort out our problems together. We must be of one mind and of one voice. This is not always possible among human beings. But we must not let petty disagreements divide us.

The Inuit were once independent and proud people. That is why we have survived. That strength, that independence, and that pride must surface again. We must prove to Canada that the original citizens of this country will not lie down and play dead. After all, the Inuit have been described by the United Nations as a people who refuse to disappear.

I am a native of North America

Chief Dan George

In the course of my lifetime I have lived in two distinct cultures. I was born into a culture that lived in communal houses. My grandfather's house was eighty feet long. It was called a smoke house, and it stood down by the beach along the inlet. All my grandfather's sons and their families lived in this large dwelling. Their sleeping apartments were separated by blankets made of bull rush reeds, but one open fire in the middle served the cooking needs of all. In houses like these, throughout the tribe, people learned to live with one another; learned to serve one another; learned to respect the rights of one another. And children shared the thoughts of the adult world and found themselves surrounded by aunts and uncles and cousins who loved them and did not threaten them. My father was born in such a house and learned from infancy how to love people and be at home with them.

And beyond this acceptance of one another there was a deep respect for everything in nature that surrounded them. My father loved the earth and all its creatures. The earth was his second mother. The earth and everything it contained was a gift from See-see-am . . . and the way to thank this great spirit was to use his gifts with respect.

I remember, as a little boy, fishing with him up Indian River and I can still see him as the sun rose above the mountain top in the early morning . . . . I can see him standing by the water's edge with his arms raised above his head while he softly moaned . . . "Thank you, thank you." It left a deep impression on my young mind.

And I shall never forget his disappointment when once he caught me gaffing for fish "just for the fun of it." "My Son" he said, "The Great Spirit gave you those fish to be your brothers, to feed you when you are hungry. You must respect them. You must not kill them just for the fun of it."

This then was the culture I was born into and for some years the only one I really knew or tasted. This is why I find it hard to accept many of the things I see around me.

I see people living in smoke houses hundreds of times bigger than the one I knew. But the people in one apartment do not even know the people in the next and care less about them.

It is also difficult for me to understand the deep hate that exists among people. It is hard to understand a culture that justifies the killing of millions in past wars, and is at this very moment preparing bombs to kill even greater numbers. It is hard for me to understand a culture that spends more on wars and weapons to kill, than it does on education and welfare to help and develop.

It is hard for me to understand a culture that not only hates and fights his brothers but even attacks nature and abuses her. I see my white brothers going about blotting out nature from his cities. I see him strip the hills bare, leaving ugly wounds on the face of mountains. I see him tearing things from the bosom of mother earth as though she were a monster, who refused to share her treasures with him. I see him throw poison in the waters, indifferent to the life he kills there; and he chokes the air with deadly fumes.

My white brother does many things well for he is more clever than my people but I wonder if he knows how to love well. I wonder if he has ever really learned to love at all. Perhaps he only loves the things that are his own but never learned to love the things that are outside and beyond him. And this is, of course, not love at all, for man must love all creation or he will love none of it. Man must love fully or he will become the lowest of the animals. It is the power to love that makes him the greatest of them all . . . for he alone of all animals is capable of love.

Love is something you and I must have. We must have it because our spirit feeds upon it. We must have it because without it we become weak and faint. Without love our self esteem weakens. Without it our courage fails. Without love we can no longer look out confidently at the world. Instead we turn inwardly and begin to feed upon our own personalities and little by little we destroy ourselves.

You and I need the strength and joy that comes from knowing that we are loved. With it we are creative. With it we march tirelessly. With it, and with it alone, we are able to sacrifice for others.

There have been times when we all wanted so desperately to feel a reassuring hand upon us . . . there have been lonely times when we so wanted a strong arm around us . . . I cannot tell you how deeply I miss my wife's presence when I return from a trip. Her love was my greatest joy, my strength, my greatest blessing.

I am afraid my culture has little to offer yours. But my culture did prize friendship and companionship. It did not look on privacy as a thing to be clung to, for privacy builds up walls and walls promote distrust. My culture lived in big family communities, and from infancy people learned to live with others.

My culture did not prize the hoarding of private possessions, in fact, to hoard was a shameful thing to do among my people. The Indian looked on all things in nature as belonging to him and he expected to share them with others and to take only what he needed.

Everyone likes to give as well as receive. No one wishes only to receive all the time. We have taken much from your culture . . . I wish you had taken something from our culture . . . for there were some beautiful and good things in it.

Soon it will be too late to know my culture, for integration is upon us and soon we will have no values but yours. Already many of our young people have forgotten the old ways. And many have been shamed of their Indian ways by scorn and ridicule. My culture is like a wounded deer that has crawled away into the forest to bleed and die alone.

The only thing that can truly help us is genuine love. You must truly love us, be patient with us and share with us. And we must love you—with a genuine love that forgives and forgets . . . a love that forgives the terrible sufferings your culture brought ours when it swept over us like a wave crashing along a beach . . .

with a love that forgets and lifts up its head and sees in your eyes an answering love of trust and acceptance.

This is brotherhood . . . anything less is not worthy of the name.

I have spoken.

Our Lost Innocence

Bruce Hutchison

On the first day of July 121 years ago, in an ugly, half-built capital beside the Ottawa River, the new nation that the Fathers of Confederation introduced to the world was an uneasy union of British and French settlers. Bonfires were lit in the towns and villages of four shabby little colonies from the Great Lakes to the Atlantic. Primitive cannons boomed, rockets flared in the sky, and bands played. Neither many foreigners nor the sponsoring government in London were convinced that such an artificial, gimcrack union could long endure. And the founders' dream of extending their creation to the Pacific was dismissed as pathetic, even absurd. But the dream became reality: the Pacific was reached and the country offered both haven and opportunity to hundreds of thousands of people from distant lands who built her cities, defined her culture and shaped her destiny.

Dutiful

For most of the first 80 years after Confederation, Canada was the disciplined, dutiful and predictable offspring of British colonization. The country grew and prospered on a tide of migration that was largely from Northern Europe, predominantly from Britain. In the past 40 years, immigrants from the wider world have transformed the nation's appearance and personality beyond anything envisaged by its founders. In the coming decades, Canada's very survival depends upon more massive immigration—and on learning to construct a cohesive society out of many diverse communities that rival each other in size and ambitions.

Troubled

Having lost our innocence, we did not celebrate Canada Day last week with the gusto we once exhibited. Instead, on this anniversary, our nation was troubled, cranky; worried about the preservation—even doubting the existence—of the distinct identity that emerged from Champlain's hovel at Quebec almost four centuries ago.

Why all the commotion in politics today, the uncertainty in private business, the misgivings among rich and poor alike? They are pertinent questions, and now, in the month of our 121st birthday, we should consider them. We should reassess, without flattering or belittling ourselves, the true state of the contemporary organism unforeseeable to the fathers of the confederacy.

Any national reappraisal invokes historical experience. A person of my age recalls that in his boyhood, Canada remained a colony by law and mentality, submissive to the all-wise statesmen of Britain, lacking any control over foreign affairs and—generally content with this status—wearing its inferiority complex like a ragged secondhand garment.

Not until the bloodletting of the First World War did a truly sovereign nation begin to replace the colony. From then on, Canadian society—in its introverted pursuit of happiness—vastly improved the lot of the average citizen, became more compassionate and generous, less racist, lavish in public service and so jealous of individual rights that it ultimately guaranteed them by a charter.

Laments

We have a living standard, measured by quality, not just materially, as high as any ever achieved by man. Yet, again and again, gloomy prophets utter laments for the nation, usually because it has not turned out to suit their personal tastes. And, although no lament is needed for a nation that keeps growing in wealth and self-respect, we must also examine the darker side of the national experiment and count the mistakes. Those have been egregious and dismal since the years of national euphoria following the Second World War.

Influence

That conflict left our land undamaged and our economy doubled in a devastated world hungry for our goods. We could sell anything, at almost any price. We proclaimed ourselves a middle power and, as honest broker, exercised real influence at the United Nations. Drinking this heady wine, we supposed that easy and quite unnatural times would never end. In our quiet but profound social revolution we unbalanced our budgets, piled up deficits and debts mountain-high for our children or grandchildren to repay, inflated the currency and lurched into a spasm of hubris that was thoroughly un-Canadian.

Still, the nation's finances are not its worst problem. Much more serious, in a wider and often-neglected perspective, is our Canadian state of mind. As a people, we have failed to discern, except in passing platitudes, the impact of the new world around us, the universal revolution fuelled by a dissonant blend of wealth and poverty; of Asia's economic power and Africa's starving millions. The forces behind this revolution are without precedent.

Dependent

Nor have we fully grasped the extent to which the dissolution of the British Empire has left us more than ever dependent on our own strength and the protection of the United States, although some Canadians reassure themselves with crude xenophobia and visceral anti-Americanism—not an attractive characteristic.

We solemnly agree that the world is changing and our nation must change with it. But most of us are determined to avoid inconvenience in our private lives if we can; change, after all, is for the next generation.

Meanwhile, over us all dangles The Bomb, on a chewed thread, although the human race so far has elected to poison the planet rather than blow it up. Canadians may be powerless to cure the world's madness, halt the inflow of foreign poisons or preserve the planetary climate, but there are formidable tasks within our control. We can prevent our people from ravishing our own environment, overcutting the forests, overfishing the oceans and we can stop living on our nation's capital like a householder who buys champagne and caviar while the roof leaks and the foundation sinks. Repairing the house and cleaning the air, water and soil will cost more and entail higher taxes than any government will admit. Yet we demand lower taxes, lower deficits and greater benefits from the state. Compared to these tasks the adjustment of Canadian industry to the brutal competition of the new world and the fairer distribution of wealth between regions and classes are relatively simple.

Task
But the largest task of all is not simple and we have hardly begun to comprehend it, much less master it. For the first time, with its birthrate falling, Canada risks a decrease in population. Massive immigration will be needed to maintain a strong, independent community. By our untidy but workable methods of accommodation and compromise, we have learned since the Second World War to manage a dual state while at the same time absorbing with reasonable fairness and humanity tens of thousands of immigrants from Europe and Asia. But in the next century, our descendants will have to manage and reconcile a multicultural society on a scale beyond our imagining.

Then will come the supreme test of Canada's realism, morality and genius. For, lacking sufficient numbers and the strength of unity, we cannot hope to possess half a continent in a crowded, desperate world. Nature will not forever tolerate a vacuum so huge and full of treasure. The alternatives decreed by history are inescapable. Canada must betray the grand dream of its founders or achieve its finest hour.

STUDENT HANDBOOK

For the Student

The activities and questions on the following pages act as an overall guide towards more active reading, writing, speaking, and critical thinking.

Author Biographies and Entry Points

The author biographies act as brief sketches of the writers' lives with particular focus on their academic and literary accomplishments. They will help you to place the writers in a specific time and place as well as direct you to further readings, both for pleasure and for independent research.

The entry points invite you to "enter" into the specific literary works beyond the initial reading and reaction. They will involve you even more actively in exploring the characters, the conflicts, the feelings, the themes, and the style of each of the selections. The entry points may encourage you to respond personally to crucial and sometimes even controversial issues suggested by the selections. They may also lead you to probe those same and related issues through extensive discussion, role-playing, reading, and creative writing projects—by yourself or with others. In all cases, once you have "entered" the works, your active involvement becomes paramount. The literature becomes *your* "territory" as both your creative and critical thinking skills evolve.

Responding Personally

The questions in this category ask you for a personal response. You won't need any special knowledge to answer them as the potential for response lies within you. Questions and activities here encourage you to imagine yourself in particular situations and to respond through speaking, writing, and role-playing in a creative manner.

Sharing Thoughts: Small Group Activities

The questions and activities in this category encourage you to explore various issues and situations with other people in your class. Working together as a small group, you will initially "brainstorm" the issue, allowing each member of your group to express an opinion without judging that opinion. After sharing all your thoughts in this open manner, your group will continue the discussion and work in collaboration with each other towards a response based on reason, examples, logic, and critical thinking. You may have to consider opposing points of view in reaching a shared, consensus opinion.

Shaping Thought: General Themes

The general themes encourage you to view the underlying messages in the selections in this anthology and in the recommended readings in the Resource List in a broader manner. They will encourage you to read further and to detect important patterns of thought within various short stories, novels, plays, poetry, and nonfiction prose. You will find the themes will provide ideas for oral presentations; seminars and debates; literary insight essays; and, long-term independent study projects.

Shaping Thought: Thematic Activities

The questions in this category ask you for a more objective response. In many cases, you will already have valid opinions on many of the issues presented and, with some initial brainstorming, you will be able to come up with many strong arguments and ideas to support your initial claims. You may want to form small groups to explore some of these initial responses with other members of your class.

Following your initial responses, you may wish to read further into the selections in this anthology or the recommended readings in the Resource List—or, you may wish to do some independent research in your local or school library. Your library's vertical files would be particularly useful in your research. Your research will allow you to articulate the best possible response by supporting your initial arguments with facts, detailed examples, causes and effects, and appeals to various, published authorities. As with the "General Themes" category, you will be able to shape your thought in a variety of formats: oral presentations, argumentative papers, seminars and debates, literary insight papers, and independent study projects.

The Medium Aids The Message: Understanding Style and Structure

The late Marshall McLuhan, a distinguished Canadian scholar and communications expert, once said that "the medium is the message." He wanted us to see that the *way* something is presented influences our initial response to it. Understanding the medium—the style and structure in which a work is written or presented—helps us to understand our own initial response to it and also helps us to comprehend the "message" or content of that work more clearly. The questions and activities in this category will encourage you to explore the style and structure of various forms of writing and to relate your ideas to the content of the writing. In your explorations, you may work alone, with a partner, or with a small group.

A Note on the Writing Process

As you probably already know, most writing does not just come out of your head and onto a piece of paper as a complete, perfect product. It doesn't matter if you're writing manually on a desk or using a typewriter or computerized word-processor, your first "copy" will probably not be your last "copy" or finished product. When responding to any of the "Entry Points" or "General Activities and Questions," you should realize that your first response may be vague, awkward, tentative, and even downright messy. There is *nothing* wrong with that! In fact, that may be the most natural response—for even the most professional of writers! Writing is an exploratory *process*—it takes certain risks on your part, it takes commitment, and, yes, it takes time. Time to evolve into that final, "more perfect" product that you can really feel proud of. Don't be too hard on yourself if, at the start, your writing seems messy and awkward. If you understand that writing is a natural process that takes risk, commitment, and time, you will improve. You will become a more organized, clearer, more lucid, and more confident writer. Knowing the process will help you to reach this goal and to be the best writer you can be.

The writing process is a flexible and recursive one: that is, some steps may be repeated or some may be skipped, to be returned to later. Since each writer has his/her own individual learning and writing style, the following steps may be of use to you:

1. *Pre-writing:* — selecting your topic and narrowing its focus
   — brainstorming the topic alone, with a partner, or with a group
   — targeting your audience and your purpose
   — developing your ideas through conferencing and researching

	— organizing your material leading to an outline and potential thesis
2. *Writing:*	— bringing your outlined ideas together in draft form, using conventional sentences and paragraphs
	— conferencing with your peers and teachers
	— evaluating the content, style, and structure of the first draft as you seek suggestions for improvement
3. *Post-writing:*	— revising the content of the draft
	— adding needed and relevant material
	— deleting weak, redundant, or irrelevant material
	— moving phrases, sentences, and paragraphs to other locations
	— checking for unity and coherence
	— conferencing with peers and teachers (editors)
4. *Proofreading:*	— checking and double-checking your paper to make it error-free in terms of the mechanical conventions: spelling, punctuation, diction, grammar, standard English usage of words, phrases and sentence formations, apostrophes, hyphens
	— conferencing with peers and teachers (editors)
5. *Evaluating:*	— final checking of your final draft or "product"
	— having your peers and teachers react to and discuss your final product with suggestions for improvement
	— looking at your final product *critically* with an eye towards improvement

Remember at all times that your peers and your teachers can be your best friends in your own evolution as a clear and confident writer. You're not alone on this winding, but satisfying, road!

Author Biographies and Entry Points

WHAT I LEARNED FROM CAESAR
Guy Vanderhaeghe

The Author
Born in 1951 in Esterhazy, Saskatchewan, GUY VANDERHAEGHE studied at the University of Saskatchewan and the University of Regina. Published in various literary magazines and anthologies, he won the Governor General's Award for *Man Descending* in 1982, from which "What I Learned from Caesar" was selected for this anthology. His first novel, *My Present Age*, was published in 1984.

Entry Points
1. In the opening paragraph, the narrator claims: "But the pastures we flee, no matter how brown and blighted—these travel with us; they can't be escaped." Is this an effective opening for a short story? What psychological truth do you think the author wants you to have immediately? Do you agree with this "truth"?

2. What is the narrator's view of the Saskatchewan countryside in which he grew up? How did this land help mold his and his father's thinking?

3. "He was let go." How does his father react to the news of his dismissal from his company in 1931? How do his son and wife react to his sudden unemployment?

4. Why does George Vander Est feel so offended when his boss says in his parting words, "Good luck, Dutchie!"? Probe this situation carefully. In his place, how would you have felt?

5. Why did George Vander Est want to forget his Belgian past? Was he wise in doing so? What were the consequences of this deliberate "escape"?

6. Why does the narrator call his father a "remade man," not a "self-made" man? What is the significance of the two photographs of his father? Explain fully.

7. "And for the first time in my life I was ashamed of him."
   (a) Why was his son so ashamed of his father?
   (b) Why was George Van Est so ashamed of himself?
   (c) Are either of them justified in these feelings of shame? Explain.

8. Evaluate the role of the narrator's mother in this story.

9. What did school and the study of Latin signify to the thirteen-year-old boy as he began high school? What did high school signify to you before you started it? What does it signify now?

10. "I'm not sure why all this happened to him . . . But I needed a reason then." Why did the boy need a reason for the tragedy that befell his father? What did the boy learn from Caesar? Explain the narrator's final thoughts in your own words.

11. In a diary format, describe your feelings after your mother or father announces that she/he has lost her/his job.

12. As George Vander Est's son, now an adult looking back on his father's problems, write a letter to your father expressing regret for your feelings of shame. Suggest why you felt the way you did then.

13. For interest and comparative reading on the effects on family members of a parent losing a job, read the American play, *Death of a Salesman*, by Arthur Miller or the Canadian play, *Of the Fields, Lately*, by David French.

THE HOCKEY SWEATER
Roch Carrier

The Author
ROCH CARRIER was born in 1937 in the small Quebec town of

Sainte-Justine-de-Dorchester and educated at the Université de Montréal and at the Sorbonne in Paris. He is one of the Quebec novelists most widely-read in English translation with his most popular book being *La Guerre, Yes Sir!* (1970). Twenty of his short stories were published in English under the title *The Hockey Sweater and Other Stories* (1979).

Entry Points

1. ". . . our real life was on the skating rink," claims the ten-year-old boy. How was the skating rink "real life"? Would this still be true for young Canadian boys today?

2. Why is the boy so adamant about *not* wearing his new hockey sweater from Eaton's? To what extent do you sympathize with his refusal? Evaluate his mother's reaction.

3. Why does the boy feel persecuted?

4. Although the story is apparently about a young boy's complete fascination with hockey, what other meanings do you think the author, Roch Carrier, intends? Explain your response.

5. Write a short story based on the winters of *your* childhood in Canada. Use vivid details and dialogue.

6. Write a brief essay in which you comment on Canada's "deux nations"—our two founding cultures. Have the roles of these cultures changed? Are they still influential?

THE RINK

Cyril Dabydeen

The Author

CYRIL DABYDEEN, born in 1945 in Guyana, South America, moved to Canada in 1970 where he finished his formal education at Queen's University, Kingston, Ontario. A winner of the Okanagan Fiction Prize, his books of poetry and prose include *Goatsong, Still Close to the Island,* and *Islands Lovelier than a Vision.* Recipient of many honours, he served as Poet Laureate of Ottawa from 1984 to 1987.

Entry Points

1. "He's thinking too that he, an islander who has come to this country to establish roots, must really learn to skate . . ." Comment on George's thoughts on the importance of learning to skate in Canada. To what extent do you agree with his point of view?

2. Why does Ida discourage George in his attempts at skating? What do Ida's comments on George's attempts at skating reveal about her own attitudes? In diary form, write about a time you tried to learn something and someone made fun of you. How did you feel?

3. "He wants to integrate, fully; and he believes that before long he'll be skating like the best of the native born-and-bred Canadians." Is George's goal of complete integration in the way that he is expressing it a wholly admirable one? Could George be charged with reverse discrimination? Comment fully.

4. Evaluate the behaviour of the kids at the ice-rink. How does George perceive them?

5. What is the point of George's final vision of his daughter on the ice-rink?

6. As George, write a letter to Boysie in which you explain to him why learning to skate is important to you.

7. With a partner, role-play the characters of George and Ida as they tell each other their dreams for their daughter in Canada. After your improvisation, write out your dialogue in script form and present it to the class.

8. Write a poem about skating and its significance to Canadians. You could consider skating's history as a form of recreation, transportation, or sport.

INPUT

Laura Bulger

The Author

LAURA BULGER was born in 1939 in Lisbon, Portugal, and

received her doctorate from the University of Oporto. Since arriving in Canada in 1966, she has taught at the University of Manitoba and the University of Toronto. She is currently a professor of Portuguese, Spanish, and Comparative Literature at York University. Her first book of short stories, *Paradise on Hold* (1987), was translated by herself from the original Portuguese version of her collection, *Vaivém*.

Entry Points

1. Being interviewed for a job is often a nervous ordeal. What factors make Maria's interview even more difficult? Explain fully.

2. Maria claims: "Too many qualifications might even be a disadvantage." Why does she say this? Do you agree with her strategy in applying for this secretarial position?

3. How do you respond to Jack Bumbleby, the director? What specific criticisms can you make of him on his conduct during the interview?

4. Maria thinks: "Privacy is a right in this country, she was sure of that, no one dared invade it. There are laws that protect the individual against such transgressions." Is she right? Investigate this question. Did Jack Bumbleby have the right to "ask some questions of a personal nature"? Why did she decide to co-operate?

5. Why did she read the computer print-out "in amazement" and why did the "grunts from the computer" bother her? To what extent do you sympathize with Maria's situation and feelings? Explain.

6. With a partner, role-play a job interview situation in which unfair tactics and questions are being used. After your improvisation, write down your questions and answers in script form. Perform it in class or on video.

7. What does this story tell you about the relationships between *some* men and *some* women in the work force? How can we correct such behaviour? Discuss your ideas and make recommendations within a small group.

A CLASS OF NEW CANADIANS
Clarke Blaise

The Author
Born in 1940 to Canadian parents in Fargo, North Dakota, CLARKE BLAISE grew up there, and in the Southern United States, the urban North, and Manitoba. He is the author of two novels, *Lunar Attractions* (1979) and *Lusts* (1983) and, along with his wife, writer Bharati Mukherjee, wrote an autobiographical journal recounting a year spent in India, *Days and Nights in Calcutta* (1977). "A Class of New Canadians" was selected from a collection of his short stories, *A North American Education* (1973).

Entry Points
1. How does Norman Dyer perceive himself? How does he think his class of new Canadians perceive him? How do *you* think they perceive him? Account for any discrepancy.

2. In thinking about his students, Norman Dyer says, "I love them . . . They need me." Does Dyer actually love them? Do they need him? Explain your response fully.

3. Throughout the story, Dyer reveals reverse discrimination. Support this statement with three references from the story. What is motivating Dyer to think this way?

4. What goals or dreams do Dyer's students have? Why is Dyer critical of them? Evaluate their goals and Dyer's criticism.

5. As you witness what he does with Miguel Mayor's letter, what is your final opinion of Norm Dyer?

6. You are Norm Dyer. In your diary, explain why you are teaching this class of new Canadians and why they love you.

7. You are one of the students in Norm Dyer's class. In a letter to a friend, write about your opinion of your teacher in the class for new Canadians.

8. You are Norm Dyer. Keep a diary while you are on holiday in a country where you do not speak the language OR while you are taking a second-language class yourself. How do these experiences affect you and your views?

9. With a partner, role-play Mr. Dyer and one of his students. The student is telling Mr. Dyer about his goals for the future. Write out the dialogue you've improvised in script form. Perform it for the class or on video.

10. Write a short composition on either
    (a) your ideas of an excellent teacher
    or (b) the best teacher you ever had.

DETAILS FROM THE CANADIAN MOSAIC
C.D. Minni

The Author
C.D. (DINO) MINNI was born in Bagnoli del Trigno, Isernia, Italy, in 1942, immigrated to Canada as a child, and grew up in Vancouver. His short stories, articles, and reviews have appeared in numerous literary magazines and anthologies and have been broadcast on CBC Radio. A reviewer for *The Vancouver Sun* since 1977, his first collection of short stories, *Other Selves*, was published in 1985.

Entry Points
1. Most of this story takes place in an unnamed city on the coast of British Columbia. What "details" from the Canadian mosaic does Minni emphasize?

2. How does nine-year-old Mario feel about leaving Italy? What are his first impressions of his new land?

3. "Hey dummy! Cat got your tongue?" Why did the three boys pick on Mario? Explain the motivations behind children who bully others. How would you have reacted if you were being bullied?

4. (a) How does Mario begin to change? Is this kind of change inevitable in a country like Canada? Explain.
   (b) "By the end of summer, he was Mario at home and Mike in the streets." Explain the full implications of this statement. What possible problems might these separate identities cause?

5. Comment on the meaning or significance of the final four paragraphs in italics, the thoughts of the adult Mario/Mike as he views the festive "Italian-Canadian community" event.

6. Are you satisfied with the ending? Conclude the story in a different way.

7. Have you ever been made to feel like an outsider? Write a diary item that describes your feelings. How did you cope with those feelings? How do you feel about this mistreatment today?

8. Write a short composition in which you describe your own details from the Canadian mosaic, that have personal meaning for you.

9. Write a short story in which a character who is being picked on stands up to the bully or bullies. Use inner and outer dialogue.

THE GLASS ROSES
Alden Nowlan

The Author
ALDEN NOWLAN (1933-1983) was born in Windsor, Nova Scotia, and dropped out of school at the age of twelve to work on farms, in lumber camps and sawmills. He later worked as a journalist and editor with several New Brunswick newspapers and in 1968 became writer-in-residence at the University of New Brunswick. Among his many collections of poetry, *Bread, Wine, and Salt* won the Governor General's Award in 1967. "The Glass Roses" first appeared in *Miracle at Indian River*, a collection of his stories published in 1968.

Entry Points
1. The story is set in a Maritime lumber camp. What major impressions does Alden Nowlan want us to have of this locale? What specific details contribute to this impression in the first two paragraphs?

2. What are fifteen-year-old Stephen's major impressions of the lumberjacks playing cards?

3. Analyze Stephen's relationship to his father.

4. Stephen's father claims that "You got to start actin' like a man if you want to hold down a man's job."

   (a) Does Stephen's father really explain what acting "like a man" means? How would you explain his making such a statement?

   (b) Do you think it is a wise statement for a father to make to his son? Explain.

   (c) How does Stephen react to his father's statement? How would *you* react?

5. What is the relationship between Stephen and Leka, the "Polack"? Why was Leka always referred to as the "Polack"? What effect does the author seek by using this racist term?

6. Explain the symbolism of the glass roses. Given the context of the story, why is "The Glass Roses" a suitable title?

7. Why does Stephen's father "despise" Leka? Analyze thoroughly and elaborate on your response. Evaluate Stephen's father's motivations.

8. After Leka apologizes to Stephen, Stephen thinks: "In his world, men did not tender apologies." Why does Stephen think this way? In a small group, discuss your definitions of men and how you think men should behave. Is this behaviour different from that of women?

9. In your opinion, is Stephen's father a "real man"? Explain.

10. The story ends somewhat inconclusively. Continue writing the story towards a more definitive conclusion. What ultimate decisions will Stephen have to make concerning how he will act towards others when he becomes a "man"?

SCHOOL, THE FIRST DAY

Barbara Sapergia

The Author

Born in 1943 in Moose Jaw, Saskatchewan, BARBARA SAPERGIA received her B.A. (1964) from the University of Saskatchewan and her M.A. (1966) from the University of Manitoba. She has written for CBC radio and television, for the stage (*Lokkinen* and *Matty and Rose*), and for various periodicals and anthologies. Her poetry collection, *Dirt Hills Mirage*, was published in 1980. "School, the First Day" is excerpted from her first novel, *Foreigners* (1984), about Romanian immigrants in southern Saskatchewan in the early years of this century.

Entry Points

1. This story, which takes place in 1913, is actually an excerpt from *Foreigners*, a novel set in Saskatchewan about Romanian immigrants. What problems with school is Nicu Dominescu experiencing?

2. What does your school do now or what should your school do to help students like Nicu to feel more comfortable? Discuss your ideas and recommendations with a small group.

3. During the baseball game at recess, Nicu feels ashamed. Why? Do you remember a time when you felt ashamed? Write a diary item recounting the experience and exploring your feelings. How did you overcome these feelings?

4. "I'm not going to school any more," Nicu says to his father. Have you ever felt the same way? Explore your own feelings. What arguments does his father put forward to convince his son of the importance of school? To what extent do you agree with his arguments?

5. Write a short story based on your worst day in school. If possible, use vivid details and dialogue as this story does.

6. Write a brief essay in which you argue convincingly the importance of education in young people's lives in Canada today. Use clear examples to prove your points.

HUNKY

Hugh Garner

The Author

HUGH GARNER (1913-1979) was born in Batley, England, and immigrated with his parents to Toronto in 1919. His life as a youth in the poorer working-class areas of Toronto eventually found expression in his most famous novel, *Cabbagetown* (1968). A prolific writer, he wrote 100 short stories, 17 books, and hundreds of articles and radio and TV scripts. *Hugh Garner's Best Short Stories* won the Governor General's Award in 1963.

Entry Points

1. What impressions do you first have of the work environment of the Ontario tobacco fields?

2. What are your first impressions of
   (a) the speaker, George?
   (b) Stanislaw Szymaniewski, who calls himself "Hunky," and "a poor D.P." (displaced person)?
   (c) Why are they working on this tobacco farm? What are their goals and ambitions?

3. What kind of employer is Maurice Vandervelde? State your opinion of his treatment of his employees.

4. As you discover more about "Hunky"—his childhood background and his actions on the farm—how do your first impressions change or evolve?

5. Although he was born in Poland with the proper name of Stanislaw Szymaniewski, he has for some reason adopted the name of "Hunky," which is a derisive slur. How and why did this probably come about? What is your reaction to this word?

6. What is George's opinion of Stanislaw marrying Marie, Vandervelde's eighteen-year-old daughter? Do you agree with his assessment? Elaborate on your response.

7. What is your personal response to George's final action in vindicating Hunky's hit-and-run death?

8. As George, write a diary item in which you express your grief over your new friend's untimely death.

9. Assume you are a farm union organizer. Write a speech protesting the labour conditions on Vandervelde's tobacco farm. Be specific in your criticisms and recommendations for improvement.

10. For interest and comparative purposes, read two other novels on migrant workers: the American John Steinbeck's *Of Mice and Men* and *The Grapes of Wrath*.

THE BROKEN GLOBE
Henry Kreisel

The Author
HENRY KREISEL was born in Vienna, Austria, in 1922, but immigrated with his family to England in 1938 when the Nazis threatened to invade his homeland. He was interned in England for 18 months during World War II as an "enemy alien." He came to Canada in 1940 and studied at the University of Toronto. Since 1947, he has taught at and been Vice-President of the University of Alberta. He has published two novels, *The Rich Man* (1948) and *The Betrayal* (1964), and a collection of short stories, *The Almost Meeting* (1981), which includes "The Broken Globe."

Entry Points
1. Nick Solchuk left Three Bear Hills in Alberta to become a geophysicist living in London, England.
   (a) How does Nick Solchuk view himself now?
   (b) How does he view his past life in Alberta?
   (c) What is your opinion of Nick Solchuk at the start of the story?

2. According to Nick Solchuk, what are some of his father's beliefs and what shaped them?

3. Solchuk says of his father and himself: "We—we had—what shall I call it—differences." Outline those "differences" and suggest reasons for them. Would it have been possible to reconcile those differences? Make suggestions.

4. What are the narrator's first impressions of the Canadian West?

5. Why do you think Nick Solchuk asked his friend to visit his father?

6. Why is the broken globe such an important object in this story?

7. Nick Solchuk's friend says of Nick's Ukrainian-born father: "It was impossible not to feel a kind of admiration for the old man. There was something heroic about him." Why does he express these feelings? Do you agree with his assessment? Do *you* admire the old man? Explain.

8. Write a short story in which a teenager and a parent have a difference of opinion over an issue taught at school. Use inner and outer dialogue to advance your plot.

9. Debate: "Schooling acts as a disruptive force on family values and beliefs." Argue for or against with specific examples from your readings or your own experiences.

10. Compare the father of this story with the father in "School, the First Day." Write a short composition comparing their attitudes towards school and the impact on their sons.

THE STORY OF NIL
Gabrielle Roy

The Author
GABRIELLE ROY (1909-1983) was born in St. Boniface, Manitoba, but in 1952 she settled in Quebec City where she lived until her death. A prolific and highly-regarded writer, her works have been translated into more than 15 languages, and three of her works have won the Governor General's Award for fiction: *The Tin Flute* (1947); *Street of Riches* (1957); and, *Ces Enfants de ma vie* (1977).

Entry Points
1. What special qualities does six-year-old Nil possess? Have you ever known anyone with similarly special qualities? Elaborate.

2. How is the young teacher affected by Nil? How are others around him affected? What does the teacher learn from her student?

3. Why does the young teacher have such contradictory feelings about her chosen career? Is she justified in her feelings?

4. "Of course I don't claim that Nil performed a miracle." What is a miracle? In your opinion, did Nil perform miracles?

Explain with references from the story.

5. Was her decision to bring Nil to sing at the old people's home "too cruel," as the teacher claims? Discuss the pro's and con's of her decision and final assessment.

6. Was the decision to allow Nil to sing at the psychiatric hospital a good one? Explain your response.

7. Explain the Ukrainian-born Paraskovia Galaida's role and influence in the life of her son, Nil. What is the final effect of the story's ending on you?

8. "The Story of Nil" is taken from Gabrielle Roy's award-winning *Children of My Heart*. How is Nil a child of the heart?

9. Write another incident in which Nil's angelic voice causes another "miracle."

10. In a small group, list musicians, singers, or performers who have evoked great feelings in you. Can the ability that some performers have to move you be considered miraculous? Discuss with your group.

11. As a student learns from a teacher, a teacher learns from his/her students. Write another story in which a student teaches a teacher a valuable lesson.

THINGS IN THE SILENCE
Harold Marshall

The Author
HAROLD MARSHALL has been an editor of several journals, newspapers, and other publications in Barbados, British Columbia, and Manitoba. He emigrated to Canada in 1956. He now works for the Winnipeg School Division and is also engaged in researching 17th century Barbadian history. His story, "Things in the Silence" appeared in *Other Voices* (1985).

Entry Points
1. What are the "Things in the Silence" that Arthur Chesterfield Waldron sees and thinks about as his train moves across the Canadian prairieland? What is his attitude to these "things"?

2. "Of things that mattered and things that didn't." As Waldron's mind wanders over his past, what things mattered and what things didn't? How does Waldron view his entire life?

3. Describe the relationship that develops in the conversation between Waldron and seven-year-old Mary. What does Mary reveal about adults and the beginnings of bigotry?

4. Comment on Mary's mother's behaviour.

5. In his final moments of life, Waldron thinks: "He had to escape and go back to where he did not have to experience his minority and his subservience. But even as he thought about it, he felt the guilt of his reason." Explain these statements and comment on their apparent contradiction.

6. In a diary format, write about your personal reaction to Waldron's final train ride and his death.

7. With a partner, role-play the characters of Waldron and Mary's mother. As Mr. Waldron, explain to Mary's mother why Mary wasn't disturbing you. Write out your improvisation in script form and present it to the class. If possible, videotape your performance.

8. For another view of the Canadian railroad's treatment of black employees, read Barbara Sapergia's play, *Matty and Rose*.

A REAL LIVE DEATH
Katie Funk Wiebe

The Author
KATIE FUNK WIEBE, born in Laird, Saskatchewan in 1924, now lives in Hillsboro, Kansas, where she teaches at Tabor College. Her publications include *Women Among the Brethren* (1979) and *Bless Me Too, My Father* (1988). Her story, "A Real Live Death" was first published in *Liars and Rascals: Mennonite Short Stories* (1989).

Entry Points
1. "Death came in bunches that year, like grapes on a vine." What is the young Saskatchewan girl's reaction to

(a) her Russian grandmother's death?

(b) Dorothy's father's death?

(c) the United Church minister's death?

What does she learn through these three deaths about "real death" and dying? What is your reaction to these deaths?

2. Why does the girl imagine the figure in the coffin at the Russian church funeral is her own mother? What does this incident reveal about the girl?

3. How does the young girl view the New Testament Easter? What is it that she doesn't understand about her own religion?

4. Explain why there are differences of opinion about Hallowe'en between herself and her parents. Are such misunderstandings common? Can you recall a similar difference of opinion with your parents? How did you overcome it?

5. Explain the significance of Glycera Zbitnoff's illness and recuperation in the girl's growing understanding of life and death within her own religious tradition.

6. In your own words, explain the paradox and appropriateness of the title.

7. Using your own observations or reflections on your own experiences, write a first-person story that deals with the death of a loved one.

8. In a personal essay, expand on the statement: "Life was a gift, not a hostile force that tried to kill us off, one by one." Use specific examples of life's "gifts."

9. As comparative reading on a child's growing awareness of life and death, read W.O. Mitchell's prairie classic, *Who Has Seen the Wind?*.

VAIVÉM

Laura Bulger

The Author
See "Input," p. 250-51, above.

Entry Points

1. "Vaivém" is a Portuguese word with a number of interesting meanings: to-and-fro motion; up-and-down motion as in a teeter-totter; coming and going of people; (figuratively) changes in fortune; (militarily) a battering ram. Given these various meanings, show how "Vaivém" is an appropriate title for this story.

2. The speaker, a grandfather, seems to be pulled between two worlds.

   (a) What attracts him to Canada? What complaints does he have about his "new" land? To what extent do you think his complaints are justified?

   (b) What does he like about his "old" land, Portugal? What does he find to criticize about it? To what extent do you sympathize with his complaints?

3. How are his children and grandchildren going to be different from him? Look up the word "assimilation" in the dictionary and apply it to the grandfather's thoughts and feelings.

4. How do you interpret the final line, "I got used to it, you know." What ideas and feelings are being expressed by this brief statement?

5. Using the same techniques of inner dialogue and contrast as seen in Laura Bulger's story, write your own story of "vaivém" in which a character expresses apparently contradictory "up-and-down" emotions about a place or another person.

I AM A CANADIAN

Duke Redbird

The Author

A Canadian Ojibway, DUKE REDBIRD was born in 1939 on the Saugeen Reserve near Owen Sound, Ontario. He completed his M.A. at York University in 1979: his thesis on the history of the Métis was published under the title *We Are Métis* in 1980. In

1981, he became the President of the Ontario Métis and Non-status Indians Association. After writing and publishing poetry for more than twenty years, he brought out his first collection of poetry, *Loveshine and Red Wine*, in 1981.

Entry Points
1. Duke Redbird is actually a Canadian Ojibway born on the Saugeen Reserve near Owen Sound. Why then does he identify himself with all the other people and things in his poem?
2. As a Canadian, are you everything that Duke Redbird is? Explain. What else are you?
3. Redbird builds the poem through a series of metaphors, wherein he compares himself directly to other objects, places, and people. Write your own poem, "I am a Canadian," using metaphors.
4. Create a collage from old Canadian magazines and newspapers that portrays the many faces of a Canadian.

SELECT SAMARITAN
Robert Finch

The Author
ROBERT FINCH was born in 1900 in Freeport, Long Island, and was educated at the University of Toronto and the Sorbonne. He became a Professor of French at the University of Toronto. Two of his collections of poetry won the Governor General's Award: *Poems* (1946) from which "Select Samaritan" is taken, and *Acis in Oxford* (1961).

Entry Points
1. A "parody" is a piece of literature that mocks or criticizes people and their actions through unworthy imitation. How is "Select Samaritan" a parody?
2. How is the title "Select Samaritan" a contradiction in terms?

3. The couple who want to adopt the two children claim, "we don't care about race." Is this true? What do they care about?

4. The couple claims that "any kids we take will be in clover" (lucky). Do you think the adopted kids would be lucky to have these people as their parents? Explain your response.

5. Role-play the couple as they are told by the agency that their application for adoption has been rejected. Write out your improvisation in script form.

THE IMMIGRANTS
Margaret Atwood

The Author

MARGARET ATWOOD was born in 1939 in Ottawa of Nova Scotian parents and grew up in Toronto (1946-1961). She received her B.A. from Victoria College in 1961 and her A.M. degree from Harvard in 1962. Winner of the Governor General's Award for poetry for *The Circle Game* (1966) and for fiction for *The Handmaid's Tale* (1986), she has written a number of books of poetry and major novels, including *The Edible Woman* (1969), *Surfacing* (1972), *Lady Oracle* (1976), and *Bodily Harm* (1981). In 1972, she produced a provocative "thematic guide to Canadian Literature" entitled *Survival*.

Entry Points

1. According to the poem, what motivates the immigrants to come to an "unknown land"? Are their expectations realistic? Explain.

2. An American author, Thomas Wolfe, once said: "You can never go home again." What did he mean by that statement? Why, according to the poet, can't the immigrants go back to the "old countries"?

3. As an early immigrant to Canada, write an item in your journal describing your voyage across the sea and your first impressions of Canada.

PROVINCIAL
Miriam Waddington

The Author
MIRIAM WADDINGTON, born in Winnipeg in 1917 and educated in Ottawa, Toronto and Philadelphia, worked for many years as a social worker before becoming a professor of English and Canadian Literature at York University in 1964. Author of a critical study of A.M. Klein (1970), she has published eleven books of poetry, including *Driving Home* (1972) from which "Provincial" was selected for this anthology.

Entry Points
1. What are the poet's attitudes towards her childhood on the Canadian Prairies? How do you know?
2. Why does the poet mention the famous cities she has visited?
3. The word "provincial" often has negative connotations meaning someone or someplace that is small-minded or narrow in views. Why then does Miriam Waddington use this word as the title of her affectionate poem on her own childhood?
4. Write a poem using vivid details about places and people in your own childhood.

GREAT-AUNT REBECCA
Elizabeth Brewster

The Author
Born in Chipman, New Brunswick, in 1922, ELIZABETH BREWSTER was educated at the University of New Brunswick, Radcliffe College, the University of Toronto, and Indiana University. She worked as a librarian in a number of provinces before joining the English Department at the University of Saskatchewan. She is best known for her nine collections of poetry including *Passage of Summer* (1969) from which "Great-Aunt Rebecca" was taken.

Entry Points
1. How did Great-Aunt Rebecca make the past world "more real" to the poet than the present?

2. Why did the poet, raised in the modern world of "radios, cars, telephones" wish to be like her great-aunt?

3. Which one of your ancestors do you admire the most? List his or her qualities. Write a letter or a poem to the ancestor, expressing your admiration.

GRANDFATHER
George Bowering

The Author

Poet and fiction writer, GEORGE BOWERING was born in 1935 in Penticton, British Columbia. He taught in Calgary, London, and Montreal before returning to Vancouver to teach at Simon Fraser University. A prolific writer, he has published over forty books and won two Governor General's Awards: for *Rocky Mountain Foot* and *The Gangs of Kosmos* (poetry, 1969); and *Burning Water* (fiction, 1980). "Grandfather" was taken from *Touch: Selected Poems 1960-1970* (1971).

Entry Points

1. What is the poet's attitude to his grandfather? How does he gain almost mythic proportions in his grandson's mind? What words or actions reveal this?

2. Why is Canada called "apocalyptic," a word usually used biblically to indicate a divine (spiritual) revelation? Is the use of such a word justified or is it too much of an exaggeration? Explain.

3. If you have access to one, look at photos in your family album. Ask questions of your parents and relatives about your older ancestors. Write a poem or prose piece wherein you describe that relative's life with vivid, perhaps mythic, details.

EQUAL OPPORTUNITY
Jim Wong-Chu

The Author

JIM WONG-CHU, born in Hong Kong in 1949, immigrated to Canada in 1953, and eventually put down roots in Vancouver's

"Chinatown"—an experience that has become central to much of his work. He has worked as a community organizer, historian, and radio broadcaster, and is a founding member of the Asian Canadian Writers Workshop, as well as a full-time letter carrier for Canada Post. A collection of his poems, *Chinatown Ghosts*, was published in 1986.

Entry Points

1. Although thousands of Chinese worked for far less than normal pay on the building of the tracks for the Canadian Pacific Railway, none was given any of the benefits of the non-Chinese workers—for example, one of the 25 000 000 acres of C.P.R. lands to settle on. What point is Jim Wong-Chu trying to make in "equal opportunity"? Explain your response.

2. Explain the term "irony." How is the poet being ironic in this poem? Do you think the poet is correct in making the subject matter of this poem a near joke?

3. Research and summarize Canada's original Chinese Immigration Act.

4. To what extent is Canada *now* the land of equal opportunity?

INSPECTION OF A HOUSE PAID IN FULL
Jim Wong-Chu

The Author
See "equal opportunity," p. 267 and above.

Entry points

1. How has the former restaurant worker "made it"? Do you think the poet admires him and his success in Canada? Do you admire him? Explain.

2. What would you consider a successful life, one that you would be proud of?

3. Are success, money, and happiness synonymous terms?

4. You have just arrived in Canada "young and penniless"

without your family. In a letter to a friend, describe your dreams and ambitions. How are you going to "make it"?

AUTOBIOGRAPHICAL
Abraham Klein

The Author
A.M. KLEIN (1909-1972) was born in Ratno, Ukraine. In 1910 his orthodox Jewish family moved to Montreal where he lived for the rest of his life. He graduated from McGill in 1930 where he studied classics and political science and later completed his study of law at the Université de Montréal (1933). He published four volumes of poetry, including the Governor General's Award winner, *The Rocking Chair and Other Poems* (1948). "Autobiographical" is taken from his 1951 poetic novel, *The Second Scroll*.

Entry Points
1. Abraham Klein was born in the Ukraine, but was raised in the Jewish community of Montreal from the age of one. What fond memories does he recollect from his childhood on the "ghetto streets"?

2. Amongst the good and affectionate memories of his childhood autobiography, Klein mentions some negative memories as well. Name them. What effects did these images and situations have on him?

3. Why does he refer to his childhood as "immortal days"?

4. What is the "fabled city"? Explain thoroughly.

5. Write an "autobiographical" poem or short story in which you recollect your "immortal" childhood days. Use images and situations that suggest both joys and fears.

CURRICULUM VITAE IV
Walter Bauer

The Author
WALTER BAUER (1904-1976), born in Merseburg, Germany, was a widely-published author, but his books were banned under the

Nazi regime. Disillusioned with German attitudes, he immigrated to Toronto in 1952 where he first found work as a dishwasher. After attending the University of Toronto, he was hired by that university to teach German from 1958 to the end of his life. Except for a few poems written in English during the last years of his life, he wrote over seventy books (novels, stories, biographies, poetry, essays) in German. The Canadian author and dramatist, Henry Beissel, translated two collections of his lyrical poetry into English: *The Price of Morning* (1968) and *A Different Sun* (1976).

Entry Points
1. Walter Bauer was born and raised in Germany. Does he feel that he made the right decision to come to Canada? What does he regret?

2. Why does he refer several times to the dawn coming?

3. A "curriculum vitae" is a common Latin phrase meaning the course of one's life, or a resume for a job application that lists significant points of your own history. Write in poetic or prose form your own "curriculum vitae."

4. When have you said "No" when many others were saying "Yes"? What were the consequences? Would you have changed your mind and conformed if you had the chance to do it all over again?

WHAT DO I REMEMBER OF THE EVACUATION?
Joy Kogawa

The Author
Poet and novelist, JOY KOGAWA was born in Vancouver in 1935. She and her family were among the thousands of Japanese Canadians interned and persecuted during World War II, an experience she described in her award-winning novel, *Obasan* (1981). She grew up in Coaldale, Alberta, attended the University of Calgary, and studied music for a year at the Toronto Conservatory of Music. She has written three volumes of poetry, including *A Choice of Dreams* (1974), from which "What Do I Remember of the Evacuation?" is taken.

Entry Points

1. As a little girl, Canadian-born Joy Kogawa was interned along with her family in a British Columbia camp during World War II. What major details does she recollect of that experience?

2. In her mind, what role did her parents play during the evacuation out of Vancouver?

3. Why did Lorraine Life behave the way she did to Joy Kogawa and her brother, Tim? Explain. How would you have reacted to Lorraine's taunts in similar circumstances?

4. Why did the poet as a child pray to God to be "white"?

5. In letter form, write to Lorraine Life explaining to her why her behaviour towards Joy and Tim is hurtful.

6. Read Joy Kogawa's adult novel, *Obasan*, or her novel for young children, *Naomi's Road*, for her further views on the evacuation of her family and their internment. For another view, read Shizuye Takashima's *A Child in Prison Camp*, written as a diary including the author's watercolour illustrations.

IMMIGRANT

Madeline Coopsammy

The Author

Born in Trinidad in 1939, MADELINE COOPSAMMY studied in Delhi on a Government of India scholarship. She immigrated to Canada in 1968 and received her B. Ed. from the University of Manitoba. She now teaches English as a second language to non-English immigrants at Portage la Prairie, where she lives.

Entry Points

1. The poet claims that the immigrant "often wonders *why*." Why is this question constantly in her head?

2. Explain how Canada is the "land of silver dreams."

3. Look up the word "alienation" in a dictionary. How is the immigrant in the poem alienated? To what extent do you sympathize with her thoughts and feelings? Explain.

4. You have left Canada to live in another country. What would return to "haunt" you? Write a poem in which you express these things as vivid images.

GUEST WORKER BLUES
Charles Roach

The Author
An activist civil rights lawyer in Toronto, CHARLES ROACH was born in Trinidad in 1933 and moved to Canada in 1955. Trained in music, art, and philosophy, he has published a book of poetry, *Root for the Ravens* (1977) from which "Guest Worker Blues" was selected for this anthology. Under the sponsorship of the Canada Council, he has given public readings of his work in Canada.

Entry Points
1. The immigrant worker from Port-of-Spain, Trinidad, is "singing the blues" about his new life as a labourer in Canada. What exactly are his complaints?

2. Why does the "guest worker" feel that "in the land of Opportunity" his life is hard? Explain both from the economic perspective and from the emotional perspective.

3. Write a protest poem in which you point out problems in your own living conditions or in your society. Use vivid details and colloquial language.

I FIGHT BACK
Lillian Allen

The Author
Born in 1951 in Spanish Town, Jamaica, LILLIAN ALLEN came to Canada after studying and working in the United States. She now lives in Toronto where she frequently "performs" her poems that were "not meant to lie still on the written page:" A member of the Toronto group, *de dub* poets, she has published two chapbooks via Domestic Bliss, a co-operative enterprise in Toronto.

She has also released several record albums, and is also the recipient of a Juno Award. "I Fight Back" first appeared in *The Teeth of the Whirlwind* (1984).

Entry Points
1. Why is the speaker in this poem fighting back? How is she fighting back?

2. When the speaker is asked why she left the "Beautiful Tropical Beach" to come to Canada, she responds, "For the Same Reasons/Your Mothers Came." What do you think those reasons were?

3. Is the speaker justified in her anger and hostility? Explain your response.

4. Write a protest speech in which you "fight back" on an issue of concern to you. Present the speech dramatically to the class.

WINTER '84
Krisantha Sri Bhaggiyadatta

The Author
KRISANTHA SRI BHAGGIYADATTA has published two collections of his poetry, including *The Only Minority Is the Bourgeoisie* (1985). "Winter '84" appeared in the periodical, *The Toronto South Asian Review*, a small literary magazine dedicated primarily but not exclusively to giving voice to the literary expression of South Asians in North America.

Entry Points
1. What is the speaker's mood during that cold winter in 1984? What words or details lead you to your conclusion?

2. From the details given, what do you think the poet's view of the city of Toronto is? Do you agree with his opinion? Explain.

3. Write a poem using vivid details about your city or town in which your own attitudes become clear.

CULTURA CANADESE
Joseph Pivato

The Author
Born in 1946 at Tezze sul Brenta, Vicenza, Italy, JOSEPH PIVATO grew up in Toronto and graduated from York University in English and French. He received an M.A. and Ph.D. in Comparative Literature from the University of Alberta. A contributor to *Canadian Ethnic Studies*, *Canadian Literature*, and *The Journal of Canadian Fiction*, he is now teaching at Athabasca University in Alberta.

Entry Points
1. The poet asks, "where is our history in this land?" Why does he ask this question? You try to answer it.
2. "doferin e san cler" is Italianese for the intersection of Dufferin and St. Clair in the middle of an area of Toronto where many Canadians of Italian descent live. The poet also infuses into his poem a number of other Italian references within a Canadian context. What is his attitude to these products, services, and names?
3. Why does the poet entitle his poem "Cultura Canadese" instead of "Canadian Culture"?
4. Write a poem about your "culture." Think about the images or products of *your* society: neighbourhood, school, family, shopping districts or malls, church, synagogue, or temple. Where is your history?

LUCIA'S MONOLOGUE
Mary Di Michele

The Author
MARY DI MICHELE was born in Italy in 1949 and immigrated to Canada in 1955. She received her M.A. (1974) in English and Creative Writing from the University of Windsor where she studied with Joyce Carol Oates. Her books include *Tree of August* (1978), *Mimosa and Other Poems* (1981), *Necessary Sugar* (1983),

and *Immune to Gravity* (1986). A regular contributor to *Books in Canada*, she has won a number of awards including the silver medal in the Du Maurier Award for poetry in 1983.

Entry Points

1. In a "dramatic monologue," the character speaking the poem to a silent listener reveals her own personality, both her strengths and flaws. What personality traits does Lucia reveal about herself at this crucial moment of her life?

2. Why does Lucia feel that so much of her life has been wasted feeling guilty? Develop your ideas by looking at the poem as a whole.

3. Lucia's father says to her: "You younger generation don't care about anything in the past." Do you think this is a fair statement about Lucia? About yourself? About your generation? Explain thoroughly.

4. What do parents owe their children? What do children owe their parents? Argue your case thoroughly.

5. With a partner, role-play the parts of Lucia and her father as they try to communicate with each other their own ideas of life. Write out your improvisation in script form and present it to the class.

6. Write a dramatic monologue in which you talk about your parents to a silent listener.

7. Write a short personal essay in which you respond to the following questions: How did you learn to be a woman or a man? Who taught you? What influenced you?

IN MY BACKYARD
Celestino De Iuliis

The Author

Born in 1946 in Campotosto in the region of Abruzzi, Italy, CELESTINO DE IULIIS received his B.A. and M.A. at the University of Toronto and taught Italian Language and Mediaeval Literature at Syracuse University. Returning to Toronto in 1976, he became active in community affairs. His collection, *Love's Sinning Song and other poems*, was published in 1981 by the Canadian Centre for Italian Culture and Education.

Entry Points

1. Why would the boy's face "blush" when his father came to visit his teachers on Parents' Night? Explain.

2. Why is the speaker ashamed of his actions as a boy?

3. Role-play the young man asking his father for forgiveness in letter form.

4. In a small group, respond to the following questions:
   (a) What do children owe their parents?
   (b) What do parents owe their children?
   Share your responses with the rest of the class.

HISTORY'S RACIAL BARRIERS
John Barber

The Author

JOHN BARBER, a freelance journalist, has written for a number of magazines, including over thirty articles for *Maclean's*, from issues dealing with AIDS and daycare to reports on refugees and Sri Lanka. His article, "History's Racial Barriers," appeared in *Maclean's* on October 13, 1986.

Entry Points

1. According to Barber, what caused "history's racial barriers" in Canada? How and why were those barriers overcome? Do you agree with Barber's major thesis?

2. What major technique does Barber use to persuade us to agree with his central thesis that Canada has acted in a racist manner in the past? How effective is it?

3. Explain what a "humanitarian tradition" is. Do you agree that Canada now can claim such a tradition? Argue your case thoroughly, pro or con.

4. Look up "xenophobia" in a dictionary. Write a diary item that describes and explains one of your xenophobias—or the lack of them.

OPENING THE DOORS
Ken MacQueen

The Author
KEN MACQUEEN is a journalist who has written articles on free trade, Canadian-American relations, and defending Canadian Arctic claims. His article "Opening the Doors" appeared in *Maclean's* as the cover story on "The Immigrants" on October 13, 1986.

Entry Points
1. Why does Ken MacQueen begin and end his journalistic essay with brief stories of specific Canadian immigrants? To what extent is this technique effective? Evaluate.

2. Why is the "ruling majority" often suspicious of new waves of immigrants into Canada? Write a letter to the editor of a local newspaper in which you try to quell their suspicions. Use facts and appeal to authority.

3. According to the article, what are the usual consequences of increased immigration in a pluralistic society? To what extent do you agree? Argue your points in an objective manner.

4. Conservative M.P. James Hawkes believes that the Canadian population must reach thirty million by the year 2000. Why does he recommend this? Evaluate his recommendation in terms of Canada's needs. How has the government handled the topic of immigration recently?

5. In a small group, assume the role of a Parliamentary Committee on Immigration. Based on your reading of this article or on other readings you have done, make five solid recommendations on immigration for Canada for the next decade. Argue their validity with your class.

ANCESTORS—THE GENETIC SOURCE
David Suzuki

The Author
Born in 1936 in Vancouver, DAVID SUZUKI is both a geneticist and broadcaster, best known as host of the CBC's science programme,

The Nature of Things. Along with his family, he was interned in a B.C. internment camp during World War II. The Suzukis later settled in Ontario. He eventually joined the faculty at the University of British Columbia after studies at the universities of Amherst and Chicago. He has written articles for many journals and newspapers and is the author of many best-selling science books for young adults. His essay, "Ancestor—the Genetic Source" is excerpted from his biography, *Metamorphosis* (1987).

Entry Points
1. Why was the bombing of Pearl Harbour in 1941 the "single most important event" that shaped David Suzuki's life? What has been the single most important event in your life?

2. Given the events of Suzuki's early life, why does he end his autobiographical essay by stating that he "was grateful that . . . (he) was born a Canadian"? Do you agree with his conclusion?

3. How does Suzuki know that the "racial connection" to Japan matters very little to him? Why does he feel he must make this statement? Analyze.

4. As a Canadian, to what extent does your "genetic source" matter to you?

5. If you have visited the country of your ancestors as Suzuki did, write a diary item describing and explaining your thoughts and feelings about your ancestor's country.

ON RACIAL ORIGINS
Pierre Berton

The Author
PIERRE BERTON, born in Whitehorse, Yukon, in 1920, is probably Canada's best-known and most prolific writer. He has written and edited numerous articles for various newspapers and magazines, including the *Vancouver Sun*, *Maclean's*, and the *Toronto Star*, and has appeared on numerous radio broadcasts and television series such as *The Great Debate* and *Front Page Challenge*. Among his many awards are the Stephen Leacock Medal for Humour and

three Governor General's Awards for nonfiction: *The Mysterious North* (1956); *Klondike* (1958); and, *The Last Spike* (1971).

Entry Points

1. Summarize (paraphrase) in your own words why Ray Silver does not wish to comply with a government regulation asking him to name the "racial origin of his parents." Does he have a valid point or is he over-reacting? Explain.

2. Evaluate Berton's claim that the practice of asking for people's racial origins is "dangerous."

3. How are aspects of this essay ironic and humorous? Do you feel such techniques are appropriate in an essay dealing with serious matters? Why or why not?

4. You have just been asked by a prospective employer to name your "racial background." How would you handle such a question?

'I'M NOT RACIST BUT . . .'
Neil Bissoondath

The Author
Born in Trinidad in 1955, NEIL BISSOONDATH immigrated to Toronto in 1973 to attend York University where he majored in French. His stories have been broadcast on *CBC Anthology* and published in *Saturday Night*. His first collection of short stories, *Digging Up the Mountains* (1985), and his first novel, *A Casual Brutality* (1988), have both been highly-praised. He is also a frequent contributor to the *Toronto Star*.

Entry Points

1. Look up the word "stereotyping" and then explain it in your own words. Is Bissoondath justified in opening his brief article with stereotyping symbols and offensive, ugly racist and sexist name-calling? Explain his purpose in using these images and words.

2. According to the article, what is the major cause of racist behaviour?

3. What aspect of Canadian multiculturalism does Bissoondath particularly criticize? To what extent do you agree with his assessment?

4. Why is the article a powerful denunciation of "true racism"?

5. With a small group, list and discuss openly other demeaning racist and sexist expressions. With your group, write a brief essay in which you state clear reasons why such expressions should not be used.

A BLACK VIEW OF CANADA
Mary Janigan

The Author
MARY JANIGAN has written over ninety articles for *Maclean's* dealing with such issues as the Constitution, free trade, Canada-U.S. relations, immigration, and Native Peoples-Government relations. "A Black View of Canada" appeared as a feature article in *Maclean's* on January 20, 1986.

Entry Points
1. In her opening remarks, Mary Janigan quotes John Robinson as saying "Blacks have been left out of the Canadian mosaic." To what extent is this statement true?

2. What exactly is polite or "subtle discrimination"? Form a group of four or five and list examples of "subtle discrimination." Why does this phenomenon exist? How can we eradicate it? Have your group come up with four solid suggestions.

3. The Canadian "black community has come a long way in a short time." What examples does Mary Janigan present to support her statement? What must Canadian Blacks do to go even further, to progress even faster? How can Canadian society facilitate such progress?

4. Janigan uses a number of techniques to make her case an effective one: appeal to authority; use of historical allusions; use of statistics; use of repetition. Experiment with one or more of these techniques as you write a brief essay entitled "My View of Canada."

GROWING UP GREEK
Helen Lucas

The Author
An accomplished artist, HELEN LUCAS was born and raised in Saskatoon, Saskatchewan, by Greek immigrant parents. Her personal essay, "Growing Up Greek," was published in 1982 in the periodical, *Canadian Woman Studies*.

Entry Points
1. When Helen Lucas was three, she recollects that she felt she had done something wrong and would go to Hell. Why did she have such negative feelings?

2. Why can't the author state precisely where she came from? Do you sympathize with her dilemma?

3. Why is change so "frightening"? Describe a change in your life that frightened or disturbed you in some way. How did you overcome these feelings?

4. Write an imaginary letter to your mother or father explaining how you are changing and becoming different from that parent. Be specific about your changing values and new aspirations.

5. Using this essay as a model, write your own autobiographical essay and entitle it "Growing Up_____." You fill in the blank to reflect your heritage.

JEWISH CHRISTMAS
Fredelle Bruser Maynard

The Author
Born in Saskatchewan in 1922, FREDELLE BRUSER MAYNARD grew up in a number of small prairie towns. Between the ages of three and nine, she lived in Birch Hills, Saskatchewan, which became the setting of her childhood autobiography, *Raisins and Almonds* (1972), which related her unique experience as part of the only Jewish family in that town. She obtained her doctorate from Radcliffe in the United States after attending both the University

of Manitoba and the University of Toronto. She is now a free-lance writer in Toronto and devotes her time to studies in cultural trends, child care, and education.

Entry Points
1. The author begins her personal essay with the admission: "Christmas, when I was young, was the season of bitterness." Why does she say this? Why is this an effective introduction?

2. Throughout her essay, Maynard seems very conscious of her "difference" in Birch Hills, Saskatchewan: "All year I walked in the shadow of difference." Point out and explain moments in her reminiscences when she feels excluded.

3. In a diary item, describe a moment in your own life when you felt excluded from a group or an activity. Describe and analyze your feelings at that moment.

4. Why does Freidele "rebel" at the age of seven? Is she justified in her reactions? Evaluate her parents' response and handling of the situation. Was the "problem" resolved to your satisfaction? Explain.

5. When she discovers what her Christmas present actually is, Freidele begins to cry: "Nothing had changed then, after all. For Jews there was no Santa Claus . . ." Yet, at the very end, her mood changes. Explain her change of heart. What does she ultimately understand of her parents' motivations?

6. Write a personal letter to your parents expressing your gratitude for their caring and love.

7. Write your own personal essay on your memories of Christmas, Hanukkah, or another important holiday of your culture.

FINAL DANCE ON RACISM'S GRAVE?
David Suzuki

The Author
See "Ancestors—The Genetic Source," pp. 277-278 (above)

Entry Points

1. David Suzuki claims that Canada is "a bold experiment." What exactly does he mean by this?

2. Do you agree with Suzuki that "Canadians . . . are too self critical" and that "we judge ourselves very harshly"? What evidence does he provide to suggest that we should be less critical and more positive?

3. Why does he say that "kids are colorblind"? Do you agree? Provide examples from your own experiences and observations.

4. Suzuki's implication is that, if "kids are colorblind," racism is not genetically inherited behaviour. What then is the cause of racism? Explore this question with a group of four and report your ideas to the class.

5. Write a brief personal essay in which you express support for Suzuki's ideas. Use Suzuki's techniques of personal anecdotes, contrast, and emotional appeal.

THE SAGA OF THE FINE-TOOTHED COMB

James H. Gray

The Author

JAMES HENRY GRAY, journalist and social historian, was born at Whitemouth, Manitoba, in 1906. He worked as a reporter, editor, and editorialist for a number of western newspapers and periodicals, including the *Winnipeg Free Press*, the *Western Oil Examiner*, and Calgary's *Farm and Ranch Review*. His nine books, written after his retirement, include *The Winter Years* (1966), *Booze* (1972), and *Troublemaker!* (1978). His personal essay, "The Saga of the Fine-toothed Comb," is excerpted from his *The Boy from Winnipeg* (1970).

Entry Points

1. Describe and evaluate the system that the teachers of Winnipeg had devised to handle the problem of teaching children "who came into class without a word of English to their

names." How does your school system handle the same problem today? Investigate.

2. How did the children in the schoolyard overcome the language barriers? Why is the learning of foreign swear words so often popular with children?

3. Why does the author emphasize the "fine-toothed comb" and the lice problem amongst the new Canadian children? Is he in danger of creating a negative stereotype? Discuss fully.

4. "Adult Winnipeg of the era was as race-proud, bigoted, and prejudice-driven as any city on earth." How does Gray use description or supporting details to validate this statement? Do you think this is a dangerous statement to make? Why or why not? Explain fully.

5. Gray reports that, as a child, he and the other children often used highly offensive racial slurs to refer to each other. What reasons does he give for the children talking this way? Do children and adults talk this way today? Discuss fully with a group.

6. Write a speech in which you explain to children under twelve why racist name-calling is offensive and hurtful. Use vivid description and supporting details to make your points clear to the children.

THE ENEMIES OF TIME

H.S. Bhabra

The Author

HARGURCHET SINGH (H.S.) BHABRA was born in Bombay, India, in 1955, but was raised in England from 1956. He attended Trinity College, Oxford, where he gained his B.A. and M.A. in English Language and Literature (1980). He moved to Canada in the early 1980s, and has since written two thrillers, *The Adversary* (1986) and *Bad Money* (1987), under the pseudonym A.M. Kabal. His latest novel, *Gestures*, was published in 1986.

1. Why does Bhabra begin his brief, personal essay with three "facts"? Is this opening effective? What three "facts" might explain your identity or personality?

2. What aspect of Canadian multiculturalism is Bhabra criticizing? Why does he think that Canada needs "some active notion" of itself? Do you agree?

3. According to Bhabra, what exactly are "the enemies of time"? Evaluate his statement.

4. Why does Bhabra finish his essay with a line quoted from an Irish poet? Is this an effective conclusion?

5. Write a letter to the author explaining your agreement or disagreement with his views. In your letter, use or make up an anecdote from a recent experience as he does with the Canadian of Northern Irish descent whom he met on the streetcar.

THE DENE DECLARATION (JULY, 1975)

The Indian Brotherhood of the Northwest Territories

Entry Points

1. The "Dene" is what the Native peoples of the North call themselves. The "Dene Declaration" was passed in July, 1975, by the General Assembly of the Indian Brotherhood and Métis Association on behalf of the Native People in the North. What major rights are the Dene declaring? Are their demands valid ones? Explain.

2. Explain what the "Fourth World" is. What are the first three "worlds"?

3. What criticisms are directed at New World countries and, in particular, Canada? To what extent do you think these criticisms valid? Argue your case using ideas or facts gained from other literary, historical, and journalistic readings.

WE MUST HAVE DREAMS
John Amagoalik

The Author

A past director of Inuit land claims for the North West Territories, JOHN AMAGOALIK has also worked as vice-president of the Inuit Tapirisat of Canada, an organization founded in 1971 to enable the Inuit (the "people") to speak with a united voice on various issues concerning development of the Canadian North and the preservation of Inuit language and culture. "We Must Have Dreams" was first published in 1977 in *Inuit Today*.

Entry Points

1. What are John Amagoalik's dreams? Are they realistic or overly idealistic? What are his fears?

2. According to John Amagoalik, why must we have dreams? Although his intended audience is the Inuit, his own people, how are his ideas applicable to all of us?

3. To what extent does he blame the "white man" for the Inuit's problems? What does he *not* want from the white people?

4. "The will to survive is there." According to Amagoalik, what specific things must the Inuit do to survive? What qualities will be needed?

5. Using rhetorical questions to begin your essay as this one does, write about *your* dreams and aspirations for yourself and your country.

I AM A NATIVE OF NORTH AMERICA
Chief Dan George

The Author

DAN GEORGE (1899-1981), or Teswahno, born on the Burrard Reserve in North Vancouver, was a hereditary chief of the Coast Salish Indians, a logger, a longshoreman, and a television and movie actor. He appeared in the CBC production of *The Ecstasy of Rita Joe* and in a number of movies, including *Little Big Man* (1970), *Harry and Tonto* (1974) and *The Outlaw Josey Wales*

(1975). His most popular works are the lyrical prose-poem collections, *My Heart Soars* (1974) and *My Spirit Soars* (1982).

Entry Points

1. Explain the predominant characteristics of the "two distinct cultures" Chief Dan George lived in. What are his attitudes to these two cultures? Are his attitudes justified? Comment fully.

2. What does Chief Dan George find difficult to understand about the culture of his "white brother"?

3. In your own words, explain George's ideas about love. George wonders if his white brother "has ever really learned to love at all." How would you respond to his comment?

4. George says: "My culture is like a wounded deer that has crawled away into the forest to bleed and die alone." What does he mean by this extended simile? Do you agree with his assessment? Why does he make this pessimistic statement?

5. Using the technique of contrast or juxtaposition as George does, write a brief essay or poem entitled "I am a citizen of North America."

OUR LOST INNOCENCE

Bruce Hutchison

The Author

Born in Prescott, Ontario, in 1901, BRUCE HUTCHISON grew up in the Kootenay region and in Victoria, British Columbia. He has worked as a reporter and editor for the *Victoria Times*, the *Winnipeg Free Press*, and *The Vancouver Sun* where he is presently Editor Emeritus. A much admired writer and commentator, he is the author of fifteen books, three of which won the Governor General's Award for nonfiction: *The Unknown Country* (1942); *The Incredible Canadian* (1952); and *Canada: Tomorrow's Giant* (1957).

Entry Points

1. Explain the title, "Our Lost Innocence." How were we as Canadians "innocent"?

2. According to Hutchison, upon what does Canada's very survival depend? Do you agree with his conclusions? Comment fully.

3. ". . . we must also examine the darker side of the national experiment and count the mistakes." What "mistakes" have we made as Canadians since the Second World War? Can these mistakes be corrected? How?

4. At the end of his essay, Hutchison eloquently declares: "Canada must betray the grand dream of its founders or achieve its finest hour." Form a small group or four or five. In your own words, restate our founders' grand dream and then articulate five ways we can achieve our finest hour in the next century! Share your visions for the future with the rest of the class.

General Activities and Questions

1. RESPONDING PERSONALLY

Using your own personal responses, imagination, and the writing process, respond to the following activities and ideas in the form suggested.

(a) *Diary*

1. Imagine you are an immigrant newly arrived in Canada. In diary form, explain your feelings on leaving your own country and your feelings in having to re-establish yourself in a new country.

2. You are an early immigrant on a ship bound for Canada. Describe in diary form your passage over the ocean and tell your diary about your dreams and hopes for you and your family in coming to Canada.

3. You have now lived in Canada for several years and your expectations have generally been met. Tell your diary how your feelings about your new country have changed over the years.

(b) *Letter*

1. Write a personal letter to a relative who is still living in your old country. Describe with some detail your impressions of your new home. Outline both your joys and problems.

2. Write a formal letter to the editor of your local newspaper, commenting on any news story or column dealing with

immigration, refugees, racial conflicts, or multiculturalism in Canada. Take a stand!

3. Write a letter to a T.V. or radio station complaining about a program or commercial that you feel promotes negative stereotyping.

4. Write a letter praising a station for programming shows that promote racial harmony and understanding.

5. Write a personal letter to one of the characters in the short stories in which, as a friend, you try to help him/her solve his/her problem.

6. You are a young Canadian of Japanese descent. It is 1942. You and your family have been designated as "enemy aliens" and have had your property confiscated. For the duration of the war against Japan, you will be interned in a holding camp in the British Columbian interior. The Canadian government is doing this because it suspects all Canadians of Japanese ancestry of possible collusion with the enemy. As you try to clarify your values and feelings, write a letter of protest to the provincial or federal government.

7. You are a Canadian of Japanese descent, a former internee, now in your fifties. It is 1988. The prime minister has just issued a statement offering a formal apology for the government's behaviour during the 1940s and compensation for your material losses. Write a letter to a friend or relative telling him/her how you now feel.

(c) *Short Story*

1. Write a short story in which you create characters who reveal qualities of tolerance and acceptance.

2. Write a story in which a character has been assimilated into the "ways" of his/her new country. In your story, try to reveal the differences between your character's attitudes and the values of the parents.

3. You are a young child (seven or eight years of age) newly arrived in Canada. You can barely speak English. Write a first-person story in which you reveal your feelings on the first day

at your new Canadian school.

4. You are an immigrant, but you have lived in Canada for fifteen years. In the same style as "Vaivém", write a story in which you give your impressions of Canada. Reveal how you have changed and how you and your children have assimilated into the New World.

5. Devise your own conclusion to one of the short stories you have read, or continue writing the story past the author's ending.

(d) *Poetry*
1. Reread "I Am a Canadian" and "Autobiographical." Write a poem that explores your own identity. Make references through vivid images and/or realistic, colloquial language to your own roots and present neighbourhood, streets, school, and family.

2. Reread "Select Samaritan." Write a poem that reveals intolerance and bigotry through the use of irony.

3. Reread "Great-Aunt Rebecca" and "Grandfather." Write a poem in which you fondly recall the qualities and actions of one of your relatives.

4. Write a poem dealing with one or more of the themes suggested in the poetry or prose of this anthology. Relate these themes to life in your neighbourhood, school, or family. Experiment with different forms of language and rhythm: conventional, colloquial, dialect, "rap," and slang.

(e) *Scripts and Role-playing: Use of Drama and Video*
1. Write a short script in which a young teenage daughter tells her father that she does not agree with his "restrictive old country" ideas on dating and curfews. Perform your script with others in class. If possible, videotape your performance and play back on the VCR.

2. Assume the role of one of the characters in the short stories or poems. Write a short script in which your character has an argument with another character in the same work. Perform or videotape your script for the class.

3. Imagine you are an interviewer on a major T.V. talk show. Write a script of questions and answers as you interview one or more of the characters from one of the short stories or poems.

4. Write a short script in which you portray a father born and raised in another country who has seen his children slowly change over the years as they identify more and more with main-stream Canadian attitudes. One of your children has just informed you that he/she intends to marry someone who is not of your ethnic or religious background. How are you going to react? What are you going to tell your child? Perform the script with others in your class and videotape your final production.

5. Reread "Lucia's Monologue." Write a script in which Lucia and her father converse with each other. Write a "monologue" yourself in which you reveal your feelings and thoughts about your parents.

6. Through improvisation, dramatize with a group one of the short stories or poems.

(f) *Media*
1. Write a one-minute commercial that promotes the benefits of racial tolerance and harmony. Perform, tape, or videotape your commercial.

2. Design a poster or collage that depicts racial harmony.

3. Design a poster or collage that promotes Canada as a great place to live.

4. List television shows, films, videos, or songs that you think encourage or combat stereotyping. Be prepared by yourself or with a group to present solid, logical reasons for your choices.

(g) *Chart*
1. Prepare, in chart form, your own family tree. Go as far back as you can by exploring family albums, family letters and notes, and by talking to older members of your family.

2. Write a character sketch or poem based on a relative from your family tree.

2. SHARING THOUGHTS: SMALL GROUP ACTIVITIES

After forming a group of four or five, you may want to consider the following suggestions in order to create a stronger, more open, and more efficient group process.

(i) Appoint one member to be a group moderator or chair.

(ii) Appoint another member to be a recorder of ideas as they spring up from the discussion.

(iii) Go around your group, allowing and encouraging each member to contribute one statement on the issue or activity under discussion.

(iv) Go around the group again encouraging more statements. At no point during the first two rounds should anyone judge the statements made. The point is to make everyone feel comfortable with making statements and having opinions based on the knowledge they possess; the point is to create an open and positive group environment.

(v) Open the discussion and, using tact and diplomacy, support your initial statements and opinions with examples and reasons. Challenge the others in the group to do the same.

(vi) Come to a consensus on the topic by listening to the recorder's summary of the discussion. Keep in mind that opposing points of view will have to be considered as part of your shared response.

1. How would you define what a Canadian is? State specific characteristics.

2. What does the term "xenophobia" mean to you? Look it up in a dictionary. Why do you think people might exhibit xenophobic feelings? Under what conditions are they more likely to exhibit these feelings? Be specific.

3. Why do you think so many people from other countries want to immigrate to Canada? What advantages do you think they see in living in Canada? What conditions exist in many countries that make people want to leave?

4. As a group, imagine that you are trying to help a new student in your school, a newly arrived immigrant. This student has noticed that, although many of the students are friendly and welcoming, *some* of them are making fun of him. Try to help this student by explaining why some people behave that way and how to handle and cope with such negative behaviour. As a group, improvise and write a script that dramatizes this situation.

5. What are the benefits and advantages of living in a multicultural Canada? What are the difficulties? As a group, compose a short essay in which you express your ideas on these two questions using specific examples and the techniques of comparison and contrast. Group edit the final copy.

6. Present one of the poems to the class as an oral performance—some parts of the poem may be read solo while other parts may be read by partners or by a group chorus. Make an audiotape of your performance and try to incorporate music as an introduction, background, or closing.

7. As a group, script and act out one of the short stories for the rest of the class or for a school assembly. Videotape your performance.

8. As a group, respond to the comments made by one of the authors or journalists in the "Essay" section of this anthology. Write a letter to the author expressing support or disagreement with his/her opinions. Group edit the letter for final copy.

9. After reading one of the selections in the anthology, write down five questions about it you want answered. Share your questions with the teacher and with other groups in the classroom. Discuss and answer your questions with your own group and with other groups and the teacher.

10. Discuss what the following ethnocultural words or phrases mean to you. After the discussion, look up the words in a dictionary or explore them further in your library's vertical files.

affirmative action	integration	reverse discrimination
anglicize	majority group	racist behaviour
anti-racist education	melting pot	segregation
assimilation	minority group	stereotype
bias	mosaic	visible minority
culture	multiculturalism	
culture shock	prejudice	
discrimination	race	
employment equity	race relations	
ethnic group	racism	
hidden curriculum		

3. SHAPING THOUGHT: GENERAL THEMES

Refer also to the "Index of Sections by Theme" on pages 301-305.

1. The Canadian immigrant experience
   — the homeland experience
   — reasons for emigration
2. Contrasting the Canadian and American Dream
3. Survival: coping and achieving goals in an alien environment
4. The nature and consequences of prejudice and xenophobia
   — minority and majority perspectives
5. The feelings and problems of alienation and isolation
6. The joys and successes of the immigrant experience
7. The processes of assimilation: "melting pot" vs "Canadian mosaic"
8. Inner problems of identity (psychomachia): the need to disguise and escape
9. Conflict and reconciliation:
   — the advantages of a multicultural society
   — creating and encouraging tolerance and respect
10. Cultural conflicts within the family:
    — parents vs children, the nature of love and respect

— tradition vs change

— the positive value of maintaining a cultural heritage

11. Schooling—a disruptive force or a vehicle for change?

12. The effects of the physical landscape—Eden or Hell?

13. Acceptance and rejection

14. New world materialism—incentive or seduction?

15. The search for identity (political, social, psychological)

16. Idealization of the past—ancestral roots and nostalgia

17. Dreams, rage, and nightmares

18. The role of women in immigrant families

19. Relationships between men and women—changing roles?

20. Loss of innocence and ideals: Paradise Lost, Paradise Regained

4. SHAPING THOUGHT: THEMATIC ACTIVITIES

(a) *Debating*

1. Debate: "Schools create and develop pride and self-esteem in students by motivating them to search for themselves." Agree or disagree, using specific examples inside and outside the formal curriculum.

2. Debate: "Prejudice is an enemy that exists in all of us." Argue for or against, using historical, personal, and literary evidence. Choose two or three selections from this anthology as part of your supporting evidence.

3. Debate: "Assimilation means the act of gaining a new identity while losing your old one." Agree or disagree, using evidence collected from personal interviews and from two or three selections in this anthology.

4. Debate: "Multiculturalism promotes ethnic ghettoization, keeping minority groups 'in their place' and out of real power." Argue for and against, using specific evidence. Reread "I'm not racist but . . .," "The enemies of time," and "We Must Have Dreams" as you build your case.

5. Debate: "Multiculturalism promotes harmony and understanding which makes Canada a more tolerant, kinder country." Argue for or against, using specific evidence from current events or from your readings in this anthology.

6. Debate: "A person is who his/her parents are." Agree or disagree by arguing the role of heredity as opposed to the role of social conditioning in a child's development. How might a new life in Canada influence either heredity or social conditioning or both?

(b) *Explaining*

1. Explain how Canada is different from the United States in its treatment and expectations of immigrants. Are these expectations changing? Give examples from your personal experiences and from your readings of selections in this anthology to support your point of view.

2. Describe and evaluate in specific terms the "Canadian Dream." Explain why the ideals of some immigrants to Canada are not matched by the realities they encounter. How is this evident in some of the literature presented in this anthology?

3. Explain the causes and effects of alienation in people. Analyze the causes and effects with specific references to the literature in this anthology.

4. How does one define one's identity? What forces aid and what forces hinder the search for one's true self? Where does one attain one's values? Explain and evaluate the significance of the various forces in your own life or in the life of a character in a short story or poem in this anthology.

5. Compare the values and motivations of the main characters in one short story with those of the main characters of another. Then, compare those values with your own.

6. Choose any short story, poem, or essay in this anthology and clearly explain your reasons for liking or disliking it.

(c) *Exploring and Reflecting*

1. Explore stereotyping in the media today. Compare these media presentations with the attitudes expressed in the selections in this anthology.

2. Explore and reflect upon the roles of two or three female characters in the short stories and poems. Look specifically at the following selections: "Input," "The Story of Nil," "A Real Live Death," "Great-Aunt Rebecca," "Lucia's Monologue," "Immigrant" and "I Fight Back." How are some of these roles changing in today's society?

3. Compare two novels from the Recommended List in this anthology with themes emanating from the multicultural experience in Canada. Explore any differences in attitudes expressed by major and minor characters and the difficulties for people who have to deal with their "old" heritage and their "new" Canadian heritage.

4. Choose one of the listed "General Themes" and, through specific references to two or three works in this anthology, write a short literary insight essay that explores your chosen theme.

5. Good literature holds up a mirror to society reflecting all its features—good and bad. Write a brief essay exploring the extent to which two or three of the works in this anthology would support this statement.

5. THE MEDIUM AIDS THE MESSAGE: UNDERSTANDING STYLE AND STRUCTURE

1. Explore the major images and descriptive detail used in two or three poems or short stories. How do these specific images or word-pictures contribute to the overall effect of the writer's message?

2. The tone of an author's voice may be joyful or regretful (see "The Rink" or "Autobiographical"), accepting or bitter (see "A Real Live Death," "The Broken Globe," and "I Fight Back"), serious or sarcastic (see "Guest Worker Blues" and "Select Samaritan"). Choose two or more of the selections in

this anthology and explore the author's voice in putting forth an attitude on his/her subject matter.

3. Examine the diction of various poems that convey strong attitudes and emotions such as love, bitterness, hate, regret, joy, and anger. Look specifically at "In My Backyard," "Curriculum Vitae IV," "I Am a Canadian," "I Fight Back," "Provincial," "Lucia's Monologue," and "What Do I Remember of the Evacuation?" for good examples of strong emotions.

4. Dialogue is an important component of a short story. Demonstrate by specific references to the short stories how dialogue helps to reveal both character and theme.

5. An author is often influenced by the landscape—urban or rural—in which the work is placed. Explain how the landscape affects the author's characters and ultimate theme in one of the short stories. Look specifically at "The Rink," "Hunky," "The Broken Globe," "The Glass Roses," "Vaivém," and "Input."

6. Point out and analyze the points of view of two or more poems or two or more prose selections. Evaluate the effectiveness of those points of view in putting forward the author's message.

7. Evaluate the ending of one of the short stories. Are you satisfied with the way the story concluded? If you found the ending too loose or inconclusive, why do you think the author ended it that way? How would you have concluded it? Look particularly at "Details from the Canadian Mosaic" and "The Glass Roses."

8. Show how the essays and articles in this anthology use one or more of the following devices or techniques to aid their message. An example of an essay that employs the device is given as a guide to help you:
   (i)   effective introduction—"Jewish Christmas"
   (ii) rhetorical questions—"We Must Have Dreams"
   (iii) descriptive or supporting details—"The Saga of the Fine-toothed Comb"

(iv) emotional appeal—"Final dance on racism's grave?"

(v)   anecdotes—"The enemies of time"

(vi) appeal to authority—"A Black View of Canada"

(vii) contrast or juxtaposition—"I am a native of North America"

(viii) irony or humour—"On Racial Origins"

(ix) symbols—"I'm not racist but. . ."

(x)   appeal to facts—"Opening the Doors"

(xi) effective conclusion—"Our Lost Innocence"

Use the above examples as models in your own essay writing. Experiment with the techniques to make your own writing more powerful.

INDEX OF SELECTIONS BY THEME

The grouping of the literary selections under the following specific, major themes is meant as an aid in following up interconnected ideas through a variety of different works and genres. The groupings are not necessarily exclusive. Other works in the anthology may also pertain.

CHILDHOOD AND YOUTH

COURAGE AND SELF-RESPECT

DEATH AND RESPONSE

FAMILY RELATIONSHIPS

HUMOUR AND IRONY

LOVE

PROTEST AND INJUSTICE

LOSS OF INNOCENCE: IDEALS AND REALITIES

WORK

INDEX BY AUTHOR

RESOURCE LISTS

The resources listed represent a distinctly Canadian perspective on the ideas evoked by this anthology and may be useful to students as

(i) further insights into the characters and themes of the material in this anthology;

(ii) comparative reading;

(iii) resources for independent study, essays, and oral/seminar projects;

(iv) reading for pleasure!

(a) *NOVELS*
Recommended for Senior Students

Apprenticeship of Duddy Kravitz, The   Mordecai Richler

Black Madonna   F.G. Paci

Black Robe   Brian Moore

Casual Brutality, A   Neil Bissoondath

Daughters of Copper Woman   Anne Cameron

Diviners, The   Margaret Laurence

Dream Like Mine, A   M.T. Kelly

Father, The   F.G. Paci

Foreigners   Barbara Sapergia

Frozen Fire   James Houston

Italians, The   F.G. Paci

Ivory Swing, The   Janette Turner Hospital

Luck of Ginger Coffee, The   Brian Moore

Obasan   Joy Kogawa

Peace Shall Destroy Many   Rudy Weibe

Rich Man, The   Henry Kreisel

Riverrun   Peter Such

Sacrifice, The   Adele Wiseman

Search for America, A   Frederick Grove

Son of a Smaller Hero   Mordecai Richler

Sparrow's Fall, The   Fred Bodsworth

Stone Angel, The   Margaret Laurence

Temptations of Big Bear, The   Rudy Weibe

Tin Flute, The   Gabrielle Roy

Under the Ribs of Death   John Marlyn

Vanishing Point, The   W.O. Mitchell

White Dawn, The   James Houston

Who Has Seen the Wind?   W.O. Mitchell

Wild Geese   Martha Ostenso

Recommended for Younger Readers

Amish Adventure   Barbara C. Smucker

Days of Terror   Barbara C. Smucker

Dreamspeaker   Cam Hubert

From Anna   Jean Little

I Heard the Owl Call My Name   Margaret Craven

Kap-Sung Ferris   Frances Duncan

Kate   Jean Little

Listen for the Singing   Jean Little

Lost in the Barrens   Farley Mowat

No Word for Goodbye   John Craig

Underground to Canada   Barbara C. Smucker

White Mist   Barbara C. Smucker

(b) *ANTHOLOGIES*

Most of the recommended books are collections of short stories, although some also contain poetry and non-fiction prose.

Basket of Apples and Other Stories, A   Shirley Faessler

Bloodflowers   W.D. Valgardson

Dance Me Outside W.P. Kinsella

Darkness Bharati Mukherjee

Digging Up the Mountains Neil Bissoondath

First People, First Voices Penny Petrone

Garden in the Wind Gabrielle Roy

Home Truths Mavis Gallant

Indian Legends of Canada E.E. Clarke

Inuit Stories Zebedee Nungak, Eugene Arima

Italian Canadian Voices C.M. Di Giovanni

Liars and Rascals: Mennonite Short Stories Hildi Froese Tiessen

Middleman and Other Stories, The Bharati Mukherjee

Neighbour and Other Stories, The Naim Kattan

Ojibway Heritage Basil Johnston

Other Selves C.D. Minni

Other Voices Lorris Elliott

Paradise on Hold Laura Bulger

Shapely Fire, A Cyril Dabydeen

Stories from Quebec P. Stratford

Stories from Western Canada Rudy Wiebe

Street, The Mordecai Richler

When Women Rule Austin Clarke

Yarmarok: Ukrainian Writing in Canada Since the Second World War Jars Balah, Yuri Klynovy

(c) *PLAYS*

Back Door William Paluk

Balconville David Fennario

Ecstasy of Rita Joe, The George Ryga

Few Things About Us, A Daniel Caudeiron

Great Hunger, The Len Peterson

Indian George Ryga

Inook and the Sun   Henry Beissel

Komagata Maru Incident, The   Sharon Pollock

La Sagouine   Antonine Maillet

Les Belles Soeurs   Michel Tremblay

Les Canadiens   Rick Salutin

Letter to My Son, A   George Ryga

Matty and Rose   Barbara Sapergia

More About Me   Daniel Caudeiron

The Rez Sisters   Tomson Highway

Rootless But Green Are the Boulevard Trees   Uma Parameswaran

Sainte-Marie Among the Hurons   James W. Nichol

Yesterday the Children Were Dancing   Gratien Gelinas

(d) *NON-FICTION PROSE*

All of Baba's Children   Myrna Kostash

Black Man's Toronto, 1914-1980, A   Donna Hill

Canadian Odyssey, The: the Greek Experience   Peter D. Chimbos

Child in Prison Camp, A   Shizuye Takashima

Continuous Journey: A Social History of South Asians in Canada
   Norman Buchignani, Doreen Indra, Ram Srivastava

Enemy That Never Was, The   Ken Adachi

First Canadians, The   Howard A. Doughty

Halfbreed   Maria Campbell

Immigrants   Robert Harney, Harold Troper

Immigrants, The   G. Montero

Immigrant Years, The: from Europe to Canada, 1945-1967   Barry
   Broadfoot

Little Immigrants, The: the Orphans Who Came to Canada
   Kenneth Bagnell

Looking into My Sister's Eyes: an Exploration in Women's History
   Jean Burnet

Man of Our Times, A   Rolf Knight, Maya Koizumi

Metamorphosis   David Suzuki

Narratives of Fugitive Slaves, The   Benjamin Drew

Raisins and Almonds   Fredelle B. Maynard

Rebirth of Canada's Indians   Harold Cardinal

Roughing It in the Bush   Susanna Moodie

South Asian Diaspora in Canada, The   Milton Israel

This Is My Own   Muriel Kitagawa

Unjust Society, The   Harold Cardinal

Voice of the Pioneer   Bill McNeil

Whatever Happened to Maggie and Other People I've Known
  Edna Staebler

Within the Barbed Wire Fence   Takeo Ujo Nakano

(e) *FILMS*

For an annotated catalogue of the following films from the National Film Board of Canada, visit your local library or write or call your N.F.B. regional office. The films are useful in providing background information and comparative components with the literature in media literacy studies.

Alden Nowlan: An Introduction

A.M. Klein: The Poet as Landscape

Autobiographical by A.M. Klein

Behind the Masks

Cold Journey

Cold Pizza

Dreamspeaker

Enemy Alien

Fields of Endless Day

Four Portraits

Franco: The Story of an Immigrant

Golden Mountain, The: The Chinese in Canada

Home Feeling: Struggle for a Community

Jews of Winnipeg, The

Journey Without Arrival: A Personal Point of View from Northrop Frye

Kurelek

Myself, Yourself

People of the Book, The

Ravinder

Red Dress, The

Rosanna: A Portrait of an Immigrant Woman

Sweater, The (by Roch Carrier)

Teach Me to Dance

This Is a Photograph

Waiting for Caroline

W.O. Mitchell: Novelist in Hiding

Credits

"What I Learned from Caesar" by Guy Vanderhaeghe from *Man Descending* by Guy Vanderhaeghe. Used by permission of Macmillan of Canada, a Division of Canada Publishing Corporation.

"The Hockey Sweater" by Roch Carrier, from *The Hockey Sweater and Other Stories*, translated by Sheila Fischman (Toronto: House of Anansi Press, 1979). Reprinted by permission.

"The Rink" by Cyril Dabydeen. Reprinted with permission of the author.

"Input" by Laura Bulger. Reprinted by permission of the author and Bramble House Inc.

"A Class of New Canadians" by Clarke Blaise. Reprinted by permission of the author. Copyright 1973.

"Details from The Canadian Mosaic" by C.D. Minni. Reprinted by permission of Guernica Editions and Dino Minni. Reprinted from *Other Selves*, published by Guernica Editions.

"The Glass Roses" by Alden Nowlan, from *Miracle at Indian River Stories* by Alden Nowlan, copyright c 1968, Clarke Irwin. Reprinted by permission of Stoddart Publishing.

"School, the First Day" by Barbara Sapergia, excerpt, Chapter 12 of *Foreigners*. Reprinted by permission of Cateau Books.

"Hunky" by Hugh Garner. Reprinted from *Hugh Garner's Best Stories*. Reprinted by permission of McGraw Hill Ryerson Limited.

"The Broken Globe" by Henry Kreisel, from *The Almost Meeting*. Reprinted by permission of NeWest Press.

"The Story of Nil" from *Children of My Heart* by Gabrielle Roy. Used by permission of the Canadian Publishers, McClelland and Stewart, Toronto.

"Things In The Silence" by Harold Marshall. Reprinted from *Other Voices*, Williams-Wallace Publishers.

"A Real Live Death" by Katie Funk Wiebe. Reprinted by permission of the author.

"Vaivém" by Laura Bulger. Reprinted by permission of the author and Bramble House Inc.

"I am a Canadian" by Duke Redbird. Reprinted by permission of the author.

"Select Samaritan" by Robert Finch. From *Poems* by Robert Finch. Copyright c Oxford University Press Canada 1946; reprinted by permission of the publisher.

"The Immigrants" by Margaret Atwood. From *The Journals of Susanna Moodie* by Margaret Atwood, copyright c Oxford University Press Canada 1970; reprinted by the permission of the publisher.